HUMAN INTERACTION IN EDUCATION

Gene Stanford
Utica College of
Syracuse University

Albert E. Roark
University of
Colorado

ALLYN and BACON, Inc.
BOSTON · LONDON · SYDNEY

Contents

Preface

If the Sixties found education in trouble, the Seventies find education in revolution. Students are in open rebellion against institutions and practices they consider inhumane. Taxpayers are revolting against the increasing costs of supporting the schools. Teachers are demanding increased salaries and an end to conditions they consider oppressive. Parents are openly questioning whether educators know what they are doing.

Although some voices can be heard demanding a return to "basic" education and traditional practices, the overpowering cry has been for a more humanistic form of education. Educators have started looking for ways to break down the rigidity and meaninglessness of many practices, and in their search they have discovered flexible scheduling, multimedia approaches, individualization, the open classroom, discovery-oriented curriculum projects, nongraded classes and team teaching.

But most of these attempts to humanize education have focused on content or structure and have ignored the *process* through which significant learning takes place, which in our view is interaction with other human beings. We have seen, for example, open classrooms in which—after a year of being in the same class—many students did not even know the names of others. We have seen attempts at individualization which allowed a student to work at his own pace, but which isolated him in a study carrel for most of the day. We have visited schools overflowing with new audiovisual equipment, but with teachers who lacked the skills to work cooperatively in sharing that equipment. We have seen teachers helping students discover through inquiry methods the social problems of the Trobriand Islanders, but who had never considered raising questions about the conflicts taking place among members of the classroom society.

Therefore, we wish to call attention to the key element in significant learning, which seems to be missing from so many of the recent attempts to change American education: that education is essentially a social process. That is, it is not something one acquires; it is something that occurs continually as a result of interaction with other human beings.

When education is viewed from this standpoint, it becomes apparent that what happens between teacher and student is more important than how much material is covered. Also, since students are themselves people and have a profound influence on one another's lives, what transpires between students is critical. Interaction between teachers and teachers and administrators is equally important, because of its effect on the personal growth of the individuals involved and because it provides a model for students. Thus, we hold that the chief functions of teachers are to engage in interpersonal relationships which are healthy and growth-producing and to provide environments which foster this type of interaction for students.

Basically, *Human Interaction in Education* is a detailed exploration of the meanings, implications and implementations of this view of education. Chapter 1 introduces the reader to our view of the nature of education and the general principles of teaching and educational objectives that derive from it. Chapter 2 provides the theoretical and empirical support for our position, drawn from the areas of psychology, communication, interpersonal relations and group dynamics. In Chapter 3 we introduce a model for understanding the development of the classroom group and how the teacher can influence the process.

Chapters 4-8 offer specific approaches to utilizing human interaction to foster significant learning. In contrast to many works which effectively "turn on" the reader to humanistic education but suggest nothing substantial he can *do*, we have attempted to give him explicit guidance and suggestions for implementing the principles we espouse. One chapter is devoted to each of the following approaches: discussion with focus on external subject-matter, discussion with a focus on the feelings and ideas of the student and the experiences of the group, role-playing and action methods, simulations and simulation games, and activities that take the student outside the classroom.

Finally, we have provided a chapter (9) describing the means for analyzing and categorizing classroom interaction. After an introductory section explaining how the instruments can be utilized by the teacher, five different approaches to measuring interaction are presented. Each approach is described either by the originator of the instrument or by an educator who has considerable knowledge of and experience in its use.

To acknowledge all the contributions that other persons have made to the contents of this book would be impossible. We are aware of the debts we owe to our colleagues and our own teachers and students who influenced our thinking and molded our present view of education— especially the students, staff and faculty at Cortez High School, 1960-1961, Phoenix, Arizona, and Marie N. Smith of Horton Watkins High School, Ladue, Missouri. Special thanks must go to the following persons for their helpfulness: Jim Bryngelson, Howard Kirschenbaum, Frank Chew, Harold Blatner, M.D., Barbara Stiltner, Anne Ramsey, Felicia Diamond, Maxwell Jones, M.D., Ann Milam, Al Thompson, Sandi Meggert, Craig Spillman, Jack E. Cousins, Don Johnson, Ron Anderson, Miles Olson, Bill May, Bob Bruce, Barbara Stanford and University Associates, Publishers and Consultants. Grateful acknowledgement is also made to the Colorado Outward Bound School, Wm. Fawcett Hill, University Associates, National Press Books, Journal of Teacher Education and the American Geological Institute for permission to use copyrighted materials.

Gene Stanford
Albert E. Roark

1

THE NATURE OF EDUCATION

The standard prescription for those afflicted with uneducation is twelve to twenty years of schooling. The school dropout rate indicates that many prefer the affliction to the cure. Concerned parents and educators have begun to take a critical look at many of the basic principles of traditional schooling practices in hopes of discovering why young people are becoming ever more contemptuous of schooling. One of these basic principles, long held sacred in American education, is that schooling—the source of education—revolves around the acquisition of facts. A less obvious, but more inaccurate, corollary to this concept is that education can be acquired without interpersonal interaction. Teachers have traditionally measured the success of their endeavors in terms of the amount of information acquired by students. In the process they have generally viewed student interaction as appropriate only if it contributed to learning the subject matter.

Traditional educational practices, as well as some innovations, tend to discourage interaction. Some of the most obvious examples include language laboratories where each student is plugged into his own recorder jack and many of the "teaching machines" with which each student works in almost total isolation. Individualized instruction is often "individualized" only in terms of the rate at which the student is expected to work, and tends to isolate the students from each other. The most blatant examples, however, are in the traditional practice of "each student doing his own work," and the view of talking during class as detrimental to learning. In fact, most classroom regulations tend to be designed so as to restrict or circumscribe student interaction in the classroom as though it were inherently harmful.

GENERAL PRINCIPLES OF EDUCATION

This book takes the position, in contrast to the traditional ideas about education described above, that human interaction is the single most important ingredient in education, and that schooling practices should be devised to enhance rather than suppress interaction. Our position rests on three basic principles, which should serve as the foundation for any attempts to humanize education: education is a social process, significant learning occurs through human interaction, and education must include self-knowledge and self-understanding.

Education Is a Social Process

The old saying that "All that is learned in school is forgotten, but the education remains" represents a much wiser conception of the essence of education than viewing it as solely the acquisition of information. Those familiar with learning and retention curves are aware that most subject matter is forgotten at frightening rates and that only a small percentage of the knowledge originally acquired is retained even one year later. In fact, we *assume* that people will forget what they have learned and without hesitation make provisions for relearning and re-training. Yet, we assume with equal confidence that a person will remain educated even if he has forgotten most of what he learned in school. Obviously, we seem to believe that something happens to a person in the process of becoming educated besides the acquisition of information. If we view education and schooling from a traditional subject-matter orientation, taking into account the contradictions, we are left with the feeling that neither the process nor the outcomes of education are clear.

However, by viewing education as essentially a social process most of the mysteries associated with it dissolve. From this viewpoint education is not something one acquires. It is, instead, a continuous process which occurs as a result of interaction with other human beings. Considering the process of education as essentially social does not deny the importance of information or skill training, but it does change the position they occupy in the process. The key to the type and quality of the educational experience is shifted from the information involved to the human interaction involved. Social interaction and social learning become the essence of education while traditional subject matter becomes an ingredient in the interaction.

It would be easy to assume from the preceding that we are minimizing the importance of subject matter. This is not our intention at all. Our intention is to remove the emphasis in teaching from information giving and to place it on human interaction. In the process we do not want to lose the content of subject matter. However, instead of the traditional approach to education which places subject matter at the center of schooling processes and places the people involved on the periphery, we are advocating that students be the prime concern in education and that what has traditionally been known as subject matter come next.

The concept that the "medium is the message," proposed by McLuhan (1966) and McLuhan and Fiore (1967), is another way of viewing our belief that education is essentially a social process. (See also Sidwell, 1969, and Postman and Weingartner, 1969.) Simplistically, it can be stated that the social interactions (medium) have the most impact, not the subject matter (content). No one will deny that the content as viewed traditionally is the subject matter. Claiming that the medium (message) is the social interaction which takes place in school is bound to raise cries of protest. Nevertheless, this concept seems to be essentially correct. It is true that students read books, view films and are periodically subjected to assorted other gadgets introduced into the process by innovators, but essentially students learn what counts from each other and learn what society expects from the teachers. Thus their social interactions become the medium through which they learn. And, if McLuhan is correct that the medium is the message, we must examine their social interactions—not the subject matter—to determine what messages they are receiving. Only then will we be able to ensure they receive messages which promote growth consistent with our objectives.

Significant Learning Occurs
Through Human Interaction

Significant learning is that learning which has meaning and importance in the life of the learner. To have meaning and importance, what is learned must affect that person's life or his potential to live life. Such learning usually occurs through human interaction, because we derive meaning from our relationship with other humans (Rogers, 1969). It is not that one person tells another the meaning of something, but instead that meaning is derived from the reactions of the persons involved. An obvious example is when a person reads that he will be discriminated against and remembers and understands this, but discovers its real meaning only when the actual discrimination takes place.

Our principle—that significant learning occurs through human interaction—is based in part on the thesis that experiential learning ("learning by doing") produces significant behavior change. Introduced by John Dewey and others, this thesis has been well substantiated and, indeed, has become almost a cliché. Our position goes one step further, however. We believe that experiential learning is essential, but that what is learned exerts its influence on the conduct of the learner through social interaction. We contend that meanings beyond those of rudimentary survival originate in social interaction. Therefore a student may "learn" by doing a project in solitude, but its significance to him is acquired only through his interaction with other persons.

Interaction which produces significant learning can take many forms. A teacher may tell his students that he does not have class favorites, and then give preferential treatment to some members of the class. What the class learns from this is that he has class favorites and does not want them to know it. A different type of learning is involved when a 200-pound high school football lineman is told that he is too small to play at a large university. A still different type is involved when a popular, attractive girl finds out that a boy she would like to date prefers someone else. The ghetto student who, through discussions with his counselor, realizes that he has an opportunity to go to college has learned something he will never forget. All of these examples involve learning in interaction with other persons. The learning is significant because it will affect the way the people involved will conduct their lives.

Education Must Include Self-Knowledge and Self-Understanding

If educators have erred by assuming that the information, not the social process involved, is the essence of education, they have compounded their error by concentrating on environmental information and ignoring self-knowledge and self-understanding. "Know thyself" is ancient advice which has been virtually disregarded in modern educational practices. In most American schools only guidance programs have concentrated on this aspect of education. Yet there is perhaps no more important factor in leading an effective life than an adequate self-concept based on accurate knowledge and understanding.

Self-knowledge refers to a knowledge of one's needs, behavioral tendencies and values. It also deals with an understanding of our impact on the world and other people. This is the kind of knowledge that lets us predict our behavior, the impact it will have on the environment and our reaction to the behavior. With this kind of knowledge a person is in a much better position to act in ways beneficial to himself and others.

The question of values and how one should lead his life has traditionally been the domain of the home and the church. Questions of personal identity, sex education and career development have been handled in the home with perhaps some help from the family pastor. But as we all know, these institutions have been less and less able to deal effectively with the nation's youth, and so schools are being expected to assume those responsibilities.

THE GOALS OF EDUCATION

Traditional educational goals have been based on a number of faulty assumptions: 1) there is a fixed body of knowledge which must be transmitted directly to students, 2) we know specifically what students should learn better than they do, and 3) subject matter is worth knowing for its own sake. These statements are part of the mythology of education now, although they may have been legitimate at one time. In the seventeenth and eighteenth centuries social conditions and communication facilities were such that schools needed to concentrate on providing knowledge directly to students. Students were expected to learn about life outside of school and to go to school to learn those things which man considered the domain of the educated. Therefore, if one was to be educated he had to attend an institution where knowledge beyond that generated in everyday life was available. The current situation is obviously not even similar, let alone identical, yet educators persist in retaining the same schooling model.

In our view, the current situation calls for man to have three major competencies or abilities if our society (perhaps even mankind) is to survive. First, man must learn to live with others in a humane way—that is, man must be humane. Second, man must learn the skills necessary for effective living. Third, man must learn to live in his physical world in a way that benefits both him and the world. Educational objectives and practices should be based on these three broad goals. Traditional concepts of subject matter objectives have validity, in our view, only as they contribute to the three main objectives.

Producing Humane Persons

Ashley Montagu (1970) has stated:

> The greatest of all talents, and the most important for man, is the talent for humanity. And what is talent? It is involvement. And the talent for being humane operationally means the involvement in the welfare of one's fellowman ... The most basic of all opportunities is the right to growth and development as a human being who has been deeply involved in the love of others, for the health and identity of the person consists in the meaningfulness of his interrelationships (p. 50).

Montagu's description contains the essence of the concept of a humane person. A humane person is not just a person who is interested in his fellowman and kind and loving toward him. A humane person is one who is involved in enhancing the welfare of his fellowman and who places the welfare of his fellowman on a par with his own welfare. A humane person does not have to view his involvement with others as self-sacrificing, but instead derives satisfaction from his contribution to the welfare of others.

Enhancing Human Effectiveness

Human effectiveness is, in our view, the ability to know and satisfy one's personal needs to the extent possible in one's environment. This conception of effectiveness includes the ability to relate effectively with other human beings when appropriate as well as to support oneself financially. The effective person is one who is able to cope with himself and his environment in self-satisfying ways and who exhibits a minimum of self-defeating behavior.

Improving Man's Relationship with His Environment

Man's impact on his environment has been increased drastically by his burgeoning numbers. In addition, man has acquired unbelievable "leverage" through his machines and explosives. The result is that man now has the ability to make Earth uninhabitable through "normal" living. Man also has the power to transform Earth into a veritable paradise. How long he will continue to have a choice is debatable, but the urgency of the situation is not. If man does not learn to live in a mutually beneficial way in his physical environment he will cease to live at all.

PRINCIPLES OF TEACHING

To be of any practical value, the principles and goals of education outlined above must be translated into teaching and schooling practices. The section which follows presents three assumptions regarding teaching which we consider necessary to implement those goals. These assumptions form the basis for the specific teaching strategies which we will introduce in later chapters.

Providing Relationships and Environmental Conditions

Teaching is essentially providing relationships and environmental conditions which facilitate increased differentiation of personal perceptions and accurate integration of new data into personal perceptions. This view of teaching is based on phenomenological psychology (Combs and Snygg, 1959; Combs, Avila and Purkey, 1971). This position assumes that a growth tendency exists in humans and that the goal of all behavior is self-enhancement. That is, a person always acts in the best way he knows, according to the way he sees the situation. However, under threat a person is likely to distort perceptions of himself and his environment. A person's behavior increases in effectiveness as his perceptions of the environment become more detailed and include more relationships. Personal effectiveness is therefore a product of our personal perceptions, and education for human effectiveness thus becomes a process of providing the conditions under which more adequate perceptions will be developed.

Facilitative relationships are characterized by trust and openness. Building trust and openness and maintaining these conditions in a classroom require that the teacher behave in this manner himself as well as having other necessary qualities.[1] The basic prerequisite is that the teacher be genuine or congruent. Basically this means not being phoney or putting on a front. But, it also requires that the teacher be appropriately self-disclosing and willing to be human rather than "professional." Research (Berenson and Carkhuff, 1967) has demonstrated that genuine expression of feelings is facilitative of personal growth in interpersonal relationships, while incongruence is destructive.

The second basic quality or ability required of the teacher in a facilitative relationship is empathy, the ability to perceive and feel with another person as if he were the other person. It means that a teacher is able to see things as the students do and to understand them as they do. An empathic relationship does not require agreement, but it does require the ability to "walk in the other person's moccasins" and let him know that you too can see and feel from that perspective.

Caring for or prizing a person unconditionally is also a necessary ingredient in a facilitative relationship. Unconditional positive regard has become a popular term for this type of caring because it conveys clearly the feeling that the caring is not based on specific conditions. While it does *not* mean approval of all behavior, it does mean that the

---

1. Rogers (1969) has been the source of most current ideas regarding facilitative relationships. See Appendix, pp. 297-299, for a summary of research on facilitative relationships in the classroom.

pupil is cared for simply because he *is* and not because he is something or does something.

The relationships established in the classroom need to lead to students feeling free from threat so that they can be free to explore, experiment and fail. Threat leads either to distortion of activities for protection or to fear of disapproval, punishment and failure. In either case student activity becomes defensive and restricted. The environment also needs to provide challenge, confrontation and the data by which the challenges can be met.

The combination of safe, secure personal relationships, solvable or unsolvable problems, and data or methodologies by which these problems can be attacked and possibly solved promotes positive self-concepts and encourages the acquiring of new knowledge and skills. The student learns about himself and derives meaning from his environmental manipulations through personal relationships. The provision of new data along with problems to be attacked provides a basis for continuing experiential learning, which in turn provides additional data for interpersonal interaction. This is basically the process of life and is never ending.

The Teacher as a Participant in the Educational Process

A basic assumption regarding American education is that there is a fundamental difference between the goals and procedures of teachers and those of students. It is assumed that ideally teachers' goals are centered on changes in the students—usually called learning, attitude or character building and skill development. Students' goals, it is assumed, are to change or to be changed as much as possible through those processes defined as learning and development.

The consequences of the presumed differences between student and teacher goals are dramatic. Teachers are supposed to change others (or, in more humanistic terms, to facilitate change), with no concern for self-change. Students are supposed to change themselves or be changed, with little regard for change in others. If teachers were participants in learning, it would tend to reduce the problem of student disregard for each other and to foster a community of learners who care for each other. The present practice tends to set the students apart from each other as well as from the teacher. Who has not watched a student gleefully answer a question in class that another student failed, with complete disregard for the other student's feelings? Or seen students hoard materials needed by others in order to win the reinforcement race?

This misconception of teaching has many implications. Perhaps the most obvious is that teachers and students are set apart in any activity which has to do with academic learning. Students immediately assume that they must guard against being abused by unfair work demands, grades and being made to appear stupid. Teachers assume that students must be taught, that they are probably not very interested and that it is the teacher's responsibility to ensure that they learn. Hence students feel they must resist for self-protection and teachers feel they must push if they are to do their jobs. Thus a cold war is already being waged before teachers and students even know each other.

Further, the traditional distinction between teachers and learners leaves students without a model to follow in their efforts to learn. Students are deprived of observing an experienced learner and benefiting from his methods and approaches. This can lead to misconceptions of how knowledge is acquired and illusions concerning the amount and type of knowledge possessed by the teacher.

Our viewpoint is that teachers and students should have the same basic goals, and that differences, if any, should be in emphasis and methods. By this we mean that in any given educational endeavor all participants should share the same basic goals even though there may be a division of labor and wide variations in procedures and specific objectives. By being a participant the teacher constructively lowers the barriers between teacher and student and increases the probability of cooperative effort, thus making it easier for students to identify with teachers and with school. Teachers should still take responsibility for the classroom but they will do it as participants in a community of learners engaged in a joint learning venture.

Positive Approaches to Discipline

Discipline is perhaps the greatest concern of beginning teachers. Fear of losing control of the class probably underlies most concerns about discipline, but fear of the loss of self-esteem and the respect of others are probably also very important. In addition, administrative pressures and demands contribute to the beginning teacher's worries about discipline.

It is unfortunate that a society which depends primarily on voluntary cooperation of its members for survival teaches its children through involuntary, authoritarian, coercive methods. The implication of this contradiction is frightening: the educational system is undermining the ideals and practices of our political system and society. How can a student be expected to learn to be democratic, much less be skillful in democratic practices, in a totalitarian institution?

The ideas presented here are designed to help the teacher create an environment among people which is psychologically healthy and conducive to all types of learning. The first principle is participation; the second is sound management; and the third is positive reinforcement.

Student participation in discipline is not new but it has rarely produced satisfactory results because of the way it has been utilized. Everyone can think of fiascos involving hall monitors, student courts and the like. The basic reason for these failures is that the systems were not, as a rule, based on true student participation. At best (at worst?) they have involved student participation in punishment. Their purpose was still to enforce the system's rules as these rules were defined and established by the system. True participation requires that the students participate in all phases of the discipline from the making of the rules to the enforcement of them.

The teacher who does not manage the classroom usually has problems that extend way beyond discipline. Discipline is affected because a well-run class usually has more to offer students, has fewer opportunities for deviant behavior, tends to be more interesting, keeps students busier and usually encourages behavior that is incompatible with deviant behavior. The result is that student-teacher confrontations are less likely, and when they do occur there is usually a positive alternative to the student's misbehavior. Thus sloppy classroom management can be said to encourage discipline problems. It is not a matter of running an authoritarian classroom: it is a matter of running a classroom well.

We advocate positive reinforcement of desirable behavior and extinction of undesirable behavior to deal with the problem of deviant behavior. Positive reinforcement refers to the providing of a reward or favorable result as a consequence of desirable behavior. Punishment or aversive control should not be used, but this does not mean that limits are not set or that other forms of influencing behavior are not considered desirable. Positive reinforcement is seen as a much more desirable approach than punishment, for various reasons. One is that when a behavior is stopped via punishment there is no way to predict what behavior will take its place. Often the behavior that replaces the undesirable behavior is even less desirable. By using the various forms of positive reinforcement, this problem can be eliminated. Another undesirable effect of punishment is that it often has adverse effects on the other class members. For example, they may learn to fear the teacher, become inhibited or begin to dread the class. Most important, it may have a damaging effect on the student who is punished. His ability to learn may be impaired by anxiety or he may lose interest in the class. Skinner (1968) contains a particularly good discussion of the undesirable effects of punishment as a means of eliminating unwanted behavior.

Behavior is extinguished (i.e., ceases to occur) if it is not reinforced. This applies to desirable as well as undesirable behavior. Extinction is preferred to punishment as a means of eliminating deviant behavior because it does not have the detrimental side effects of punishment. If a student is punished for his behavior in class, the negative consequences mentioned above are likely to occur. However, if the reinforcers of the behavior are removed the behavior can be eliminated without these problems.[2]

THE GOALS OF THIS BOOK

To implement the principles of education and achieve the goals we have all-too-briefly described above will be a formidable task for the teacher of the 1970s. How can this book help with that task? Are we suggesting a new teaching methodology—a new bag of tricks—or are we advocating a whole new curriculum that we hope will replace the three R's? In a sense we are doing both.

On the one hand, we see human interaction as the most promising

2. Since it is beyond the scope of this book to present a thorough discussion of behavior modification techniques in discipline, several additional readings are suggested:
Madsen, C.H., Jr., and Madsen, C.K. *Teaching discipline: behavioral principles toward a positive approach.* Boston: Allyn and Bacon, 1970. Mager, R.F. *Developing attitude toward learning.* Palo Alto, Calif.: Fearon, 1968. Sarason, I.G., Glaser, E.M., and Fargo, G.A. *Reinforcing productive classroom behavior.* New York: Behavioral Publications, 1972. Skinner, B.F. *The technology of teaching.* New York: Appleton-Century-Crofts, 1968.

approach to teaching any subject matter—from a highly traditional curriculum in basic reading skills to an innovative, discovery-oriented approach to biology. Therefore, we have provided a wealth of specific teaching activities that can be used as the methodology for facilitating learning of any subject matter. In this way we hope to influence the *process* of education.

On the other hand, we also see human interaction as forming the basis of a new *content* of education. If, as we have postulated, the goals of education should be to produce more humane and effective persons and improve man's relationship with his environment, the content of education must shift from external subject matter to the social and psychological development of the student himself. We have no illusions about convincing educators to make this shift overnight, but we do feel strongly that schools must stop looking for new approaches for reaching the same goals and start implementing new goals based on a realistic view of the needs of people and society.

Even "humanistic" educators have been guilty of failure to see beyond traditional subject matter goals. The early innovations in affective education, for example, emphasized too much the use of feelings to improve insight into literature and history, rather than using history and literature as the means for helping students understand and deal with their feelings.

Innovators must ultimately break out of the confines of traditional curriculum, and shape a new curriculum which will deliberately and directly improve students' understanding of themselves and others and their relationship with their environment. To this end we have suggested, in later chapters, a number of teaching strategies and activities that have no connections with traditional subject matter, but which are designed to implement the new goals of education we have proposed.

References 1

BERENSON, B.G., and CARKHUFF, R.R., *Sources of gain in counseling and psychotherapy.* New York: Holt, 1967.

COMBS, A.W., AVILA, D.L., and PURKEY, W.W. *Helping relationships: basic concepts for the helping professions.* Boston: Allyn and Bacon, 1971.

COMBS, A.W., and SNYGG, D. *Individual behavior: A perceptual approach to behavior.* (Rev. ed.) New York: Harper, 1959.

McLUHAN, M. *Understanding media: The extensions of man.* New York: McGraw-Hill, 1966.

McLUHAN, M., and FIORE, Q. *The medium is the message.* New York: Bantam Books, 1967.

MONTAGU, A. Just what is "equal opportunity"? *Vista,* 1970, **6**, No. 1, 23-25 & 56.

POSTMAN, N., and WEINGARTNER, C. *Teaching as a subversive activity.* New York: Delacorte Press, 1969.

ROGERS, C.R. *Freedom to learn.* Columbus: Merrill, 1969.

SAMPSON, R.V. *The psychology of power.* New York: Pantheon Books, 1966.

SIDWELL, R.T. Cooling down the classroom: Some educational implications of the McLuhan thesis. In Stoff and Schwartzber (Eds.), *The human encounter: Readings in education.* New York: Harper, 1969.

SKINNER, B.F. *The technology of teaching.* New York: Appleton-Century-Crofts, 1968.

TRAUX, C.B. Self-disclosure, genuineness, and the interpersonal relationship. *Counselor education and supervision,* 1971, **10**, no. 4, 351-354.

2

THE THEORETICAL BASIS FOR INTERACTIVE EDUCATION

If you are like most of the teachers and teachers-to-be that we work with, the very word *theoretical* in the title of this chapter is enough to make you shudder. "Why do I continually have to read about theories?" you're probably wanting to know. "Why can't someone just give me practical advice on what to do in the classroom?"

We agree that too many books about education are filled with abstract ideas and no concrete suggestions on how to implement those ideas. For that reason we have loaded Chapters Three through Nine with a wealth of specific teaching strategies. But we also believe that "there is nothing so practical as a good theory." Sound contradictory? Perhaps. But the fact is that unless you know *why*, you can never know *what* you should do. Sure, you can lead your students through a few exercises or revamp your lesson plans to include some new approaches. But without a secure theoretical base, you may end up confusing students with activities that teach contradictory attitudes or concepts, or merely parading before them a series of clever but useless gimmicks.

For interactive education to be successful, the teacher needs to know the basic theories on which it is based. We did not think up our teaching activities "cold" and did not choose them simply because they seemed likely to grab the attention of students. Rather, we suggest activities that are directly linked to a particular view of the nature of man that we think has validity, to psychological principles that have been confirmed through research, to theories of communication and to some definite ideas about what constitutes healthy interpersonal relationships. We think, therefore, that for the how-to-do-it material which follows this chapter to have optimal usefulness for you, you should be well aware of the theoretical base on which it rests. You will then be better equipped to implement and extend our suggestions in your own work.

PSYCHOLOGICAL FOUNDATIONS OF INTERACTIVE EDUCATION

To some extent, all our acts, especially those that involve people, are influenced by our conception of the nature of man. Therefore, our approach to teaching is directly tied to our view of man. For this reason we have chosen to discuss briefly three psychological theories—that is, statements of what man is—which have enormously influenced us personally and education in general, and then to discuss the synthesis of these theories on which this book is based.

Psychoanalysis

Our society has been virtually transformed by psychoanalytic concepts, and it is a rare person who is not at least superficially acquainted with the basic ideas in Freudian psychology. Since there is no way to deal briefly and adequately with the entire realm of psychoanalytic theory, we are limiting our discussion to some basic assumptions about man's psychological functioning:

1. MAN IS REACTIVE IN DEPTH. Behavior is not determined simply by the external stimuli to which one is exposed or by the goal one seeks, but is also extensively influenced by internal stimuli. These internal stimuli may be primarily instinctual, such as the sex drive or anger, or they may

be the result of ego or superego demands. In addition, id, ego and superego conflicts exert a powerful influence on behavior. The main point is that man is a *reactive* being, not a *proactive* being. That is, his behavior is determined by the stimuli to which he is subjected, and not by a decision to act in a certain way. In the psychoanalytic scheme, one can conceptualize man as being pushed and pulled by a variety of internal forces while at the same time being influenced by his environment.

2. MAN IS A PRODUCT OF HIS HISTORY. This principle is the very foundation of psychoanalytic therapy, which relies heavily on the exploration and understanding of past events in order to interpret and correct present behavior. The person's present behavior is seen as being significantly influenced by his psychosexual development and the past events of his life. For educators, the two most important implications of this principle are that a) we cannot fully understand a child's behavior until we know his history, and b) the effects of what happens to a child in school extend far beyond the immediate situation in ways perhaps neither understood nor intended.

3. MAN IS UNCONSCIOUS OR MINIMALLY AWARE OF MANY STIMULI TO WHICH HE IS REACTING. Human behavior is influenced by forces to which the actor is not consciously attending, and human beings have an active psychic life of which they are unaware. Often conflicts develop between the contents of the unconscious and the conscious wishes and values held by the person, and these conflicts can lead to unexplainable and at times contradictory behavior. In order to reconcile unconscious and conscious thought processes and defend against conscious awareness of unacceptable material, man has a variety of defense mechanisms which distort or deny to awareness all unacceptable thoughts, feelings and motives.

The implications of these three characteristics of man for teachers are profound. For example, the question, "Why did you do that?" which is asked so often in school, is impossible to answer, since no one is completely aware of all the forces acting on him at any one moment. Also, teachers have direct access to only some of the variables which influence student behavior—or their own. Finally, teachers must learn to expect behavior which does not seem reasonable in view of the situation, since man reacts to both internal and external stimuli. Dealing with behavior in terms of only what teacher and student are consciously aware is thus bound to fail and at other times to be only minimally satisfactory.

Behaviorism

To many persons, behaviorism is little more than white rats, Skinner boxes and salivating dogs. Actually the term encompasses a wide range of schools of thought, starting with the early work of Pavlov and Watson and extending through that of Guthrie, Hull and Skinner. However, in the midst of the diversity we can perceive some commonalities:

1. MAN IS A REACTIVE BEING. His behavior is influenced entirely by environmental conditions, not by any decision on his part. Hence, behaviorism stresses external stimuli and observable behavior and deemphasizes or ignores acts of will or physical determinants of behavior.

2. MAN IS A HISTORY OF HIS REINFORCEMENTS. All that man is has been determined by which of his behaviors have been rewarded and which have been extinguished through lack of reward. If this be true, man can be viewed as a *tabula rasa,* a blank slate, waiting to be shaped and molded through reinforcement.

The behavioristic view of the nature of man has been violently resisted by many persons, who feel that it is degrading and reduces humans to the level of animals. Others have protested its mechanistic and deterministic character, stating that man is neither completely knowable nor completely predictable. The most serious criticism of behaviorism has been that it ignores the question of values—that it does not provide any guidelines as to what man *should* be, but only provides the means through which man can be shaped into whatever someone *wants* him to be. The ethical question of who has the right to do the shaping is usually not considered of great importance to behaviorists.

Despite the criticisms of behaviorism, we all apparently acknowledge many of its general concepts in everyday life, as revealed in the attention we give to rewarding good behavior and punishing undesirable behavior—whether it be in our children, our dogs or our students.

Behavioristic approaches have much to offer teachers. Whereas psychoanalytic theory tells a teacher to expect irrational behavior and behavior of essentially unknown causes, which is difficult to control or modify, behaviorism states that behavior can be managed through the manipulation of either the stimuli in the presences of which the behavior occurs or the reinforcers of the behavior. It further states that behavior which is not reinforced eventually ceases. Therefore, the teacher whose students do not behave in desired ways has the concrete task of removing reinforcers of the undesirable behavior and providing reinforcers for more desirable behavior. Whereas psychoanalytic theory implies that teaching is a difficult task, behaviorism views teaching optimistically as primarily the arrangement of contingencies of reinforcement (Skinner, 1968).

The Third Force

Third force psychology is partially a reaction to both behaviorism and psychoanalysis. Proponents of third force psychology consider that behaviorism has erred in overlooking man's ability to direct his own life and that psychoanalysis has erred in paying too much attention to man's emotional disturbances and not enough to his healthy aspects. The stress in third force psychology is on expanding human potentialities. For this reason it is often labelled "humanistic" psychology. The following concepts characterize the major tenets of this position:

1. MAN IS PROACTIVE. Man is able to act upon his environment as well as react to it. The influence of environmental and genetic determinants is acknowledged, but man is assumed to have the ability to modify himself and his environment in directions of his choice.

2. MAN IS BASICALLY GOOD. A central theme throughout all third force psychology is that man is basically good. Man's behavioral and developmental tendencies are viewed as good; any restriction or warping of man's capabilities is viewed as bad.

3. PERCEPTION IS CRITICAL. Since man is considered to be capable of initiating action and is not simply at the mercy of the stimuli in his environment or of the forces operating within him, it follows that man's perception of *what is* is crucial. Perception and the organization of

perceptions have been of considerable concern to humanistic psychology throughout its history.

4. THE HUMAN CONDITION IS A LEGITIMATE CONCERN OF PSYCHOLOGY. In addition to—or perhaps because of—the emphasis on man as a proactive being, actively taking part in shaping his destiny as well as living it, third force psychology is directly concerned with values, purposes and the quality and nature of interpersonal relations. Considerations of dignity, love, good and evil, aesthetics and all other questions regarding the human condition are viewed as central to psychology. This view brings psychology directly into the arena of everyday human life.

For teachers, third force psychology does not provide ready-made techniques or principles which, if followed, guarantee success. Instead, it provides a challenge. The challenge is whether teachers can furnish the conditions in which students can develop to their maximum potential as human beings. To aid in this task, some techniques are suggested, some research findings are offered and a developing body of theoretical knowledge is available, but the teacher is clearly told that the responsibility is *his* as a human being involved in the lives of other human beings. The message is both implicit and explicit: *help man become that which he can become.*

A Question of Synthesis

We have borrowed liberally from each position in the formation of our own beliefs. From the insights of the Freudian position we freely acknowledge that there is at least a continuum of awareness and probably something that can be labelled an unconscious. We accept that we are partially motivated by unconscious forces and that all is not necessarily what it appears to be. And we recognize forces related to sex, aggression and other drives which we cannot completely account for by conditioning, perception or choice.

We also believe that the conditions under which behavior occurs and the consequences of that behavior can affect future behavior. Yet, unlike the aficionados of operant conditioning, we believe that behavior is only influenced, not determined, by its contingencies.

This is basically a humanistic position, undergirded by phenomenological concepts, as described in Combs and Snygg (1959), but not disregarding other sources of human understanding. Essentially we fall in the middle of the third force position, with perhaps more emphasis than some on self-concept theory, with less emphasis than many on existential thought and with openness to input from any source which will enable us to behave more effectively. Because of the heavy emphasis we place on self-concept and related principles of psychology, these ideas will be expanded in the remainder of this section.

Self-Concept

Personal identity is an illusive commodity. We all know who we are, yet we constantly seek reassurance and welcome information which confirms or exceeds our beliefs. Further, we identify ourselves in many different ways depending on the circumstances. At a PTA meeting we may identify ourselves as teachers, but at the university we may say we are students. Under still other circumstances we may refer to ourselves as Elks, parents, Chicanos, middle-class and so forth. We complicate the picture even more by qualifying these basic concepts—saying, "I am a good parent," or, "I am a militant Chicano teacher." Underlying these various identities is a stable, pervasive concept of ourselves which is never completely overshadowed by role or situational demands. However difficult it may be for us to define, we all have a concept of ourselves as a person which is broader and more basic than the concepts we have of ourselves in specific circumstances or roles. This all-important concept is our self-concept.

The simplest definition that can be given for self-concept is that it consists of all that we perceive ourselves to be. It is the organized belief system and feelings we have regarding who we are, how we should behave, how we appear and where we belong. These basic beliefs and feelings regarding our identity are arrived at through a process of organization and integration of an infinite number of progressively more minute and isolated self-perceptions. For example, a person, let us say Joe Riley, may on a given day and at a given moment see himself as a father, plumber, man and sailing enthusiast who is fixing a flat on his boat trailer. For the moment Joe will have a perception of himself as a flat fixer, but this perception will be relatively minute and isolated from his other perceptions of himself and probably contribute little to his self-concept. His view of himself as father doing something for his son, however, would probably be central to his self-concept.

A person has a concept of himself in every situation which is determined by what he is experiencing at the moment and the beliefs he brought to the situation. The beliefs we have of ourselves vary in importance and in their relevance to our self-concept. The beliefs and feelings we have regarding our sex role are more central to our self-concept than those regarding our spelling ability, and both of these may be more important than our concepts of ourselves as bean bag tossers. The crucial element is the organization of these diverse and fragmented beliefs and feelings into a basic self-concept of ourselves as persons. This self-concept is "the most important single factor affecting behavior" (Combs, Avila and Purkey, 1971, p. 39).

The development of the self-concept is a gradual, never-ending social process in which we learn about ourselves through interaction with others. Basically, we do this in two ways: 1. We compare ourselves with others, either directly or indirectly. Rosemary, for example, looks around the room and notices that she is the only one who hasn't finished the test and concludes that the others can work faster than she can; this is *direct* comparison. Jake, on the other hand, looks up the high-jump records and concludes that he is not one of the best high-jumpers in the state; this is *indirect* comparison. 2. We also learn about ourselves from the reactions of others to us. Each time someone interacts with us it contributes something, however slight, to what we believe about ourselves. Every interaction with another person allows us to learn a little more and thus alters our self-concept somewhat, although often imperceptibly. In a sense, we cannot escape both seeing ourselves in comparison to others and through their eyes as reflected in their reactions to us.

Since the self-concept is learned, it can be altered or enhanced through learning opportunities. When we combine this with the idea that the self-concept is a direct determinant of behavior, the implications for education are obvious. We have an obligation to ensure that students have an opportunity to interact extensively in ways that will provide them with accurate feedback and other information about themselves. The activities in Chapter Five—Facilitating Self-Disclosure, pp. 140-144, and Facilitating Feedback, pp. 151-156—provide many opportunities for students to acquire self-knowledge and improve their self-concept. Role playing, as discussed in Chapter Six, also leads to insight and increased self-understanding. However, we also have a responsibility to guard against students' having experiences that lead them to form negative self-concepts through repeated failure and comparisons that continually denigrate them. Inevitably, some such experiences will occur, but we must ensure that they are offset by success experiences.[1]

Perceptual Field

Everything that we are aware of, including ourselves, constitutes our perceptual field. By necessity we act in accordance with our perceptions of ourselves and our environment. We do not avoid touching a stove because it *is* hot, but because we *think* it is hot. There is ample research which indicates that the same thing holds true about self-perceptions; we act in accordance with how we see ourselves, and dramatic changes can be brought about in behavior by changing a person's self-concept (Combs, Avila and Purkey, 1971). The influences of self-concept on school achievement have also been thoroughly documented (Purkey, 1970).

All aspects of our perceptual field do not have an equal influence on our behavior. Since we can attend to only a limited number of stimuli at any one instant, those to which we are attending most have the greatest influence on our behavior. For example, if we are in a room with twenty students, those to whom we are talking at the moment will have the greatest influence on what we say. In any given situation our behavior will be influenced most by our self-concept and then in descending order by those aspects of our environment psychologically closest to us, i.e., those aspects we most closely identify with or feel have the most relevance to ourselves.

The quality of our perceptions is determined by: 1. the richness or amount of information in our perceptual field, 2. the degree of meaningful differentiation; e.g., the prospector who can distinguish between worthless rocks and valuable ore as opposed to the person who sees only rocks, 3. the accuracy and freedom from distortion of perceptions. Perception is not, obviously, the simple act of being aware, but includes the organization and meaning given to those things in our awareness. The overall quality of our perceptions is also influenced by selective attention. Since we can attend to only a small portion of the available stimuli at any one moment, it is vital that we attend to relevant elements. Since what is perceived is also, to an extent at least, dependent

1. See Labenne and Greene's *Educational Implications of Self-Concept Theory* (1969) for a more complete treatment of this topic.

on our behavior, it quickly becomes apparent that perception and behavior are interdependent, with the quality of one influencing the quality
of the other in a never-ending manner.

Most perceptual psychologists regard reality as that which is perceived by each person and consider that each person's behavior is
dependent on his perceptions. Therefore, we have only our own perceptions or our perceptions of others' perceptions to determine reality.
From this standpoint learning is the process of determining the meaning
of experiences, and involves both the acquisition of new information and
establishing its meaning (Combs, Avila and Purkey, 1971). In summary,
learning occurs primarily through experiencing directly or indirectly
through the reflected learning of others (Combs and Snygg, 1959). Consequently, a person's concepts of self and reality are a combination of
meaning drawn directly from experience and of meaning inferred from
the appraisal of others.

Under any circumstances, reality is what we perceive it to be. In a
classroom, there are as many realities as there are persons, and the
personal meaning of what occurs will be at least somewhat different for
each person present. We cannot assume that our (the teacher's) concept
of reality even approximates anyone else's. After making an assignment,
you may walk over to a student to be helpful and plan to do the same
for every student in the room. The students' perceptions of your behavior, however, may be quite different: the student you approach may feel
embarrassed and put down, believing you think he is too dumb to
understand; his best friend may get mad because you are picking on
him; and many of the rest of the class may resent your showing him
special attention. Each of these perceptions is reality to the persons
holding them. The only way to unravel the misunderstanding is through
a frank, open discussion which allows everyone to check his perceptions
against the perceptions of others.

Meaning and Learning

We feel that it is helpful to assume that there are two basic types of
meanings: personal meaning, which is a unique meaning available only
to an individual person, and consensual meaning, which is meaning
arrived at by pooling the perceptions of relevant persons in regard to a
particular object or event. Personal meaning can be communicated to

another person, but it can never be shared. If it is truly shared, it then becomes consensual meaning, since human beings are unique and therefore cannot have identical thought processes.

Consensual meaning is usually tied to a referent such as the standard measures of length, weight and time provided by the National Bureau of Standards of the U.S. Department of Commerce. Most referents are not nearly so precise or as generally accepted as those of the Bureau of Standards, and this leads to misunderstandings and psychological distance between people. Consider the concept of democracy. People simply do not have an agreed-upon referent for democracy, which leads to sincere persons using the word to refer to quite different governmental practices. It is difficult to avoid conflict when these differences involve emotional issues or vital concerns. Personal meanings must remain unique, but satisfactory interpersonal relationships and communication depend upon generally accepted consensual meanings.

Learning is essentially a question of determining meaning, and achieving increased differentiation, clarity and accuracy in our perceptions. These processes occur through experience, increased information and human interaction. The importance of human interaction in this process has been underscored by Combs, Avila and Purkey (1971): "The discovery of meaning . . . can only take place in people and cannot occur without the involvement of persons. This is the human side of learning (p. 91)."

The most important meanings are those which have to do with the relationships of the self-concept to the rest of the perceptual field, because these are the meanings with the greatest impact on behavior. "Any information will affect a person's behavior only in the degree to which he has discovered its personal meaning for him" (Combs, Avila and Purkey, 1971, p. 92).

In teaching, then, the most important issue is not how much information or what skills a student has acquired, but what personal meanings he has acquired and the implications of these meanings for his behavior. Therefore, teaching by necessity must be individualized, since personal meanings are necessarily individual. Yet, since discovery of personal meaning requires human interaction, approaches to "individualized instruction" that continually isolate students from one another must be avoided.

What might be required are learning teams formed of students who share the same goals. Groups of five or six students could develop team objectives consistent with the individual objectives of the members of the team. The group could work together until their objectives were achieved, then disband and form new groups to achieve a new set of objectives. This would allow the teacher to interact effectively with large numbers of students, provide for the discovery of personal meanings and promote student-to-student interaction in a constructive way.[2]

Not only must learning involve human interaction, but it must be based on direct experience. Meaning drawn directly from experience is more likely to be accurate and relevant than meaning acquired abstractly or second-hand through the experiences of others. These concepts imply a "learn by doing" approach to teaching: 1. that students should have an opportunity to interact with one another so that they can learn through the interaction and check out their perceptions, 2. that they should experience, insofar as possible, what they are learning, so that the perceptions and meanings are their own, and 3. that students should be engaged in problem solving which can be directly translated into a search for personal meaning.

To emphasize the importance of "learning by doing" from this theoretical standpoint, let us examine a sophomore geography class in an inner-city high school. Traditionally students would perhaps read about mountains and rivers and some of the demographic considerations of geography. Reading would be supplemented by movies and illustrative materials such as maps and pictures. Field trips and guest speakers would be used to supplement classroom activities. A class with all of these things and an energetic, creative teacher could be a very pleasant and valuable experience.

If, in addition to these ingredients, however, the students could get personally involved with each other, the teacher and the subject matter, learning could be dramatically improved. Students should be encouraged to look at a particular aspect of geography and try to determine its meaning for them. Once they selected an area which they felt had some particular meaning for them, they should be encouraged and provided with the means by which they could test it out, check to see if the meaning indeed does exist or in some way act on the environment in a positive fashion. For example, students could form a committee to look into erosion or litter in their neighborhood or the possibilities of mountain recreation areas for students such as them. By becoming partici-

2. For additional suggestions on how teachers and students can plan together, see Carl Rogers' *Freedom to Learn* (1969) and John M. Lembo's *When Learning Happens* (1972).

pants in the environment, they acquire a personal interest in and commitment to the subject matter.

The teacher's tasks are to facilitate interaction, provide direct experiences when possible and help students select problems which are indeed problems for them. By direct involvement and experience in solving real problems, the student is able to learn gradually how he affects his environment and his life. In effect, what happens is that the boundaries between school and "real life" are lessened. See Chapter Eight for an extensive discussion of this process.

Self-Concept and Motivation

Humanistic psychology assumes a general psychological as well as physical growth force in humans. Self-enhancement is seen as the ultimate goal of every act. Indeed, it can be argued that man has no choice but to act in a self-enhancing manner (Combs, Avila and Purkey, 1971).

Schools, by and large, have not capitalized on this striving for self-enhancement as a motivating force. If curricula were so designed that students felt self-enhanced by performing the prescribed activities, the problem of motivation in schools would be largely eliminated. Also, if we accept that everything we do is done for self-enhancement, we need to recognize that teaching is primarily a matter of providing opportunities and not a question of "motivating" students through incentives, force or threats of punishment. Assuming that we always act in the most self-enhancing manner possible means we must also assume that students also act in the most self-enhancing manner possible under the circumstances. Deviant behavior can therefore be considered a result of the lack of appropriate avenues for self-enhancement.

BASIC CONCEPTS IN COMMUNICATION

Communication is often conceptualized as a process of imparting or exchanging new information, when actually this constitutes only a small part of communication. Most of communication deals with social interaction and communicating with feelings, attitudes and relationships of the persons involved. Words are excellent means of imparting new information, but they are limited in their ability to sustain social interaction. In social interaction there are always many messages, *beyond* the words, which enhance, modify and at times replace words in communicating.

Obviously what we say to our students about subject matter is not the only information we give them, and indeed may be the least important. The teacher who avoids speaking to, standing near or touching a student is communicating loudly and clearly that he does not consider the student to be of much worth, despite what that day's social studies lesson may say about equality in America. It is also apparent that we say things about the subject matter which we do not intend to say and that we say these things through means other than words. Tone of voice and posture clearly reveal attitudes toward subject matter, even if a teacher tries hard to be "objective" in his choice of words.

One of the most difficult situations to handle is receiving contradictory messages at the same time from the same person. As teachers this is likely to happen even under the best of circumstances because of the multiple demands of the role we are asked to play and the large numbers of people we communicate with simultaneously. The possibility of the wrong students getting the wrong message is excellent. Also, there is the possibility of students misreading your attitude toward the situation as being your attitude toward them. The opposite is just as true: we have very few opportunities to find out what the students are thinking and feeling, so we are likely to misread their messages. Indeed, the most harmful element in most classrooms is probably the lack of understanding on a personal level that exists between everyone.

Communication is influenced by many factors—both positive and negative. The following are some of the most common modifiers of communication.

Expectations

Think back—perhaps it was only today—when someone had promised to meet you and was late. As you stood on that street corner, becoming more and more impatient, how many people did you see who resembled the person you were expecting? We tend to perceive what we are expecting and tend to distort reality to fit our expectations. While the results of "expectation distortion" are detrimental to communication, they can be amusing.

A counselor teaching a class in family living had just finished a lesson on homosexuality when she was approached by a student. The conversation went something like this:

STUDENT: "Do you have a book on careers?"

COUNSELOR: "No, I don't think I have any books on the subject."

STUDENT: "Well, I just wanted to take a look at what I could do when I get out of high school."

COUNSELOR: "What did you say you wanted a book about?"

STUDENT: "Careers."

COUNSELOR: "What?"

STUDENT: "Careers."

COUNSELOR: "Oh, careers. I thought you said *queers.*"

As teachers we must continually guard that our expectations do not lead to distortions in our perceptions of what students are saying. Similarly, we must try to determine if students' expectations are adversely influencing their perceptions of what we are saying. Inaccuracies in communication may sometimes be humorous, but they are detrimental to learning and must be avoided if possible.

While distortions in communication cannot be eliminated, their detrimental effects can be reduced markedly through perception checks. By perception check we mean comparing our perceptions with those of the other persons involved and trying to arrive at a common understanding of what is being discussed. For example:

MS. MEYERS: "I don't understand why you are all so mad."

JAMES: "Well, you would be mad too, if you were gypped out of a credit."

MARION: "It wouldn't have been so bad if Ms. Parnelli's class didn't get credit."

MS. MEYERS: (*Perception Check*) "Let me make sure I understand. You are upset because you feel you were unfairly deprived of a credit and this was made worse because Ms. Parnelli's class got credit. Is that correct?"

CLASS MEMBERS: "That's right, and we don't think it is fair."

MS. MEYERS: (*Second part of perception check*) "That's not how I understand what happened. Maybe we can combine what we know and get it straightened out . . ."

Personal Needs

Personal needs also influence communication significantly. Maslow (1968) stresses the influence of needs on cognition and states that if we do not have to find qualities in a person or situation that will gratify our own needs we can gain a "much clearer and more insightful perception and understanding of what is there (pp. 41-42)." Maslow further states that need-motivated perception shapes things in a purposeful fashion designed to contribute to the satisfaction of the need. If, for example, we have a strong need to be liked, we may see only those cues in a situation that fill this need and ignore the hostile elements.

However, the influence of needs on communication does not stop with perception. Our responses and what we choose to respond to are also influenced by our needs. Imagine it is Friday and you are anxious to finish a unit before a three-day weekend. Attempting to be democratic, however, you ask the class if they would rather finish the unit or work on their individual projects. Two students say they want to finish the unit; two or three others mumble that they have important things to do; and most sit glumly. You say, "Well, good, I think that we should finish the unit too." Later in the teachers' lounge you comment, "I'm sure glad the class voted to finish the unit. It will make next week a lot easier." Both your perception of what happened and what you responded to were influenced by your own need to finish the unit. A perception check, such as described in the example of Ms. Meyers and her class, would help to clear up this failure in communication.

Threat

Threat has a negative effect on communication because it affects perception. We defend against threat through distortion and denial of perceptions, which in turn lead to inaccuracies in communication.

In our view the distortion or denial occurs to protect our self-concept. We tend to alter our perceptions to fit our self-concept when what we are perceiving, if admitted into our thoughts as experienced, would tend to devalue us (Samovar and Rintye, 1970). This process occurs whether we are experiencing our own behavior or that of someone else. For example, persons who feel that sex is a sign of immorality may be so threatened by sexual feelings that they will never admit them to conscious thought. Likewise, we have probably all been aware of persons who seem oblivious to obvious emotions in others. The net effect of denial or distortion in communication is usually to reduce its effectiveness and to reduce the satisfaction of the persons involved.

An interesting example of denial and distortion was provided by Uvaldo Palomares, noted educator with a special interest in communication. In a workshop attended by one of the authors recently, Dr. Palomares told of conducting research into the way teachers react to students of different skin colors. He discovered that teachers tended to talk to lighter-skinned students more often than to darker students, to touch them more often and to stand closer to them. One teacher who participated in the study could not believe that she was treating dark-skinned students differently. She saw herself as democratic, fair and totally devoid of prejudice, and vehemently denied the behavior the research revealed. In an attempt to prove that her score was inaccurate, she asked to be taught the scoring procedure and to view her videotape and score it herself. Only when confronted directly by the evidence of her behavior was she able to break through the denial that had been protecting her self-concept. Needless to say, she was quite shaken by this new knowledge about herself.

It is obvious that threat is a primary obstacle to learning. If—either because of the nature of the topic or the circumstances under which it is introduced—a student feels that the new information poses a threat to his self-concept, he will protect himself by refusing, in one way or another, to perceive the new information. This helps explain why, for example, students can be totally unchanged by twelve years of training designed to eradicate their "nonstandard" speech patterns. They interpret the language arts teachers' attempts to teach them "good" (i.e., white middle-class) language patterns as a criticism and a demand that they deny a part of themselves.

Threats to self-esteem come from many sources in the classroom. Evaluation by the teacher is among the most serious. Low grades, failure experiences and disapproval from the teacher are virtually always interpreted as a threat to the student's self-concept. For this reason, the teacher must thoughtfully consider the detrimental effects that grading can have on students and on effective learning.[3]

3. A number of alternatives to traditional grading procedures are spelled out—in a most readable fashion—in *Wad-Ja-Get? The Grading Game in American Education* by Kirschenbaum, Simon and Napier (1971).

Rejection and ridicule by other students is another significant source of threat in the classroom. Students have the potential to be cruel and insensitive on occasion—as well as to provide support and understanding to one another. Therefore, the teacher should take deliberate steps to develop in his students the interpersonal skills they need to make one another feel comfortable in the group. In Chapters Four and Five, we provide a sequence of activities to accomplish this goal and thus reduce the threat level in the classroom.

Trust

Trust is a key variable in communication because it directly influences the amount of defensiveness present and, through defensiveness, the quality of communication. Trust in a relationship is influenced by the personal security of each person, the certainty each has of the other's intentions and by the proportion of good to bad intentions assumed to exist among the participants. In turn, trust influences the amount of threat and consequently defensiveness present; a high trust level decreases defensiveness, while a low trust level increases it. Defensiveness leads to deteriorating communication through distortion and denial, as discussed previously. As a rule, any threat and attempts to control or evaluate will increase defensiveness, while spontaneous and empathic interaction will decrease it (Gibb, 1961). However, a high trust level may keep defensiveness down even though the intent of the interaction is obviously control or evaluation, while a low trust level will keep defensiveness up regardless of intentions.

A highly trusted teacher who is well-known to students may ask them to do a series of activities that are blatantly manipulative, evaluative and personally threatening without leading to distrust or defensiveness. On the other hand, a teacher who is not trusted may raise defensive behavior by a simple change in classroom activities including an offer of a day off. The influence of trust on the amount of defensiveness in a relationship is hard to exaggerate.

The importance of trust between a teacher and student and among students has led us to devise a number of trust-building exercises based on the principle that trust can be increased by increasing the personal security of each participant and by increasing the knowledge each has of the others' intentions. These are presented in detail in Chapters Four, Five and Six.

Security and Openness

A secure person is confident of his identity, his worth, and his acceptance and desirability in personal relationships. In short, he knows himself, accepts himself and feels sure of his place in the world. Security reduces defensiveness because no situation is perceived as constituting a personal threat. Adversity becomes merely a challenge, a problem to be solved or another mountain to climb, rather than a threat to personal esteem or position.

Personal security improves communication because when we are secure we are willing to "hear" more messages accurately and completely, and also because when we are secure we *send* better, more complete messages. Openness allows us to send messages about ourselves and our feelings clearly and directly so that the receiver does not have to guess at our intentions or feelings. This tends to reduce ambiguity and opportunities for distortion and probably also leads to a reduction in threat level. As Jourard (1964) states, "I think it is almost self-evident that you cannot love another person, that is, behave toward him so as to foster his happiness and growth, unless you know what he needs. And you cannot know what he needs unless he tells you (p. 3)." Openness in communication improves the quality of communication through increased information and through increased clarity in what is being said.

Messages Beyond Words

All movement and sound serves a communication purpose in addition to whatever other purpose it might have. As an illustration, let us consider a brief encounter between a professor and a student in the hallway of a university classroom building. A class has just taken place in which the student has presented a particularly good paper. As everyone files out the professor calls the student by name. The student stops and the professor walks quickly toward him. As he reaches the student, he stands close to him (some two feet away) in a relaxed manner and asks if he would have time to make a presentation to another class which could benefit from his ideas. The professor's tone of voice is friendly and low-pitched, with the stress being primarily on the personal pronouns. As the conversation ends, they part and both seem pleased.

What happened? We know a student was asked to make a presentation to a class. The context hints that this was a way of acknowledging a good job and perhaps expertise. We can infer, though, that the professor was trying also to convey personal acceptance and regard for the student as well as equality—by walking toward the student, standing close, talking in a low tone of voice and stressing the student as well as his ideas. Words were rather unimportant; the student would have received the same basic message if he had been asked to go play golf the next day.

Basically we have been talking of two languages: the language of words which is conveyed through auditory channels, and the language of body motion which is conveyed through visual channels. The extensions of these languages, such as body posture, accent, skin tone, and rate of speech, odor and other factors are also important. If we are content in everyday life with an awareness of only the words involved in communication, then we must realize that they are only a small part of the message and are not adequate to explain fully what is transpiring in social interaction.

Body language is the term applied to communication through non-verbal means by Fast (1970). Birdwhistell (1970) and Argyle (1969) present much more sophisticated analyses of this process and draw attention to the interactive aspects of different channels of communication. They point out that we communicate through symbols (words) which have meaning to the persons involved; this is the province of *linguistics*. The way the words are said also serves a communication function (tone of voice, timing of speech, accent, and other factors); this is the province of *paralinguistics. Kinesics* deals with communication through body motion such as gestures, eyebrow movements or movements of the mouth. *Parakinesics* deals with body stance, changes in the skin and general categories of behavior such as clumsiness. Birdwhistell combines paralinguistic and parakinesic modalities into a single system which he calls *paralanguage*. Although these distinctions can be very confusing, analysis of communication from this approach provides us with more useful data than would an overly simplified approach, however attractive it might be.

Before reading further, have a meal with another person and insist on placing your silverware next to his plate. Don't say anything, just continue to place your silverware next to his as if it were the natural thing to do. What happened? It's likely that you made your friend very uncomfortable because you invaded his "territory." The concepts of territoriality and proxemics have been advanced to explain human interaction which seems inadequately treated by conventional means (Hall, 1959, 1966; Ardrey, 1966; Sommer, 1969; and Argyle, 1969). The main idea in both concepts is that space and distance serve a communication function, and if we are unaware of what is involved it can be detrimental to a relationship. For example, if we insist on talking to a person at a greater distance than he is accustomed to, we can expect him to become uncomfortable and start moving toward us to reestablish a "normal" distance. On the other hand, if we insist on standing closer than eighteen inches in our conversations with casual acquaintances, we can also expect repercussions (Argyle, 1969).

The concepts of proxemics (distance) and territoriality are difficult to separate meaningfully, although at some point they do deal with different aspects of behavior. Ardrey (1966) presents an intriguing picture of human motivation and interaction in terms of man's need for control over geographic space. He contends that man's need to control a certain territory is biologically determined and cannot be eliminated. The interaction between behavior in terms of the distance at which social interaction is taking place and the human need to control a certain amount of space is especially evident if we are talking of close human interaction such as that which occurs in the classroom. We need to make sure that we do not make students uncomfortable by placing them "too" close to others or by violating their personal space. Open discussion and heightened awareness on the teacher's part are the best safeguards against problems in communication arising from space and distance.

Meaning and Understanding

The assumption that words have meaning, and consequently that it is important to use words with the correct meaning in the correct way if we want to communicate, causes many problems in communication. In contrast to the assumption that words have meaning, we hold that meanings are personal and assigned to words only by the people who use them. "Words do not have meaning—people do (Berlo, 1960, p. 174)." For example, let us consider the meaning of two sentences:

> Rte opu sennoklaw?
> My mother is tall.

In all likelihood, the first sentence doesn't make sense to you; it certainly doesn't to us. There is nothing in our experience symbolized by these words; that is, no meaning has been assigned to them. In the second sentence, we assume we know what the words mean because we have had many experiences symbolized by these words. But this is precisely where the problem starts. We have not all had the same experiences and we are using identical words to stand for similar but *not* identical experiences. This sloppy arrangement is necessary since no two people have exactly the same experiences, and no one ever has the same experience twice. Nevertheless, it means that communication can never be considered perfect and no one can ever expect to fully understand another, since the meaning which one person has assigned to a word will not be identical to the meaning assigned by the other person.

Psychological Distance and Meaning

We have proposed five categories of psychological distance in terms of meaning: Theoretical, Abstract, Objective, Personal Cognitive and Personal Experiencing (pp. 268-274). In terms of psychological distance, Theoretical is the most distant and Personal Experiencing is the closest.

For example, if we asked you for the theoretical meaning of love, you might say, "Love is the mutual attraction and feeling of caring that accounts for family solidarity and the formation of societies. It is ultimately explained by the chemical reaction that occurs between living organisms who have very similar reactions to stimuli with high survival value." However inadequate, we now have a theoretical explanation of love. If we asked you to define love, you would more likely define it abstractly: "Love is a feeling of tenderness and caring so strong we are willing to put another's welfare before our own." This is an abstraction, although it may be based on your own feelings and experiences. If in our pushy way we said, "Yes, but when have you seen love?" you might reply, "When Martha stayed up all night making a dress for her girls to wear in the Christmas play, even though the dresses were worn only ten minutes." And we might press further, "But how about *you;* don't you feel love?" To which you might reply, "Yes, every time I see my little boy coming home from school, I just want to hold and hug him, and I feel really glad."

When describing Martha's actions you were giving us an *objective* meaning; that is, a meaning attached to a particular behavior that could be observed by others and agreed or disagreed with. When you described your feelings, you were telling us about a *personal* meaning as you *experience* it. It is impossible to say that one of these meanings is more correct than another.

The basic difference in the preceding definitions is one of psychological distance. Theoretical explanations are the fabric by which we unite bits of experience into comprehensive explanations. Psychologically they are impersonal and distant. Theories, abstractions, and objective referents can be verified by opinions of others and are thus open to consensual agreement. But personal meanings are open to *our* scrutiny only; *we* are the sole judge.

The question of personal meaning seems to be at the bottom of much misunderstanding, difficulty and ineffectiveness in education. So often we miss the meaning the student intended to convey or his meaning is simply beyond our experience. The whole question of relevance could be restated in terms of personal meaning. Students are finding it hard to find a significant personal meaning in "subject matter." But the problem has another side. We often speak as if the subject matter has the only "real" meaning and the students' personal meanings ("opinions") are irrelevant or secondary at best. The effect over a long period of time, especially for students with different experiential backgrounds from the teacher, is to drive them away into a world where their meanings are nearer those of their environment and accepted as having worth.

THE DYNAMICS OF HUMAN RELATIONSHIPS

Ultimately the goal of communication is human interaction. Communication makes interaction possible and provides the participants with a means by which they can affect each other. The adequacy of communication determines the extent to which each person is able to send and receive messages accurately and completely. Therefore, it is obvious that the quality of communication influences the quality of the interaction. However, good communication does not guarantee good human relations.

The characteristics of interactions which determine their quality are difficult to identify. However, it is becoming apparent that we have a choice in the way we deal with people. We can exploit them and treat them as nonhumans, or we can love them and treat them as our brothers. The nature of our future existence depends on our choice. It is a particularly crucial choice for teachers.

Research indicates that the average teacher engages in as many as 100 interpersonal interactions each day (Jackson, 1968, p. 11). If we combine this with the amount of time spent in school, the results are staggering: school people—teachers, students, administrators—spend about 1,000 hours per year interacting with one another. Our relationships in school are important—if only in terms of sheer quantity! Man's search for the key to human relationships has yielded equivocal results. Certainly, as long as there are wars we cannot say we have an answer. Yet there seems to be hope in some of the insights of research in social science and in the thoughts of philosophers such as Martin Buber.

I-Thou and I-It

Buber (1958) describes two basic types of relationships: *I-Thou* and *I-It*. The I-It is the typical subject-object relationship. It is the usual way of dealing with people or objects in terms of their usefulness, category or connection. I-It is not a mutual interhuman relationship. A necessary condition is the subject-object dichotomy, in which the person (I) remains distinct from the other (It) and views the other as necessarily separate from himself. This type of relationship necessarily considers the object of the viewer in terms of the utility possessed for the viewer. That is, the implication in this type of relationship is that one person exists for the use or satisfaction of another. We are, in effect, tools or good for the benefit of another; this is the normal relationship between most people. The obvious alienation and lack of identification implied in this arrangement is often overlooked or passed off as reality. The I-It relationship, while not intrinsically bad, and necessary in everyday life in order to transact the routine business of existence is, nevertheless, at the base of all exploitive relationships.

In contrast to the I-It relationship, Buber (1958 and 1965) proposes an I-Thou relationship—one which is entered into with the whole being and which "is characterized by mutuality, directness, presentness, intensity, and ineffability" (Friedman, 1965, p. 12). I-Thou is a participatory relationship in which one does not regard another person or thing as a category or tool but as a being of essence. The other is seen as the transcending of distance through a living relationship which at least momentarily allows one to open and admit another. It need not, and cannot, last forever; but to be human one must take part in I-Thou relationships. I-Thou is not restricted to interhuman relationships, but as Buber (1965) states, the interhuman relationship is unique: "the participation of both partners is in principle indispensable" (p. 75). Interhuman implies the encounter of one person with another. It is a meeting in which the participants are confirmed as humans and the interaction between them is uniquely human. The overall meaning is to be found in what the persons mutually live together.

We could explain I-Thou relationships between persons as a matter of psychological functioning of a person or persons. But it seems to be more, as Buber (1965) states: "When two men converse together, the psychological is certainly an important part of the situation ... the hidden accompaniment to the conversation ... whose meaning is to be found neither in one of the two partners nor in both together, but only in their dialogue itself, in this 'between' which they live together" (p. 75). Human interaction and communication are the keys to man's fulfillment and existence; man is inextricably bound up in man and, as Buber states, the meaning is to be found in the 'between' we live together.

Interdependence

Interdependence is different from both exploitation and dependence. Exploitation implies using someone to his or her detriment, and dependence implies being helped to our detriment. In interdependence, the welfare of one is bound up in the welfare of all. The person who is being helped expects to help in return, but more important, he expects the helper to benefit by helping. Also, the helper expects himself to benefit by helping. The situation is one in which it is impossible to separate the welfare of one from another. The intentions of everyone are considered positive, and psychological interaction therefore becomes mutually enhancing.[4] Interdependence, from this view, thus becomes both a product of positive interpersonal interaction and a condition facilitating positive interaction.

The classroom should be a small community of learners engaged in activities particularly suited to meeting their learning needs. This community is one in which *all* participants share in *all* necessary functions. We envision a classroom of active participants who are all responsible for themselves as well as for the contributions they can make to the welfare of others. Decisions should be made by those most directly concerned with the decision and having the best data that can be brought to bear in the decision-making process. All participants have equal rights as persons, although they may have different functional roles. Students and teachers move from role to role as necessary to most effectively approach the problems involved in living close together and to accomplish the tasks involved in purposeful learning.

Conditions Which Foster Growth

Helping relationships are formed on a broad base of facilitative conditions (Carkhuff and Berenson, 1967; Carkhuff, 1969). These conditions provide the base from which other helping activities are launched. Generally recognized facilitative conditions are presented in the classic paper by Rogers (1958) and elaborated in slightly different form by Carkhuff and Berenson (1967). The core conditions are *empathy, positive regard, congruence* and to a certain extent *concreteness of expression.*

Empathy means to understand another person from his or her own frame of reference and to be able to feel with him. This ability to understand another well enough to see the world as he sees it seems essential in helping relationships. We need to listen to see how it looks and feels to another so that it is "as if" we were there. Empathy can be

4. See Harris (1969) for an extensive treatment of this concept.

approached intellectually as the ability to predict another's feeling or response or as a close feeling with another.[5]

Positive regard has been known by many terms, including *unconditional positive regard, respect* and *caring.* The concept as we see it refers to a concern for the person because he *is* a person. This caring cannot be altered, enhanced or diminished by what the person does. That is, there are no conditions by which the person must live in order for us to care for him or care more for him. This caring or concern carries with it an inherent respect for the person as he is, irrespective of his actions. It does not mean that we have to put up with anything the person does. It simply means, "I respect you as a person and care for you as a person; nothing you can do will ever change that. I reserve the right, however, to expect you to intervene in my life sphere in a way that is mutually self-enhancing."

Congruence means, simply, communicating to the other person what you genuinely mean and feel at the moment. Genuineness has been used as a synonym for congruence because to many people it conveys the essence of the concept better than the word congruence. Being genuine in a relationship means that we are being ourselves without elaboration or facade or withholding. Does it mean I tell a child that I am mad at him when I am? Yes. But won't this damage the child? What makes you think that he doesn't already know you are mad? We communicate in many ways other than verbal, a point discussed earlier. Being genuine means that all our messages say about the same thing. The message thus becomes easier to read and we avoid placing the receiver in the dilemma of receiving contradictory messages.

There is less evidence to support concreteness as a core facilitative condition than in the case of the other three conditions, but there is sufficient evidence to consider it and call for more research. Concreteness means saying what we mean as concretely and specifically as possible. Communication is facilitated by using concrete words that are not likely to be misunderstood. It also means that we try to use words that are more likely to be in the vocabulary of the person to whom we are speaking. Hence, to a group of third-graders or salesmen, it is better to say, "Darnit, I mean it!" than, "On the issues presently being considered, I intend to remain adamant."

5. See Dixon and Morse (1961) for elaboration on this theme.

The Teacher as a Person

When people are relating to each other, their personal characteristics cannot be separated from the characteristics of their relationship. A case could probably be made for saying that it is the people who count, and not any particular aspect of the communication or interaction, but this is probably no more helpful than saying the relationship is what counts.[6] In teaching, subject matter knowledge and teaching skill are obviously also central variables, but the fallacy in looking for different skills or variables still remains. The various functions cannot be separated from the person performing them. The effect of what is done is invariably modified by the personal impact of the person performing the action. Two teachers can do exactly the same thing and get quite different results.

Thus we are faced with a dilemma to which there are no simple answers. If we consider teaching a mystery and say that there are born teachers and nonteachers, we are saying that a person cannot learn to be a teacher—and we are thus faced with a dead-end situation. Our task would then be merely to find the "born" teachers and encourage them to apply for the job. On the other hand, if we presume that teaching is a series of techniques that can be learned precisely, we are ignoring the interactional aspects of teaching; and we know from experience and research that teaching is just not that simple (Mason and Blumberg, 1969). The answer seems to lie somewhere between these two black-and-white extremes. Our position is that the quality of the interaction between teacher and student is the critical variable but not the only variable. To a certain extent, some people are "naturally" able to establish relationships based on empathy, congruence and unconditional positive regard. And to a certain extent, prospective teachers can be trained in the skills necessary for establishing this kind of relationship.

A teacher attempting the approach to education we are advocating will find the demands of the task to be quite different from those encountered in the usual approach to teaching. Perhaps the characteristic most necessary to implement this approach is that of personal freedom. By personal freedom we mean a freedom to be oneself in a role-free manner. This doesn't mean that one does not have a role as a

6. Perhaps the best attempt to combine these positions has been made by Boy and Pine (1971) in a very full, short treatise primarily focused on the person of the teacher. Other good works on this topic include Moustakas (1966) and Jersild (1955).

teacher or student, but it means that one has to learn to interact first as a person and secondly as a teacher, and further that this interaction is based on the demands of the situation and our perception of them at the time. It means that we need to give up the security of knowing what is right based on what the role implies for our behavior. It also means giving up the security of being able to rely on external direction or authority for the basis for our decisions and behavior. Without this personal freedom no structural changes in schools or changes in curriculum will make basic changes in the educational process. Freedom must first be present in the people involved if actual changes are to take place. Creating freedom, or perhaps more accurately the illusion of freedom, through curriculum or schedule changes does not materially affect what happens unless the teacher has the personal freedom to act differently. If we are concerned with changes in interpersonal interactions, these must come about by changes instituted directly by each person involved. Even if a teacher has the sanction of external authority, he is still not free to make changes until he has the personal freedom which will allow him to make the necessary changes.

There is the potential for considerable, personal threat involved in close, interpersonal interactions. Stepping out of the role of teacher in relating with students and colleagues and beginning to relate personally can be extremely threatening. The safeguards and distance provided by relating as a teacher first and a person second are suddenly removed. Teachers contemplating an interactive approach to teaching should expect some time for adjustment and to have to handle unexpected threat and anxiety aroused by interactions that would not likely have occurred in a more impersonal approach to teaching.

For example, in a true participatory decision-making process, a teacher may suddenly find that his own opinions are no more important than anyone else's. However laudable this sounds theoretically, it is a rude shock to the teacher who has been granted the authority position for years. Secondly, as students' independence increases, the good feeling that teachers get from people needing them is suddenly diminished drastically. One of the authors remembers vividly a scene in a teachers' lounge when a teacher who had been away on an accreditation team visit returned for the first time. He taught in a manner very similar to that described here, and his students had acquired considerable personal independence in their class. He related that he was eager to be back and see how things were going. He said that his class had greeted him warmly, but then with some anguish and some levity he reported that they were not particularly relieved to see him back and that they actually had done just as well when he was gone and did not particularly need him. The mixture of pride and of nervous laughter was obvious in his comments.

The teacher's personal security can also be threatened by receiving feedback from students for the first time regarding his relationship with them. It can be very gratifying if the relationship is what the teacher expected it to be, but it can be very threatening if the teacher is not used to this kind of frank, open discussion of interpersonal relationship. Also as students become free to interact, more and more of their inner doubts, fears and emotions surface, and these can be threatening, especially if they are feelings of inadequacy, hostility or unaccustomed love. If the teacher is too threatened by these emotions and their open expression, it is doubtful that a highly constructive, interpersonal interaction can be maintained.

The teacher must ensure that he or she as a person will feel comfortable and be effective in the kinds of interpersonal relationships required by interactive education. We are not implying that the teacher be some sort of psychological superman. Rather, we are stating that the teacher must first of all have developed the personal freedom to act independently of a role or predetermined course of action. The teacher must be able to make judgments and accept responsibility for these judgments. In the process he must be able to engage in close, constructive interpersonal experiences without becoming insecure and threatened to the point of diminishing personal effectiveness. Secondly, specific interpersonal relationship skills and communication skills are necessary in addition to the personal qualities of the teacher. These skills, involving empathy, genuineness and other communication and interpersonal skills, can be learned and learned systematically (Carkhuff, 1969).

This is not to say that a teacher whose personal characteristics are antithetical to the skills involved will be able to acquire the skills without changing. But it does mean that the skills can be specifically practiced, studied and learned. The process of making these changes and acquiring these skills need not be an interminably long process or a particularly complicated one.

References   2

ARDREY, R. *The territorial imperative.* New York: Atheneum, 1966.

ARGYLE, M. *Social interaction.* New York: Atherton Press, 1969.

BERLO, D.K. *The process of communication.* New York: Holt, 1960.

BIRDWHISTELL, R.L. *Kinesics and context.* Philadelphia: University of Pennsylvania Press, 1970.

BLAKE, R., MOUTON, J.S., BARNES, L.B., and GREINER, L.E. Breakthrough in organization development. In R.T. Golembiewski and A. Blumberg (Ed.), *Sensitivity training and the laboratory approach.* Itasca, Ill.: R.E. Peacock, 1970.

BOY, A.V., and PINE, G.J. *Expanding the self: Personal growth for teachers.* Dubuque, Iowa: Brown, 1971.

BUBER, M. *I and thou.* Trans. by R.E. Smith. New York: Scribner's, 1958.

BUBER, M. *The knowledge of man.* London: George Allen and Unwin, Ltd., 1965.

CARKHUFF, R.R. *Helping and human relations.* Vols. I and II. New York: Holt, 1969.

CARKHUFF, R.R., and BERENSON, B.G. *Beyond counseling and therapy.* New York: Holt, 1967.

COMBS, A.W., AVILA, D.L., and PURKEY, W.W. *Helping relationships: Basic concepts for the helping professions.* Boston: Allyn and Bacon, 1971.

COMBS, A.W., and SYNGG, D. *Individual behavior: A perceptual approach to behavior.* (Rev. ed.) New York: Harper, 1959.

DIXON, W.R., and MORSE, W.C. The prediction of teaching performance: Empathic potential. *Journal of Teacher Education,* 1961, **12**, 322-329.

FAST, J. *Body language.* New York: Evans, 1970.

FRANKL, V.E. *Psychotherapy and existentialism.* New York: Simon and Schuster, 1967.

FRIEDMAN, M. Introduction. In M. BUBER, *The knowledge of man.* London: George Allen and Unwin, Ltd., 1965.

GIBB, J.R. Defensive communication. *Journal of Communication,* 1961, **11**, 141-148.

HALL, E.T. *The silent language.* New York: Doubleday, 1959.

HALL, E.T. *The hidden dimension.* New York: Doubleday, 1966.

HARRIS, T.A. *I'm O.K., you're O.K.* New York: Harper, 1969.

JACKSON, P.W. *Life in classrooms.* New York: Holt, 1968.

JERSILD, A.T. *When teachers face themselves.* New York: Teachers College Press, 1955.

JOURARD, S.M. *The transparent self.* New York: Van Nostrand, 1964.

KIRSCHENBAUM, H., SIMON, S.B., and NAPIER, R.W. *Wad-ja-get? The grading game in American education.* New York: Hart, 1971.

LABENNE, W.D., and GREENE, B.I. *Educational implications of self-concept theory.* Pacific Palisades, Calif.: Goodyear Publishing, 1969.

LEMBO, J.M. *When learning happens.* New York: Schocken Books, 1972.

MASLOW, A.H. *Toward a psychology of being.* Princeton: Van Nostrand, 1968.

MASON, J., and BLUMBERG, A. Perceived educational value of the classroom and teacher-pupil interpersonal relationships. *Journal of Secondary Education,* 1969, **44,** 135-138.

MOUSTAKAS, C. *The authentic teacher.* Cambridge: Doyle, 1966.

OTTO, H.A. New light on human potential. *Saturday Review,* 1969, **52** (51), 14-17.

PURKEY, W.W. *Self concept and school achievement.* Englewood Cliffs, N.J.: Prentice-Hall, 1970.

REIS, P. Talk to 1972 Denver Vocational Guidance Institute, Denver, Colorado.

ROGERS, C.R. *On becoming a person.* Boston: Houghton Mifflin, 1961.

ROGERS, C.R. *Freedom to learn.* Columbus: Merrill, 1969.

ROGERS, C.R. The characteristics of a helping relationship. *Personnel and Guidance Journal,* 1958, **37,** 6-16.

RUESCH, J., and WELDON, K. *Nonverbal communication.* Berkeley: University of California Press, 1956.

SAMOVAR, L.A., and RINTYE, E.D. Interpersonal communication: Some working principles. In R.S. Cathcart and L.A. Samovar, *Small group communication.* Dubuque, Iowa: Brown, 1970.

SKINNER, B.F. *The technology of teaching.* New York: Appleton-Century-Crofts, 1968.

SOMMER, R. *Personal space.* Englewood Cliffs, N.J.: Prentice-Hall, 1969.

3

GROUP DEVELOPMENT IN THE CLASSROOM

Group ·development in the classroom is perhaps the least studied and understood aspect of schooling practices. One of the reasons is that in the traditional approach to teaching very few groups actually develop in the classroom. Instead, classrooms are usually filled with aggregates of students and one teacher. Research has demonstrated that aggregates and groups produce different types of classroom learning and behavior (Gage, 1963; Minuchin, 1965). For our purposes, an *aggregate* is defined as a gathering of persons who maintain interpersonal distance, do not directly examine their interpersonal interaction, do not have a common task and are not interdependent.

A *group* differs from an aggregate in several ways: 1. groups have close personal interaction, 2. groups examine their interaction whenever appropriate, 3. groups have a group goal in addition to individual goals, 4. group members are interdependent in group tasks and often in areas outside of the specific purpose of the group, 5. group members tend to emphasize a "we" feeling when referring to the group. Although a more precise definition would be necessary if we were contemplating research, the preceding characteristics will serve to form a base for the succeeding discussion.

Groups have not been the rule in traditional schooling practices because of the emphasis on the teacher as an information dispenser and students as information receptacles. This approach has also commonly emphasized individual accomplishments, and de-emphasized cooperative endeavors. The result has been a highly competitive system which emphasizes individual rather than group attainment.

Theoretical speculations regarding group development are numerous, but research has been scant. The reasons for this at first surprising situation become clear after a moment's reflection; group development is a fascinating subject, but one next to impossible to research except through costly, time-consuming observational techniques. Nevertheless, some provocative and useful research has been done. Anderson (1969) reviewed five studies related to group development which have added to understanding of the stages through which groups progress. Watson (1969) presents a thorough, well-documented study, in which group communications are analyzed in relation to group development. Boyd (1967) was able to show that groups of elementary school students also move through theoretically predictable phases. The concept of developmental trends in groups has been supported by Bales and Strodbeck (1960), Philip and Dunphy (1959), and Fisher (1970). In addition, Lubin and Zuckerman (1967) provide partial support for the contention of developmental trends in training groups. Runkel *et al.* (1971) were able to support Tuckman's (1965) two-stage theory of group development using classroom groups.

The preceding studies are difficult to interpret, but promising. Individually they do not have very great significance for education, but collectively they demonstrate that the concept of developmental stages in groups can be empirically validated. Further, they indicate that specific verbal, affective and decision-making behaviors can be associated with specific stages in group development. More convincingly the indications are that these developmental trends hold in general across different small group types and participant age levels. The implications of these studies and others which support the developmental concept of group interaction is that group interaction at any particular time cannot be completely explained or interpreted without taking developmental factors into consideration.

BEGINNINGS AND ENDINGS: LIFE CYCLES IN GROUPS

"To every thing there is a season, and a time to every purpose under the heaven:

A time to be born, and a time to die; a time to plant, and a time to pluck up that which is planted . . ."

—Read by Carl Hayden upon his retirement from the United States Senate.

As Carl Hayden so poignantly stated at his retirement, there is a time for everything in life, however difficult it may be. And so it is in groups. They begin, more or less serve their purpose and end. Some seem to

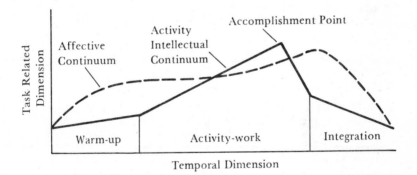

FIGURE 1. CHARACTERISTICS OF CLASSROOM ACTIVITY

have only a beginning and an end with no purpose. Others, like Carl Hayden, seem to serve usefully interminably, but all eventually end. The two most difficult phases in a group's life are the beginning and ending. The beginning is fraught with anxiety of what is to be in the group and with fears of success and failure; the ending is a mixture of regret over leaving and anxiety over a new beginning.

Group life runs a nearly perfect parallel to all life in the nature of its development. Hollander (1969) discusses the cyclical concept of group life and contends that there is a high degree of similarity between group development, especially as expressed in psychodrama, and almost all other human activity. He proposes three basic periods in a group's life or any human activity which are particularly important to teachers and education. He also proposes two continua which are of considerable importance in classroom or study groups. Figure 1 is an integration of Hollander's concepts derived from psychodrama groups and our concepts derived from classroom discussion and work groups.

As can easily be seen, the resemblance between the two curves and a normal curve of distribution is very high. Looking at the temporal dimension from the warm-up to the integration phase first will allow discussion of the other characteristics in terms of this dimension.

Warm-Up Phase

The warm-up phase is the period of time necessary for students to become accustomed to, and tuned into a new situation; it also includes the time necessary to become physically and psychologically prepared

TABLE 1. WARM-UP PHASE ACTIVITIES

Stage 1	Stage 2	Stage 3
Separation from involvement in previous activity	Becoming accustomed to new activity and tuning into situation	Becoming involved in and preparing for new activity

for the ensuing activity. Although from a temporal standpoint these activities are not discrete, for purposes of illustration the warm-up phase can be subdivided into three parts, as Table 1 indicates.

The warm-up phase in education is often referred to as "getting them settled down." However, this is only a small part of the warm-up phase—the first part—and having students settled down does not mean they are warmed up to work. It may only mean that their involvement with a previous activity has diminished, or that it is of a passive and not easily observable nature. In any event, before they are ready to work, students need to become accustomed to the new situation and to become primarily responsive to the stimuli in the new situation—that is, to be "tuned in." This tuning in is very important because unaccustomed situations tend to raise anxieties and produce distorted perceptions for a variety of reasons. The familiar question, "Do you get the picture?" represents a layman's approach to a perceptual check to make sure the listener is responding to the appropriate gestalt.

The final portion of the warm-up phase is of a very diverse nature because it is often the final step before actually starting the main activity. Therefore, what occurs in the involvement and preparation stage of warm-up depends a great deal on the nature of the ensuing activities. Students may, for example, sharpen pencils, check directions, work sample problems or get necessary materials. Often it becomes evident that students have not completed the warm-up phase before activity begins when they engage in inappropriate and disruptive behavior which is so only because other students no longer need to ask, "What page?" and borrow pencils and paper.

Often teachers feel frustrated and angry when students do not get involved as quickly as they want them to. (We know of one college professor who calmly started to take off his shirt in front of his class in order to get their attention!) There seems to be no point in getting perturbed at students; for all practical purposes some warm-up is inevitable. The first task is to divert students' attention from what they *were* doing. As the man said when people commented on how hard it must be to get his mule to obey if he had to hit him over the head with a two-by-four each time: "He is very obedient, and obeys even whispered commands, but it is hard to get his attention." So it is with classes. The games and exercises found in this book can be very effective warm-up devices. Generally activities or strong stimuli such as brief recordings, pictures or puzzles are effective if they are not intrinsically so interesting that students don't want to leave them. If the stimulus is directly associated with the day's activities, so much the better, but this is not necessary—the function of the stimulus is to distract the students from what was on their minds when they came into the room. After the students have been distracted from previous activities and "tuned in" to the current focus, they are ready to become involved in the day's activities.

Activity Phase

Getting students to work is a perpetual struggle for some teachers. It seems that while this is a major goal of many teachers, and one they stress the most, it still remains a problem. It doesn't seem possible to divide the activity phase with the same degree of confidence with which the warm-up phase was divided. One reason is that progress of the activity phase depends to a great extent on the task being performed. However, two stages seem identifiable and one point during the activity phase usually stands out. The stages are outlined in Table 2.

Although these stages will not always occur, or be pronounced, during any one class period, they are typical of the activity phase. Generally the duration of the building stage (stage 1) will be longer by far than the consolidation stage (stage 2). The accomplishment point (see Figure 1) is usually of short duration and consists primarily of an awareness that the task is going to be accomplished during the prescribed limits or that a different course of action will be necessary. In either case, the sense of urgency and immediacy declines and activity takes on a more relaxed pace. Most teachers are well aware of these stages in the activity phase and recognize them easily if the activity itself

TABLE 2. ACTIVITY PHASE STAGES

Stage 1	*Stage 2*
Organizing work, outlining activities, followed by initial productive work; work toward goal is in progress. Product-related activity is the rule-some group maintenance as necessary to proceed. Divergent and then convergent.	This is a convergent summarizing stage. Results are consolidated. Review and polish. Clean-up. Consolidate gains.

does not disguise them or prevent them from occurring. The final stage is usually one of wrap-up and consolidation or checking, and is usually of short duration.

As you can see in Figure 1, the work continuum and the affect continuum are not identical. In the usual class group it is easier to get task-related emotion than it is to get task-related activity. Also, in the typical class, task-related activity is stressed more than task-related affect, so that there is typically more task-related activity than affect. The most relevant concept here, however, is that the emotional involvement continues to build after the task has been completed, or at least remains very high. This means that for students to be ready for another task, they must have time to dissipate the emotion built up regarding the previous task.

The main advantage of being aware of these stages is knowing that students do not respond well if they are asked to do activities that do not correspond to the stage they are in, or to start a new activity if a fairly significant accomplishment point has not yet been reached. Therefore, if teachers have several tasks they want accomplished, it would generally be to their advantage to schedule the most complex or lengthy activity last.

Integration Phase

The integration phase is a troublesome period for teachers because often they do not have a rationale for it beyond summarizing the content of

TABLE 3. INTEGRATION PHASE

Stage 1	Stage 2	Stage 3
Reporting personal meaning and checking perceptions of activity with others in group or entire class	Summary and pulling together; may include clarification	Discussing significance of activity for participants' future; also introduction of future activity

the day's activity. As in the case of the warm-up phase, the integration phase has three distinct stages, as Table 3 indicates. Also, as in the warm-up phase, these stages tend to overlap; the overlap is generally less, however, and more sporadic.

The integration phase is critical, although it is often ignored in the interest of covering more subject matter or finishing a project. The nature of the integration phase is often misunderstood; it is easy to consider it as a termination phase, but it is more than merely termination. This phase includes concentration on personal meaning and clarification of the personal meaning and perception of activities. This means that more than a simple summary or recap is indicated. There needs to be time to think and compare impressions before it is wrapped up. If this thinking and clarification are not complete, much of the value of the activities may be lost.

The degree to which the integration phase is completed successfully seems to be related to the amount of satisfaction students have with a day's activities. The reason for this, apparently, is that students often do not obtain from their participation a clear or complete picture regarding the relevance of a task. Often no connection at all is made, and sometimes the connection is erroneous. "I don't see what good that will do us," or, "That was sure a waste of time!" are not infrequent student comments. If a classroom has open discussion norms so that these questions can be dealt with openly, students can be helped to see meaning in the activities or their future usefulness. On the other hand, the discussion may reveal that the task *was* a waste of time, a fact which may also be important to know.

Life Cycles in the Classroom

Consideration of the overall concept of a life cycle for human activities raises several other points. One is perhaps obvious: all activities have a life cycle which is imposed upon the life cycle of longer-term activities. In school, for example, the life cycle for the day's activities is imposed on those for the week, and so forth. This is the source of many day-to-day difficulties which are often misunderstood: the class that just never seems to settle down, or other teachers thinking students you had no trouble with are impossible.

Consider this: the teacher before you teaches social studies through simulations, community projects and heated discussions. Furthermore, he takes pride in having exciting classes and turning on his students. Then you get them the next period, in Latin. Problems are inevitable. Or, what about the students who always do their geography in math and math in homemaking? These problems make sense if we look at them in terms of where students are in their life cycles regarding each activity. The swinging social studies teacher is sending his students out of class at the peak of their activity phase. However inadequate, they are going to go through an integration phase. In this case, it will probably occur in your classroom. As a solution you might consider team teaching or charging him for completing his class. The explanation of the students' doing their work in the wrong class is more complex, but probably involves personal life cycles which they have worked out for each subject that do not coincide with the school's schedule.

Student rebellion against some tasks or teachers and apparently contradictory acceptance of others may also be related to life cycle considerations. Some teachers instinctively or deliberately take these considerations into account in their teaching activities, while others do not. Student satisfaction and sense of accomplishment are also closely related to the adequate completion of life cycles in activities. An awareness of life cycles can also be helpful in judging the appropriateness of the time allowed for particular programs or sequences. One of the biggest problems is often that two hours would be an ideal time when only one is available. A final thought is that interrupting a cycle in which students are very involved, or simply not allowing time to complete it, may arouse anger or anxiety: this emotion can generally be dealt with more adequately if it is recognized for what it is and not attributed to other reasons.

STAGES IN GROUP DEVELOPMENT

In the discussion on life cycles in groups we were considering phenomena which are present in all life activities and which can be expected to occur in predictable cycles. That is, each class period, each unit of work or each discussion was considered to have its own cycle. In this section we will be discussing a very similar process but one which is by no means identical. The life cycle of a group will share many characteristics with the stages in a group's development, but the two are not the same. Group development follows a developmental course somewhat like that of an individual person, starting with infancy and growing to maturity. Along the way, presumably, irreversible changes take place, and life style and skills are developed. Progressive or cumulative changes are the prime concern, and not cyclical occurrences, during the development process.

While we can say with assurance that any group will have a relatively complete, even if abbreviated life cycle, the same cannot be said about developmental stages. In fact, most groups do not progress beyond the very first stages. Life cycles will occur whether we like it or not; we can improve them and use them to our advantage, but we cannot eliminate them. If we accept birth, we might as well accept death because birth and death are indivisible—in between there may or may not be growth or activity but there will be an in-between. Group devel-

opment deals with the in-between in a group's formation and dissipa-
tion. Little may develop in the in-between, as has been the case of some
committees on which the authors have served, but what happens may be
understood and facilitated through an understanding of the process.

A large number of theoretical formulations exist regarding the
stages groups go through. There is some similarity in these formulations
but they are by no means redundant. About the only stage on which all
agree on is the beginning stage. One of the reasons for differences in the
theories is that they have been formed using different types of groups as
referents and different types of data. Another reason is that for the most
part the theoretical concepts have been developed from informal observation or participation in groups. Because of the limited usefulness of
presenting a large number of models of group development, each developed for a specific purpose, our presentation will be focused on a
general model developed specifically for classroom use.

Several general models have been proposed elsewhere; Mahler
(1969), Schmuck and Schmuck (1971), and Hansen (1971) are examples.
However, these models are not sufficiently developed to provide a thorough framework for teachers. The model proposed here is a seven-stage,
three-dimensional model (see Table 4). The stages refer to progressive
changes in the way the group functions. The dimensions are those
dimensions or group characteristics from which we determine the stage
of group development and which we feel are most influential in determining the overall functioning of the group.

The following outline may help place the discussion of the model in
context.

Stage 1: Beginning

Stage one is characterized more by the need for orientation than anything else, and much of the activity centers around this need (see Bales
and Strodbeck, 1951; Tuckman, 1965; Fisher, 1970). Initially, the orientation need takes the form of questions regarding belonging. (Schutz
(1958) uses the term *inclusion* to designate this phase of his three-stage
theory which characterizes the next step as *control* and the final step as
affection.) Some of the first questions are, "Is this geography?" "Is Mrs.
Shantymeyer teaching this section?" "Is this Mr. Fiero's section of metal
working?" In other words, these are the most basic questions of orienta-

TABLE 4. STAGES OF GROUP DEVELOPMENT

	Interaction Pattern	Process & Focus	Communication
STAGE 1. BEGINNING	Randomness or leader-centered; pairing & sub-grouping	Confusion; searching; protective & seeking allies	Guarded; constricted; topic- & situation-centered
STAGE 2. NORM DEVELOPMENT	Erratic, tentative; usually leader-centered or leader-directed	Testing limits; seeking answers; trial balloons; leadership	Security-oriented; situation-centered; little self-disclosure
STAGE 3. CONFLICT	Erratic; centers on one person &/or pair, depending on issue; or random	Confrontive; hostile; anxious; conflict	One-way; distorted; labeling; some self-disclosure, usually in anger or retaliation
STAGE 4. TRANSITION	Less erratic; patterns develop; less centered on leader	Vacillate between task & group concerns; focus on new norms & personal feelings	Self-disclosure & feedback-more open & less labeling
STAGE 5. PRODUCTION	Based on task at hand; usually work-dictated	Cooperation; group leadership; group is a *group; we* identify	Open, within limits of disclosure, feedback & intimacy norms
STAGE 6. AFFECTION	Group-centered but moving to individual in focus	I-Thou interaction often; intimacy norms changed to more intimacy	More self-disclosure & risk; positive feedback
STAGE 7. ACTUALIZATION	Pattern appropriate to task; usually group-centered	Flexible; moves from task to person to group as appropriate	Open, constructive, accurate-based on *being* rather than needs

tion. The student is trying to find out if he belongs here. Often a very embarrassed student finds that he has been in the wrong class for a day or two—evidence of the importance of these simple questions.

Once the very basic questions of orientation are answered, the students start asking the same type of question in more sophisticated ways. Questions of compatibility soon come up: "Gee, I wish Suzy weren't in this class"; "Rick is going to raise the curve, I just know he is!"; "These kids sure seem smart and act like they know this already. Maybe I should transfer to a slower section"; "Mrs. Hackenschidt doesn't look as bad as the kids say she is." These are questions of belonging regarding compatibility and competence. They are very important, and students often spend a great deal of their energy in the first weeks, to the dismay of teachers and counselors, trying to ease their doubts and find more compatible classes.

After the questions based on initial impressions come the long-range questions: "I wonder what this class is going to be like," or, "I wonder if she is going to be really tough." These questions are usually followed by the same type of questions regarding others in the classroom. What the other students are like and what they think of each other become central concerns. All students wonder how they fit with the others and how well they will be accepted. The class is an aggregate at this point and has not had an opportunity to develop a social structure or norms for interaction. Consequently, students are searching for cues regarding appropriate behavior and others' reactions to them.

During this initial observation period students will be forming impressions of the class and of one another, and drawing conclusions from these impressions. The amount of trust present at this time will have a great influence on how the students perceive one another and the total situation. The first reactions and interpersonal interactions will be constricted and guarded, but if the trust level is high interactions will open up. Trust is perhaps the key ingredient needed for constructive interaction to occur at this point (Gibb, 1964; Friedlander, 1970). If the students see the environment as hostile, seeking allies, counteracting the hostility, flight and protective behavior are likely to predominate. If they see the environment as nonthreatening and trustworthy, interaction is likely to take on more friendly, open, nonaggressive forms, with less energy spent in seeking allies. The latter type of interaction sets the stage for group development, whereas the former does not.

The interaction pattern during this first stage is usually random or leader-centered. The reasons for this are that group norms have not developed and a social structure does not exist specific to the class. The teacher is usually seen as the only recognized authority to whom the entire class has to respond. Therefore, the interaction tends to be either chaotic or teacher-centered. As the students begin to know each other, or if they already knew each other before this class, they tend to form pairs and some of the interaction takes place between these pairs. Often there is some subgrouping during the latter parts of this stage, or if previous acquaintanceships promote it, early in the stage. As a rule, however, the class remains chaotic unless the teacher provides leadership in promoting orderly interaction.

Stage one is a critical stage in group development because it sets the mood for the class, and students' expectations and feelings about the class begin to form early in this stage. If the class spends too much time in this stage, expectations of nonproductive behavior will begin to form and anxiety and disillusionment will begin to appear. Therefore, it is important that the teacher try to meet the needs of students in this phase as soon as possible. Orientation should have high priority until orientation needs have been met. Precise descriptions of the class, meeting times, textbooks and other such data should be available in written form and explained adequately. Next, the students should be told what is expected in terms of class requirements and procedures. Whenever possible, this should also be in written form supplemented by verbal explanations. Anxiety and distractions common in this stage interfere with a clear understanding of material presented at this time, and a teacher should expect to have to go over these materials several times. It sometimes helps to know that, initially at least, this is an inevitable part of the warm-up cycle for the entire class.

Interpersonal orientation and trust building must also be given immediate attention. In order for students to trust one another and the teacher, they need to know one another. Based on this premise, we recommend games and interaction exercises designed to foster self-disclosure and feedback appropriate for people who are just getting acquainted. Teachers can speed the process considerably by modeling self-disclosure through providing relevant appropriate personal information. The way the teacher responds will be noticed by the students, and if the teacher uses reflective listening techniques and responds to the personal meaning of students' statements it will not only be helpful at the time but will also promote personal interaction among them.

Stage 2: Norm Development

At this stage, the class is just beginning to become self-conscious. It is definitely still an aggregate composed of many different individuals with little communication on a very personal level and with little commitment to the class. But at this stage it is becoming apparent that they are going to have some established ways of interacting with one another. As students begin to feel the need for interaction norms and as they begin to wonder on an ongoing level what is expected and accepted and where the limits and power lie, the group is moving out of the beginning stage and into the norm development stage.

The interaction pattern at this time is generally leader-centered. The leader may, or may not, be the teacher, but the characteristics of this phase are that people are seeking direction, and they will turn at least momentarily to anyone who seems to have an answer. Whereas the first stage was characterized by questions of what-is-this and where-do-I-fit, the second stage is characterized by questions of how-far-can-I-go and how-is-it-going-to-be-done. Much of student behavior is testing at this point. The teacher's acceptance of them is tested; limits are tested; procedures are tested; relationships are tested; and leaders are tested. This is the first big step toward becoming a group. The beginning stage could have been the beginning of anything, but during stage two basic ground rules are being established which will be very difficult to change.

This stage presents the most severe test of the teacher. As this stage goes, so goes the class. If the teacher wants to have an authoritarian relationship, this is where it must be established—"start out tough and then ease up" is sound advice if you want an authoritarian classroom. But if you want a group-centered class, it is much harder to prescribe what must be done. It is imperative that the leadership be present to bring the class out of the confusion and erratic behavior of the first stage, but if in the process the norms are established that the class is not responsible for its own behavior, group development may be stopped at this point. Shared leadership and responsibility are necessary ingredients at this stage if the class is to develop into a self-regulating group. If the teacher provides for these, the interaction becomes tentative as students become leaders and leaders change. Erratic behavior becomes commonplace as new modes of behavior are experimented with or proposed.

As Tuckman (1965) so aptly points out, groups have two functions: *interpersonal* and *task*. It must be kept in mind that during stage two the class may make much greater progress in one area than another. Also, it is usually easier for the teacher to help establish task-related norms than it is to help establish interpersonal norms. If the teacher can concentrate on acceptance of student ideas and recognition of student feelings while providing the direction needed to help the class establish their own norms within acceptable limits, norms will gradually develop which allow the teacher to teach in a democratic manner. Students will gradually assume more and more responsibility for the class and their own behavior.

The teacher can be of considerable help during this period by helping students recognize their feelings and needs in the class. Time can be set aside for planning and students can be provided with samples of how classes can be organized in different student-centered ways. Many will need help expressing themselves and in making decisions. Far-out solutions will be proposed, and anxiety and emotions may soar momentarily, during which times the teacher needs to remain a steadying influence but not a dictatorial one. If a student asks if they can have beer in the classroom, the teacher needs to respond to the intent of the question and not react to squash the idea. The teacher might say,

> "John, I'm really not sure if you wanted to see what would have to be done to have beer in the class, or if you wondered what my reaction might be?"
>
> JOHN: "I think it would be a good idea."
>
> TEACHER: "Class, John has brought up the idea of beer in the class, would you like to discuss it?"

Several very important points have been made in this interaction: 1. ideas are not censored, 2. the teacher shows respect for ideas that are different, and 3. the teacher does not rule arbitrarily, but instead opens up the idea for class discussion. Through this type of interaction, the class can become accustomed to making its own rules and being responsible for its actions.

Stage 3: Conflict

In many of the models of group development, conflict is presented as the second stage. In classroom groups, however, it seems that this stage does not occur until after a fairly distinct norm-formation stage. Stages one and two are essentially dependent stages. The class, even in the development of norms, has a definite dependence attitude: the teacher and other class leaders are looked to for leadership and the "right way" to do things. By contrast, stage three is a counterdependent phase. The working through of the problems inherent in setting norms has given class members more confidence in their ability to solve problems and run the class, and now they are not sure they want to do it the way it has been set up.

Conflict arouses the anxiety of class members, and this can be a trying time for conforming students who do not like to see authority challenged or rules changed. While it may be a trying time for some students, it is an easy period for the secure teacher who can accept the struggling counterdependent themes for what they are. An insecure . teacher who does not understand group development can fall into the trap of wondering if more direction isn't needed and if his whole attempt to develop the group isn't a failure.

To group leaders this is known as "get-the-leader time": no matter what you do, it is wrong. The implication is that you don't really understand what is going on, and furthermore, the class wouldn't be in such bad shape if you had handled things better previously. Students who had previously asked for more structure now feel that there is too much structure, and students who had not wanted any structure now feel there should be more. In an analogy to human development, it is a combination of the "terrible twos," with the "me do" element showing through loud and clear, and of adolescent revolt against authority. Often the new norms, especially if they have involved working together, have aroused anxiety concerning the degree of intimacy involved. Students seeking change will often call for new votes on rules. Hidden conflicts between students will suddenly emerge. Subgroups will be formed for security reasons and new interaction patterns will emerge. Throughout this stage will be a strong feeling of "We need new leadership and new rules."

The interaction during this phase is erratic but not random and not leader-centered. Occasionally it will move from person to person and from issue to issue so fast as to appear random and fruitless, but in the long run it becomes clear that this is a time for group members to get things off their chests and to bring conflicts out into the open. As time goes by these conflicts will become clear and some polarization will take place around issues. For a time the interaction pattern will reflect this polarization as members argue back and forth trying to settle the issues.

This can be a very uncomfortable time for students unaccustomed to open conflict and expression of feelings. Consequently, some students will show a tendency to withdraw to avoid conflict or to become so anxious that it impairs their functioning in class. Also, this is a time when many thoughtless statements are made by students who have not learned how to express anger in nondestructive ways. If one student calls another a ding-a-ling for his stand on an issue in class, the teacher can help restore constructive interaction by remarks which stress the feelings involved, such as: "Carl, you seem pretty mad at Jim for his feelings about the project"; or, "Sue, you seem very upset at the way Carl and Jim are arguing." These remarks legitimize the feelings underlying the conflict or point out the effect of the conflict on other members of the class. Both are ways of turning the conflict into a constructive learning situation.

Strangely enough, this conflict and anxiety pave the way for deepening ties and more constructive working relationships. The key to this being a positive force in the life of the students and in the class's developing into a group lies in the way the conflict and hostility are handled. If the students are punished or if the conflict is not brought out into the open and dealt with as a legitimate issue, and if negative feelings are not dealt with as natural feelings, polarization can develop and hidden feelings of animosity can begin to disrupt the class. The teacher's primary task at this time is to help the students express their feelings and resolve their conflicts. Conflict resolution skills can be very helpful at this stage, but the main concern is not to get embroiled in the conflicts. The intensity of feelings will lead to self-disclosure and feedback which can be encouraged as a means of bringing the class closer together. Often this is the beginning of a true group feeling, and this stage is often followed by a very positive period.

Stage 4: Transition

This stage is often welcomed by a teacher or group leader who has had all he can stand of the bickering and conflict of stage three. It first becomes evident when the conflicts begin to be resolved in constructive ways which are actually translated into new ways of operating in the class. During this stage the intense conflicts of stage three are replaced by differences of opinion with acceptance of the differences by others. Stereotypes that members have had of each other have begun to disappear as a result of the new knowledge acquired about each other in the preceding stages. By now the members feel that they have been heard, and they are willing to move on and accept others and their opinions. Leadership becomes genuinely shared, and feelings of *we* emerge as group solidarity and cohesiveness begin to develop.

Definite positive feelings between members become apparent. Utilizing the security developed expressing negative feelings in the previous stage, members now move to consolidate and clarify their position through expression of positive feelings. Students volunteer to help each other whether needed or not, and all of a sudden the teacher is not such a "bad guy" after all. The teacher will never regain the stature he possessed in stage one, and stage three feelings may appear again now and then, but "get-the-leader" time is past. As interpersonal relationships are worked out among members, task considerations once again begin to take on a central role, which had been usurped by interpersonal considerations during the conflict stage. New norms or modifications of old norms become accepted, and the class can now devote more time and energy to work.

Communication is by far more open and constructive during this stage than in any of the preceding stages. Genuine two-way communication is apparent during much of the time. Need for protection and guarded communication is not evident, so self-disclosure and feedback become routine. Intimacy in communication becomes obvious as members say directly what they feel about each other without worrying about being rebuffed. I-Thou moments tend to increase and genuine respect for each other as persons leads to dropping of stereotypes, with communication becoming more meaningful.

Stage 5: Production

Up until stage five the class has been primarily an aggregate, but during stage four the transition was made to a group. Indeed, that was the entire purpose of stage four and the prime determinant of the activities that differentiate stage four from any other stage. Gradually, as the new norms adopted in stage four become routine and there is little regression to stage three, we can say that stage five activities are replacing stage four activities. Further characteristics of a highly developed stage five are trust, shared leadership, effective communication and a decrease in power relationships (see Bennis and Shepard, 1961). If stage five activities and modes of interacting are well-established, the teacher now becomes primarily a consultant to the class, although this is not seen as an abdication of authority. The power struggle elements of stage three are no longer dominant, and power relationships are usually replaced by personal relationships.

Most classes do not reach stage five. This stage represents the first time a group has been formed and the first time that a true *we* feeling is present, in which concern and interest is shown in *all* members of the class. At this stage group and individual goals tend to merge and involvement tends to be very high. Absenteeism is usually low and loyalty to the class is high. Very few interpersonal concerns are shown and norms are acceptable to all, or those who deviate do so in an acceptable manner. The teacher is considered a group member and participant. His authority and position are seldom questioned, but the teacher as a person is considered more important than as teacher—a complete reversal of the situation in stage one.

The most successful classes generally spend most of their time in stage five, once they reach it. As a rule this is the most comfortable stage for teachers. It represents high achievement in the traditional academic sense, and yet even a cursory acquaintance with the class demonstrates that positive affective elements are present at a very high level. The classroom is usually somewhat noisy but not chaotic. The interaction is definitely learner-centered but goal-directed and productive. The teacher serves as a resource and helps plan and develop strategies for attaining learning goals. Schmuck and Schmuck (1971) describe a similar stage which seems to differ from our concept of this stage only in the degree of student leadership and student involvement in setting their own standards. We propose that these concerns are taken care of to a great extent during the transition stage—a stage which Schmuck and Schmuck do not include in their model. Gorman (1969) enters into an extensive discussion of many of the activities that must occur before a stage five group can develop. In an excellent summary statement, Gorman writes: "The assumption here is that process communication needs to be dealt with *before effective* content communication can take place" (p. 174).

Stage 6: Affection

This is a rare stage and one that would not be considered appropriate by many teachers. Yet, it is a stage very congruent with the values being heard more and more from youth today. In this stage, the ability of the group to function as they have in stage five is still definitely present, but the goal-directed feeling so evident in stage five is lessened and in its place is found an increased appreciation of the group and of the persons in the group for their own sake. I-Thou relationships increase as task-oriented behavior fades somewhat into the background. In a sense, people rediscover each other in this stage and are fascinated by what they find. Close personal interaction is sought at every turn and task activities become secondary to relationship activities.

Norms are reevaluated as they were in stage three, but this time the motive is to change them to allow more time and energy for "getting together" and becoming personally closer to each other. Intimacy norms usually undergo a thorough revision toward more closeness. Task norms are scrutinized to see if they can be scaled down without causing conflict. This is a "good feeling" stage, and conflict is not deliberately sought and, when present, is handled with great concern for the group and the individuals involved. The group at this stage somewhat resembles a very successful family who value success among themselves and as a family more than they value external accomplishments. Individual accomplishments at the expense of the group are scorned.

Stage six is a very poor time to try to give grades. Students in stage five will approach grades reluctantly but in a businesslike way; students in stage six will approach them kicking and screaming, with loud protests of their uselessness and detrimental effects: "We have worked so hard and accomplished so much that everybody should get an A"; "Grades don't mean anything anyway; do we really have to have grades?" "Couldn't we have pass-fail?" "You grade us?" "We trust you, give us any grade you want." We have found no effective way to deal with this problem except to get a commitment from the class regarding grading procedures *before* they reach this stage. This doesn't do away with the problem, but it keeps the situation such that you can sleep at night.

In summary, while it might be said that students in stage five are willing to work themselves to death, students in stage six are willing to love themselves to death. Students in stage five are more like students have been traditionally supposed to be, but students in stage six have more fun. At the end of class and afterwards, students who ended at stage five will remember their class as a great class and will stress some of the things they did and accomplished; stage six students will remember these things also but will tend to stress isolated instances which had great personal meaning to them and the friends they made within the group. In both types of groups friendships are likely to last long after the class is over and perhaps for a lifetime. The teacher is a model and reality check as well as a resource to classes in these stages, but the teacher as a person is what the students usually respond to.

Stage 7: Actualization

Flexibility and being-oriented behavior are the hallmarks of this stage. It is a rare stage indeed; it is a safe guess that most American students have never had the opportunity to participate in a class functioning at this level. Probably most teachers have not either. Schmuck and Schmuck (1971) refer to a similar stage as the ideal level of group maturity. They write that this stage has been attained when "norms allow for a variety of individual learning styles to be expressed and accepted, and when the group has the power to change itself toward a more effective state" (p. 122). This statement can apply to stages five and six also, but the key is the ease with which the class can move from one state to another.

In stage seven individual and group needs are satisfied to the extent that higher-order needs come into play and are met on a continuous basis. The group does not feel the need for affection-related activities noted in stage six or the work-related activities prevalent in stage five. The group is as open to the expression of conflict as it is to the expression of affection, and work regains some of the appeal which was lost in stage six. Individuals and the group all work together in a process of becoming and being. Their norms become redefined in terms of human potential and human welfare as expressed in their behavior. Authenticity and awareness are at the base of their activity.

Consensus becomes an accepted way of arriving at decisions, and open dissent and agreement are taken for granted until something can be worked out. One of the authors remembers a class which, when presented with the problem of grading, solved it in the way characteristic of groups operating at this level. They decided that since theirs had been a "talking" class, they should have a talking final evaluation which would permit them to integrate and consolidate what they had learned in class. As a procedure they decided on a rotating board of classmates who would conduct an oral evaluation based on each student's understanding of the course material. To the author's surprise, their complicated procedure for determining the schedule of who was on the *two* boards necessary, and when each person was to meet a board of his or her peers, actually worked! Each student met a board and each student served on a board. The teacher was delegated the chore of compiling the evaluations arrived at by the boards and recording the grades—not exactly a position of high status.

A class at this level is rare, and represents a challenge because it means that in order to understand what is going on the teacher must be able to live personally at this level—something that precious few of us can do, and certainly something which is even rarer on an ongoing everyday basis. If as teachers we don't understand it, perhaps it tells us something about ourselves, but it also means we have to develop the confidence to step back and interfere only if we have objective evidence that what is going on is not constructive. Our discomfort with new and creative behavior is not sufficient criteria for use with groups operating at this level.

Summary and Discussion

Group development is not a well-understood phenomenon and there is scant research evidence to back up theoretical speculations. However, it is possible using studies of many different types of groups to recognize developmental stages applicable to classrooms. This section was developed using available research and the authors' experience as guidelines. No research has been done with the specific stages suggested by the authors beyond informal observation,[1] but the stages are consistent with research using similar stages.

The seven stages are not presented as discrete stages with behavior unique to each stage which will not be found in any other stage. Instead, they are proposed as stages in which behavior characteristics of that

1. A study by Barbara Stiltner (1973) tests an adaptation of the model we propose.

particular stage predominate. Groups will regress for brief periods of time to previous stages, or attempt behavior at a more advanced stage. Under stress there is a tendency to regress, and when a stage seems to be mastered there is a tendency to move tentatively to the next stage. Our observation indicates that most classes never progress beyond the transition stage (four) and never become actual groups. Instead, they operate as a work-oriented aggregate with some stage five characteristics.

The teacher plays a crucial role at all stages and it is impossible for a group to develop very far without at least the tacit consent of the teacher, and for most younger children without considerable help. How this can be given will be discussed further in the next section.

FROM AGGREGATE TO GROUP: THE TEACHER IN THE PROCESS

Working with a class in a way that will foster their development from an aggregate to a group makes specific demands on teachers and requires specific knowledge. In this section we will present briefly, almost in outline form, some of the considerations the teacher must keep in mind, and some ways the teacher can influence a class in the process of becoming a group.

Meeting Life-Cycle Needs

The first consideration that must be understood about any class is where they stand in their life cycle. At times it is impossible to determine this precisely. If so, it is best to estimate the position and start working with them as if they were slightly *less* far into the cycle than your estimate.

Table 5 presents a brief summary of the principal needs during the three main phases of a life cycle. These needs tend to hold whether we are speaking of the life cycle of an entire school year, of a student's high school years or of a single class period. These are needs that must be met if the cycle is to progress as satisfactorily as possible.

Let us use the example of a student entering junior high school. Even before he starts, he needs to know something about the registration procedures—this can be considered part of the reorientation needs of the end of his elementary school cycle or the orientation needs of the

TABLE 5. LIFE-CYCLE NEEDS

Warm-up	Activity	Integration
Involvement needs; interest needs; orientation needs; trust	Technical and information needs; organization, procedural and material needs	Discussion; clarification; integration; reorientation needs

start of his junior high school career. Next, he needs to learn to trust, become involved, interested and acquainted. As he moves into the activity-production phase his needs turn to considerations associated with the activity. (*Caution:* keep in mind that the needs of shorter cycles such as class periods and subject matter units are superimposed on those of the longer life cycle.) Toward the end of junior high, activity needs begin to take a back seat to integration needs.

Therefore, the first step a teacher should take in helping a class build to a group is to ensure that school and classroom activities are at least attempting to meet the life-cycle needs of students. This includes all life-cycle needs, from those of the students' total life (often called developmental needs) to those of the class period.

Meeting Group Development Needs

The second consideration involves an understanding of the stages of group development. To fully understand this at any particular time the teacher will also have to understand the influence of the group on individuals, and vice versa. We urge teachers to frequently discuss this problem with the students both individually and as a total class. Often a student will feel that the class seems to be progressing satisfactorily but that it isn't for him; at other times a class will feel that an individual or individuals are getting them off track, not contributing or being hurt by the class. These concerns should be dealt with as soon as possible. They can be sufficiently serious to hold up the development of the group or to be detrimental to an individual. Assuming normal progress, a class's needs will change as they progress. Also, the *needs that must be met before they can move to the next stage must be considered.*

The following outline of needs that generally predominate at each stages are presented to help a teacher in the process of building a group.

STAGE 1: BEGINNING. The main needs are for orientation and trust building. There is also a strong need for building satisfactory communication and interpersonal interaction skills in most classes. Students need to get to know each other and to "find their place" in the class.

STAGE 2: NORM DEVELOPMENT. Team building and organizational skills usually need supplementing. Classes generally need some help in recognizing the demands of the situation and in interpreting their own behavior. Stage one needs are generally still important in this stage, and these are blended with the problems associated with building satisfactory norms.

STAGE 3: CONFLICT. Conflict resolution needs and those associated with constructive dealing with hostility and confrontation are crucial. Understanding and feedback are called for in huge amounts during crisis situations. Open discussions, problem solving techniques and exercises aimed at clarifying the situation can help reduce some of the frustration, guilt and anger engendered by the frequent conflict inherent in this stage.

STAGE 4: TRANSITION. Students need help in developing leadership skills and in developing or modifying new norms. Desires to work cooperatively and to show positive feelings are often frustrated by a lack of skills in these areas, which creates a new need for skill in organizational and interpersonal areas. It is easy to ignore personal needs in this stage in order to get on with the work.

STAGE 5: PRODUCTION. This is the working stage, and most needs revolve around task-related issues. If the class is to progress beyond this stage the teacher must meet not only the needs associated with everyday task-oriented behavior but also the needs associated with making it a closer functioning and more cohesive group. For the first time the class can be considered a group, but it is a group for the performance of a task and has only a secondary interest in the welfare of individual members. To achieve this interest, class members need to get to know each other better, and this is where the teacher can help by structuring activities that focus on the person and by interacting in this manner with students at all times. It is easy to be satisfied with having gotten the class this far and forget that it is overbalanced in the direction of a task-orientation.

STAGE 6: AFFECTION. The teacher or somebody has done his job well if the group has progressed to this point, but now, if anything, the class is overbalanced toward interpersonal affection. Students' needs are centered around seeing the meaning of their activities and keeping a long-range perspective on the class. Teachers can help students examine their current activities in light of their long-range objectives. Decision and problem solving needs are also quite apparent at times.

STAGE 7: ACTUALIZATION. Understanding, friendship, challenge and freedom needs are probably dominant at this point. Interpersonal and communication skills are generally high, as are task skills and generally coping behavior, but groups operating at this level are rare and providing the understanding necessary to sustain this level of operation is difficult.

To summarize: *the second step a teacher should take in helping a class develop into a group is to ensure that the needs associated with the stage in which the class is at the present time are being met to at least a minimal degree. Then, in order for the class to progress to the next stage, the teacher should make provisions for them to acquire the skills and personal relationships needed for the next stage.*

Assuming that the teacher has adequately met the requirements of the life-cycle position and stage of development the class is in, the need for providing constructive interaction that will lead to a high stage of group development is still present. The fundamental elements in the teacher's influence are empathy, genuineness, positive regard for students and general skills of interacting and communicating. Since these characteristics, because of their importance, have been discussed at length elsewhere in this book, they will not be discussed here; but this should not be taken as any intent to diminish their importance in group development. Instead, the following section will concentrate on application of techniques.

A class is influenced by the following conditions, all more or less under the control of the teacher (we are intentionally ignoring conditions beyond the control of the teacher, such as socioeconomic status, in order to concentrate on what the teacher *can* do):

1. THE PERSON OF THE TEACHER. How the teacher is dressed and groomed are influential, although it may be hard to find out why. But a teacher in hot pants will definitely get a different reaction than one dressed conservatively. A male teacher 6'6" who weighs 250 pounds generally gets a different reaction than the average 5'4" lady. And the black teacher with an Afro gets a different reaction than the average white teacher. The teacher who smiles and is friendly gets a different reaction than a grouch, and so on. The point is that how we appear, so to speak, influences the reaction to what we do and modifies its influence on the class. We need to take this into account and at least see that it is not getting in our way; if it is, we must decide what—if anything—we need or want to do about it.

2. THE TEACHER AS A MODEL. It is important to remember that the students will use a teacher's behavior as a model of desired behavior. Hence, it is important to monitor one's own behavior closely to see that it is congruent with the behavior expected of students. Often in the press of getting things done we fall back on authoritarian methods or do not check to see that we do not become impersonal or arbitrary. Whatever behavior we desire in the classroom can be promoted by acting that way ourselves.

3. STIMULUS. This is the two-by-four board the man used to get his mule's attention. A photograph, poem, recording, newly-discovered bird's nest or any other object or activity can serve as the stimulus to get students' attention as well as to stimulate their thoughts. It is very important to try to keep the main stimulus or stimuli in the room consistent with the intent of the interaction for the day.

4. STRUCTURE AND ORGANIZATION. The way the class is physically structured, as well as how it is organized, affects the interaction materially. Sitting in circles is a start, but it is only a start. To maximize interaction students need to be grouped into smaller units all the way down to pairs, or even starting with individuals and then working up. Organization into work teams also promotes interaction. In teams students can be assigned process roles, such as observer of how the team interacts, with regular meetings scheduled for feedback to the other students. This arrangement helps students learn how to become aware of their actions on one another as well as how to observe and give feedback. By organizing in teams with team leaders, students also learn

leadership skills and effectiveness as team members. Team positions can be rotated and different teams can be formed for different purposes, so that students can get practice in different roles. Interdependence can be encouraged more through organizational procedures than perhaps any other way. Other suggestions are found in subsequent chapters of this book.

5. TASK. Although at this point we are not suggesting any tasks outside the regular subject matter, interaction for the sake of personal growth is obviously a possibility. Within the regular subject matter, however, there are many opportunities for tasks that promote interaction and involvement. History can be taught as a study of the past or as a comparison of the past and present or of the interaction between the past and present. Students can be asked to examine how they have been influenced by an historical period or how they resemble an historical character rather than to describe the period or character. They also can be asked to perform tasks that require the effort of more than one member to complete, with different segments of the tasks contributing to the completion of other segments being done by other students. This arrangement promotes interaction as well as responsibility to each other, and not just to the class or teacher.

6. DIRECTION. This is the way that most of us try to promote our goals in teaching: we tell students what we want done. Yet, *not one* of the preceding ways of promoting interaction requires that the students be instructed or told to interact. Instead, they are led to interact by the way the teacher acts, by a stimulus (say an exciting movie, or a picture of a big foot which a teacher we know uses successfully) and by the structure or organization, or task. It is also appropriate to actually tell students to interact at times. For example:

> AT THE BEGINNING OF A NEW CLASS, "Why don't you take a few minutes and mill around and get to know those students you have not already met?" Or, "Let's play the Name Game so that we can get to know each other's names. My name is Mr. Morretti. *(To student on right)* Who are you?"
>
> STUDENT: "I'm Jake Svenson." *(Students are seated in a large circle.)*
>
> MORRETTI: "First, who am I?"
>
> SVENSON: "You are Mr. Morretti."
>
> MORRETTI: "And you are?"

SVENSON: "Jake Svenson."

MORRETTI: "Okay, next." *(To next student on the right of Jake)*

JANE: "I'm Jane Marlow."

MORRETTI: "Okay, but who am I?"

JANE: "You are Mr. Morretti."

MORRETTI: "And who is he?" *(Pointing to Jake)*

JANE: "He is Jake Svenson."

MORRETTI: "Okay, once again, start with me."

JANE: "Oh, I get it, Mr. Morretti, Jake Svenson, and I am Jane Marlow."

MORRETTI: "Next."

STUDENT: "Mr. Morretti, Jake Svenson, Jane Marlow, and I am Olen Green."

REST OF CLASS *(with anxiety and groans):* "We can't do it." "All the way around?"

MORRETTI: "Sure you can. Just don't worry about it and listen carefully."

The above example includes many rather pointed directions, but it promotes interaction and closer relations because the directions were to interact and did not require the students to sit passively and absorb. The options are many—Mr. Morretti could have introduced the students himself, which would have promoted passivity and reduced interaction; or he could have had them introduce themselves, which still would not have promoted as much activity and interaction. Later, in-depth introductions of one student by another follows the Name Game quite well and serves as another step in the warm-up phase and meets get-acquainted needs.

7. SELF-DISCLOSURE AND FEEDBACK. The success of a group probably depends more on the openness of the communication in the group and of the ability to give and receive feedback than on any other factor. The teacher can model self-disclosure and feedback and can introduce exercises to encourage students to talk about themselves and their reactions to others. We believe the class needs to have some rationale for how this helps them work as a class in building a group. The Johari Window (see Figure 2) is probably the most useful tool available for explaining the effects of feedback and self-disclosure on the functioning of a group (Luft, 1969, 1970).

At the initial meeting of a group the Open area is small in relation to the other areas and hinders and constricts interaction because information needed for maximally effective interaction is not available. When a large Hidden area is present, we are forced to interact by guesswork. There is doubt in the communication and interaction and inevitably misunderstanding and disagreement. It is the presence of the large Hidden and Blind areas during the norm formation period of a class that paves the way for the conflict stage. The norms are set without sufficient disclosure and feedback to assure that they are acceptable.

	Known to Self	Not Known to Self
Known to Others	**OPEN** All parties are aware of one another's feelings and acceptance in this area and open to discussion and change. There is no need to hide or withhold feedback about this area.	**BLIND** Others can see things a person is not aware of or attending to. Can lead to embarrassment or doubt as to one's position.
Not Known to Others	**HIDDEN** This is the area we do not disclose to others for whatever the reasons, but we are aware of it. Usually maintained through distrust.	**UNKNOWN** This area is unknown but can become known by interaction, self-disclosure and feedback.

FIGURE 2. JOHARI WINDOW   (adapted from Luft, 1969, 1970, with permission of National Press Books)

Then, when the members start saying what they really feel, conflict arises because they still do not have a large enough Open area to have developed respect and concern for each other. One of the main needs during this period is for a larger Open area, especially in regard to feelings about each other and the class. The teacher can usually be of most help by acting in ways that increase the Open area and by helping students directly or indirectly to increase the Open area.

In increasing the Open area some specific things should be kept in mind. Forced disclosure is not desirable; it usually leads to threat and all its attendant problems. Also, trust usually leads automatically to self-disclosure. Feedback and self-disclosure require skills not possessed by many persons and may have to be learned as is any other activity. Often it is important for the teacher to determine whether the group could be advanced more by feedback or by self-disclosure (feedback reduces the Blind area, and self-disclosure reduces the Hidden area). *Finally, the teacher can open up communication and interaction more by responding personally and to personal meaning than through any other method.*

The preceding seven ways of influencing the process of group building operate whether the teacher wants them to or not. Therefore, it is imperative that the teacher at least recognize his effect. Also, it should not be forgotten that they operate in interaction with each other and many other variables, so it is not just a matter of learning techniques. It is more a matter of understanding what is going on to be able to determine what is needed to arrive at a more desirable interaction or to move in the desired direction.

Team building or department or faculty building toward the type of interaction described for the classroom goes through the same stages and with the same life-cycle considerations. There are variations, to be sure, but the requirements for building an effective work team are not materially different from those for building an effective classroom group. The leadership problems are probably greater, and teachers and administrators may find it more difficult to open up their mode of communicating, but the principles—and the benefits—remain the same.

References   3

ANDERSON, A. R. Group counseling. *Review of Educational Research,* 1969, **4,** 209-226.

BALES, R. F. and STRODBECK, F. L. Phases in group problem solving. In C. Cartwright and A. Zander, *Group dynamics research and theory.* (2nd ed.) New York: Harper, 1960.

BENNIS, W. G., and SHEPARD, H. A. A theory of group development. In W. G. Bennis, K. D. Benne, and R. Chin, (Eds.), *The planning of change.* New York: Holt, 1961.

BOYD, R. D. Phase analysis of groups of elementary school pupils. *Journal of Experimental Education,* 1967, **35,** 91-95.

FISHER, B. A. Decision emergence phases in group decision making. *Speech Monographs,* 1970, **37,** 53-66.

FRIEDLANDER, F. Primacy of trust as a facilitator of further group accomplishment. *Journal of Applied Behavioral Science,* 1970, **6,** 387-400.

GAGE, N. L. (ED.) *Handbook of research on teaching.* Chicago: Rand McNally, 1963.

GIBB, J. Climate for trust formation. In L. Bradford, J. Gibb, and K. Benne (Eds.), *T-group theory and laboratory method.* New York: Wiley, 1964.

GORMAN, A. H. *Teachers and learners: The interactive process of education.* Boston: Allyn and Bacon, 1969.

HANSEN, J. C. Life stages of a group. In J. C. Hansen and S. H. Cramer (Eds.), *Group guidance and counseling in the schools.* New York: Appleton-Century-Crofts, 1971.

HOLLANDER, CARL. *A process for psychodrama training: The Hollander psychodrama curve.* Littleton, Colo.: Evergreen Institute Press, 1969.

LUBIN, B., and ZUCKERMAN, M. Affective and perceptual-cognitive patterns in sensitivity training groups. *Psychological Reports,* 1967, **21,** 365-367.

LUFT, J. *Group processes: An introduction to group dynamics.* (2nd ed.) Palo Alto, Calif.: National Press Books, 1970.

LUFT, J. *Of human interaction.* Palo Alto, Calif.: National Press Books, 1969.

MAHLER, C. A. *Group counseling in the schools.* Boston: Houghton Mifflin, 1969.

MINUCHIN, P. P. Solving problems cooperatively: A comparison of three classroom groups. *Childhood Education,* 1965, **41,** 480-484.

PHILIP, H., and DUNPHY, D. Developmental trends in small groups. *Sociometry*, 1959, **22**, 162-174.

RUNKEL, P. J., *et al.* Stages of group development: An empirical test of Tuckman's hypothesis. *Journal of Applied Behavioral Science*, 1971, **7**, 180-193.

SCHMUCK, R. A., and SCHMUCK, P. A. *Group processes in the classroom.* Dubuque, Iowa: Brown, 1971.

SCHUTZ, W. C. Interpersonal underworld. *Harvard Business Review*, 1958, **36**, 123-135.

STILTNER, B. *The effect of interaction activities and teacher role on group development in junior high school classrooms.* (Unpublished doctoral dissertation) University of Colorado, 1973.

TUCKMAN, B. W. Developmental sequence in small groups. *Psychological Bulletin*, 1965, **63**, 384-399.

WATSON, E. R. Group communications and developmental processes. *High School Journal*, 1969, **52**, 431-440.

4

LEARNING THROUGH GROUP DISCUSSION

From a group of primitive tribesmen sitting around a storyteller to the modern-day housewife gossiping over the back fence with a neighbor, verbal interaction has always been an important way in which people learn. In their daily dealings with one another, most human beings interact personally thousands of times more frequently than they read or write. It is not surprising, then, that schools have always utilized some form of verbal activity as an integral part of the learning process.

TEACHER-CENTERED DISCUSSION

Until recently classroom activity was generally limited to those kinds in which the teacher was the focal point. The teacher has traditionally been considered the subject-matter authority, and it has been assumed that students learn best by listening to and talking to the teacher. The lecture method is perhaps the most obvious example of teacher-centered instruction: the teacher tells students what he thinks they ought to know, and they listen and perhaps ask questions to clarify unclear points in the lecture. As a means of conveying information, this method is relatively efficient and easier for the teacher to organize than other methods, but its effectiveness is questionable, particularly in producing the kinds of learning which we have postulated as the goals of education.

Recitation

Even when teachers have discarded the lecture method as too boring or ineffective, their methods of instruction have usually remained highly teacher-centered. Recitation, for example, is a popular alternative to the lecture method. In hopes of getting students more actively involved in learning, teachers ask a large number of subject-matter questions—usually covering a reading assignment—and call on various students to answer them. Recitation can therefore be used as an oral quiz. If students know that they are going to be questioned in this manner, teachers reason, they will be more likely to do their homework in order to avoid the embarrassment of not knowing the right answer. Yet, recitation can be useful in ways other than forcing students to do their homework. It gives them a chance to review material in order to fix it more clearly in their memory, and it shows the teacher what parts of the material need more explanation. Recitation can also have a positive psychological effect for those who give an appropriate answer by reinforcing what has been learned and building self-esteem.

Although recitation can have advantages for both teacher and student, it has the serious drawback of limiting classroom interaction to exchanges between teacher and student. The teacher asks a question and calls on a student to answer. The student replies to the teacher, and the teacher tells him whether he is right or wrong. This approach perpetuates the assumption that the teacher is the sole judge of the validity of ideas, and isolates students from one another. It also encourages students to compete with one another, to try to show one another up and to vie with one another for the teacher's attention and approval. The result is that students ignore for the most part what one another are saying, and concentrate on interacting directly with the teacher.

Inductive Questioning

In order to deemphasize factual information and to develop concepts and higher order learning, teachers have often replaced recitation with inductive questioning. In this form of interaction, the teacher asks a series of questions designed to lead students to predetermined conclusions from information they already possess (perhaps learned from a reading assignment). It is not—as is recitation—a form of testing a student's knowledge of facts, but is a way of helping him form concepts based on those facts. Often this method requires that different students in the class answer different parts of the series of questions, thus encouraging the students to build on the contributions of others in the group. Nevertheless, it has serious disadvantages. First of all, inductive questioning is based on the assumption that there is a "right" answer or concept and that the teacher not only knows what it is but also knows the best steps for arriving at that answer. Recent research in problem solving indicates that individuals have widely diverse means of forming concepts and arriving at solutions to problems, and that the process that works best for one may not work for another. Inductive questioning, therefore, must be used with care. It cannot be undertaken with the assumption that all students can be led to insight through a carefully worked-out sequence of questions. Students may need to be allowed to find their own path to the goal or draw their own conclusions from a set of data.

Another disadvantage to inductive questioning is that, like recitation, it limits interaction to exchanges between teacher and student. Although some cooperation between students may be necessary in order to build a concept, the teacher is still the focal point of the interaction and controls it tightly. Not only does the teacher determine the goal he wishes the class to attain, he also structures the means the group will use toward reaching that goal.

"Free" Discussion

Occasionally a teacher may wish to allow students to discuss a topic freely instead of testing them on facts or leading them inductively to a predetermined conclusion. Yet, disconcertingly often, the "discussion" that results consists largely of exchanges between student and teacher and continues to discourage students from talking to one another. Here is the way a typical classroom discussion often goes:

> The eighth-grade social science class in a suburban junior high school
> has been studying the effects of urbanization on American society. The

teacher wants to give the students a chance to examine freely the implications of urbanization and thus poses the question, "How would your life be different if you lived in a city than it would be if you lived in a village of 500 people?" The teacher congratulates himself for asking a question that will allow students to become personally involved with the subject matter and stretch their imaginations. He stands smiling expectantly at the class, which is seated in five rows of six desks each, facing the front of the room.

1. TEACHER: How would your life be different if you lived in a city than it would be if you lived in a village of 500 people? *(pause; Bill raises hand)* Bill?

2. BILL: It sure would be dull in a village. There'd be nothing to do.

3. TEACHER: You don't think you'd find a village very exciting.

4. BILL: No, I'd rather live in a city where there would be skating rinks and the zoo and lots of movies to choose from.

5. TEACHER: What about the rest of you? *(Sally raises hand)* Sally?

6. SALLY: It would be easier to shop in the city. You might not find everything you need in the village.

7. TEACHER: Yes, the city would have many more stores. *(Dan raises hand)* Yes, Dan?

8. DAN: I'd like to live in the small town. That way you could get to know people better.

9. TEACHER: You think you could get better acquainted with people in the village than you could in the town. *(Bill raises hand)* Bill?

10. BILL: But you could get acquainted with the people on your block in the city just as well as you could in the village.

11. TEACHER: Yes, that's probably true. *(Sue raises hand)* Sue?

12. SUE: I don't really think there'd be much difference, especially since we have television and newspapers and good communication now'days.

13. TEACHER: You think that the differences Bill and Dan and Sally pointed out really aren't too important.

14. SUE: Yeah, they're exaggerating small differences is what I think.

From one standpoint the teacher's verbal behavior is quite helpful in this example. He presents (1) a general question that allows students to respond with their personal opinions rather than have to guess what "right" answer the teacher has in mind. He encourages the whole class to contribute (5). He also reflects on and clarifies the students' responses, indicating understanding and acceptance of their contributions (3, 7, 9). And he points out relationships between the various responses (13).

However, like recitation and inductive questioning, this form of discussion isolates students from one another. Notice, for example, that Sue (12, 14) spoke to the teacher even though she was responding to contributions made by other students. The teacher is used by the students not only as the authority against whom to check the validity of their responses, but also as a sort of "switchboard" through which they direct their responses to one another. Rather than telling Bill and Dan and Sally that she doesn't agree with them ("I think you're exaggerating small differences"), Sue must use the teacher to relay this information to them, saying in effect, "Please tell Bill and Dan and Sally that I think they're exaggerating small differences." Despite the teacher's good intentions, students continue to direct their talk exclusively to the teacher, and thus are deprived of the learning that could come from interaction with each other.

GROUP-CENTERED DISCUSSION

How could the teacher restructure this discussion to maximize interaction among the students? First, he could arrange the desks in such a way that students could look directly at one another. A circle would be ideal, but a double horseshoe might be necessary if the room is small. Rather than stand in front of the group, the teacher could either sit unobtrusively with the group or remove himself from the group entirely. After stating the question, the teacher could refrain from calling on students and could redirect their comments to other students if they persisted in using him as focal point of the discussion. By contrast with the example above, here is the way a group-centered discussion would proceed:

1. TEACHER: I'd like you to spend the next twenty minutes discussing as a group the question that I've put on the board, "How would your life be different if you lived in a city than it would be if you lived in a village of 500 people?" At the end of that time, I'd like you to give me a list of ten or fifteen ways that you've agreed on. *(He settles back to observe the work of the group)*

2. BILL *(After a short pause):* Well, let's get to work. Who's got any ideas?

3. SALLY: I think one difference is that it's easier to shop in the city. You might not find everything you need in the village.

4. DAN: Yeah, I agree. And also, you'd have more to do in the city. The village wouldn't be very exciting.

5. BILL: Is someone getting these things down? We need to keep a list.

6. JANE: I'll do it. *(Gets out notebook and begins to write.)*

7. BILL: Who's got another idea?

8. PHIL: Well, a small town is more isolated from the rest of the world. You wouldn't know as much about what was going on.

9. SUE: I don't agree. I think that with mass communication even people in small towns are well informed.

10. CHAD: Yeah, that's right. I think there isn't much difference in how well informed you'd be.

11. BILL: Does everybody agree that we should leave that off? *(Murmurs of assent.)*

12. PHIL: I guess that difference really isn't too great. But people in the city *do* have a chance to be exposed to many different ideas— there's the museum and the planetarium and lectures and concerts and stuff.

13. TEACHER: You think that although perhaps you wouldn't be isolated in a small town, you'd have a chance to learn about many more things in a city?

14. PHIL: Yeah, I guess that's right.

15. BILL: Well, perhaps we should put *that* on the list.

16. SUE: I can buy that. Let's do.

17. DONNA: I know something we haven't thought of: in a small town you get to know people much better than you do in a city.

18. KAREN: Yeah, small towns are much more friendly. I lived in Martin, Tennessee, for five years when I was a kid and it was terrific.

19. STEVE: But can't you get to know people in your neighborhood in a city just as well?

The primary difference between this example and the previous one is that the students are interacting with one another instead of directing their comments to the teacher. They are answering the same question and are making many of the same points, but the teacher has removed himself from the role of switchboard and demonstrates from his behavior that he expects the students to work out the problem themselves.

Notice, though, that the teacher has not deserted the class: he watches their progress carefully and intervenes (13) when he feels that a point needs to be clarified or that a student is being misunderstood.

This type of discussion can be viewed as "group-centered" as opposed to teacher-centered. The teacher does not act as leader of the group. Rather, the leadership emerges from the group itself as it works toward the goal. The members of the group speak directly to one another, and they take responsibility for examining and evaluating one another's contributions. The task, not the teacher, becomes the focus of the group's attention, and the interaction pattern shifts from teacher-student to student-student. For these reasons we feel a group-centered discussion is superior to teacher-centered discussion for achieving the goals of education we proposed in Chapter One.

Types of Group-Centered Discussion

A group-centered discussion can be structured with either of two major purposes in mind, although these are not mutually exclusive. For most classroom discussions, the group will have accomplishing a task as its purpose. In the example above, the task was to formulate a list of ways in which one's life would be different in the city from the way it would be in a village. This was the goal the group was to achieve, and the teacher made it explicit. Other tasks might be to work a grammar exercise together, to solve a math problem, to devise a more ecologically sound means of disposing of waste matter or to list the causes of the Civil War. While the tasks vary in their abstractness and complexity, they have in common the fact that some group product results from the discussion. The group's interaction revolves around the task rather than the teacher. It is the need to attain this goal or product that determines the group's interaction—not leadership from the teacher. The teacher limits himself to setting the goal (however, many times he may wish to let the group set their own goal) and does not specify the steps which the group must take to reach the goal (as in the case of inductive questioning). In a broad sense, this type of group-centered discussion can be termed *problem solving.*

The second type of group-centered discussion has sharing as its primary goal. This type of discussion is sometimes called *open-ended* because no specific goal or product has been set as the outcome. Members pool their ideas and feelings without trying to reach a conclusion. Such a discussion is useful if the teacher feels students need a chance to vent their emotional reaction to a stimulus, which can range from a subject-matter issue to an occurrence in the classroom. It may also be useful if the teacher wants students to see the range of opinions on an issue or the range of experiences students have had, without coming to agreement on the best course of action or the best viewpoint. Often the teacher may wish to begin with an open-ended discussion in order to clear the air and expose students to a large number of ideas, and then later give the discussion a different structure by suggesting that the group work toward a specific goal or product. Thus, the two forms of group-centered discussion can complement each other. However, it is essential that the teacher have in mind which form he wishes to use and give students explicit instructions accordingly.

Benefits of Group Discussion

As an instructional mode group-centered discussion serves many of the purposes claimed for more traditional discussion methods, as well as others that teacher-led discussions rarely achieve. First of all, a group discussion gives the participant a chance to learn new information from others. He has access to their previous experiences and knowledge, as well as their insights into the subject matter. Other students may bring up points he missed or failed to consider, and they may serve to clarify for him parts of the material which he did not fully understand.

Through group discussion the student also consolidates his own learning. For most people verbalizing an idea or concept helps to fix it in the memory and aids integration with other concepts. Furthermore, the process of discussing an idea helps the student sharpen his opinions and clarify his own point of view. By getting the reactions of other students to his views, a student can test the validity of his ideas. Other students can help him see aspects of an issue that he has overlooked or can provide substantiating evidence that he has not considered.

When a classroom group works together on a task, its members can also develop skills of group problem solving, such as setting clear goals, taking responsibility to contribute, encouraging others, careful listening, cooperating and arriving at a consensus. Modern society requires that adults be able to solve problems cooperatively, but developing these skills has previously been left largely to chance by the schools. Classroom activities that simulate the kind of cooperative work required by adult society is the best way of facilitating the development of problem-solving skills.

In addition to the largely cognitive benefits of group discussion listed thus far, there are psychological benefits to the student. Through participation in classroom discussion he can gain feelings of acceptance and belonging. He perceives that his views matter to the others in the group because they need him in order to accomplish their goals. He also is given an opportunity to ventilate his feelings in a nonthreatening atmosphere. When students can express their feelings to the group, they may begin to see that these feelings are neither strange nor unacceptable, but that frequently other students feel the same way. Emotions which might distort or prevent the acquisition of subject matter are examined openly, thus freeing the student to think more rationally.

A frequently ignored outcome of group discussion is the learning of basic social skills such as respect for others, communicating unambiguously and careful listening. As a laboratory for teaching students to get along with others, the classroom discussion group is unequalled. The teacher and others in the group can help the student examine his ways of relating to other people and can support his efforts to develop more effective behavior. The cohesive nature of the classroom group, coupled with norms that are similar to those in society in general, can be a potent force in socializing the student.

ORGANIZING GROUP DISCUSSIONS

As we have seen in the contrasting examples of a classroom discussion given earlier, the teacher who wishes to utilize group-centered discussion will probably have to make changes in the way he organizes the class as well as in his own behavior. He will have to concern himself with questions such as: How large should the classroom groups be? How do I assign students to these groups? What type of seating arrangement do I use? What kind of instructions do I give the groups? What do I do while the groups are working?

Group Size

The teacher will wish to be flexible in the size of groups he employs, utilizing different size groups for different purposes. For some tasks, pairing the students in *dyads* may be most effective. When two students work together, it is likely that both will have to be highly involved. If he is working with only one other person, a student—even one who is somewhat shy—will probably be more active that he would be in a group of, say, thirty. And he is probably less likely to be afraid to contribute, since the threat level is lowered. However, dyads have the disadvantage of limiting the number of points of view that can be utilized in solving a problem. If the task requires that a wide range of opinions and information be synthesized, a group with more members is preferable. Therefore the teacher may sometimes wish to divide the class into groups of three or four students. *Triads* and *quartets* have many of the advantages of dyads—lower threat level and high involvement—while providing a wider variety of input.

A *small group* generally consists of five to ten participants. For most classroom tasks this is the ideal size. The group is small enough to allow everyone to take an active part in the discussion, yet large enough to provide a wide range of opinions and information. A group that grows larger than eight or ten becomes unwieldy. Decisions are difficult to arrive at and each individual's share of the "air time" is reduced. It becomes easier for the passive individual to withdraw and hide himself behind the interaction of others. Although there are some circumstances in which being able to withdraw from the interaction is desirable, in most subject-matter discussions a group size that maximizes each person's participation is usually preferable.

On some occasions the teacher may wish to conduct group discussions that place all members of the class in a *total group* of twenty to thirty-five students. Particularly when the issue to be discussed is some matter that concerns the entire classroom—such as a decision about sharing materials, or when to go to lunch or what subject-matter unit to work on next—the teacher will wish to work with the group as a whole. The large size of the total group will make active participation by all members more difficult and, with younger students especially, often presents a chance for distracting behavior. The teacher will need to make sure that all students are given a chance to express themselves, particularly when an important decision is being made. One way to ensure total participation in decision-making is to start with the students in dyads. When they have arrived at an answer, instruct them to join with another dyad and discuss the issue in this group of four until they arrive at an answer. Proceed to combine groups until the total class is meeting as one group.

It is obvious, then, that the size of a discussion group is determined primarily by the *purpose* of the discussion. The teacher will probably wish to use small groups of eight to ten most frequently—sometimes breaking these into dyads or triads for special purposes that require high involvement, and sometimes bringing the class together in the total group for special experiences and decision making. No rule of thumb is possible in deciding what size to utilize. The teacher simply has to experiment to determine what size works best for his particular purposes.

Assigning Students to Groups

The manner in which the teacher assigns students to groups will likewise depend on his purpose. Random assignment usually assures a good mixture of boys and girls, highly verbal and passive students, leaders and followers, and enthusiastic and reluctant learners. Studies have shown that heterogeneous groups are more likely to do well on a task than are homogeneous groups. Random assignment can often be accomplished best by using a counting-off procedure:

> * Divide the number of students in the class by the number of members you want in each small group. The result is the highest number to which students should number-off. For example, if there are thirty students in the class and you want there to be no more than eight in each small group, instruct students to number-off from one to four. Then, instruct all the ones to form one group, all the twos to form another group, and so forth.

However, especially in the early part of the term, the teacher may wish to allow students to work with people whom they already know in order to assure that they will feel comfortable in the group. This can most easily be accomplished by simply asking students to find five (or seven or three) other students with whom they want to work. Many students may be reluctant to take the risk of choosing other members or may be hurt if they are not chosen by anyone. Therefore, a sociometric device like the following is sometimes preferable:

* Give each student a card and ask him to write his name in the upper left-hand corner. Then, ask him to list two members of the class with whom he would like to work. If a student can think of only one or wants to list more than two, that is perfectly acceptable. Then, ask students to turn the cards in to you—explaining that you will keep the information entirely confidential. Using the information on the cards, you can assign students to small groups in which there is at least one person with whom they stated they wanted to work. When it is not possible to include any of a student's choices, try to assign him to a group in which at least one person chose him.

As the term progresses, you may wish to change the composition of the small groups in order to separate students who are hostile to each other or to place an inhibited student in a more encouraging atmosphere. In general, however, we suggest leaving the groups intact for as long a period of time as is feasible. As we discussed in Chapter Three, it takes any group many weeks to become well-acquainted with one another and to develop the cohesiveness that makes their work productive and enjoyable. Rearranging the composition of small groups merely to "expose" students to others in the class will probably result in less effective work and an atmosphere of uneasiness. As we will explain in detail later, there are many other means of overcoming hostility between group members or encouraging inhibited students besides changing their group assignment.

Seating Arrangements

As we pointed out in the contrasting examples of discussion earlier, the seating arrangement in the classroom can seriously affect the effectiveness of group discussions. It is axiomatic that discussion groups should sit in such a way that all members can see all other members and that all members can hear one another without the need to shout. A tight circle fills this requirement best. If the total class is meeting together, their desks should be arranged in a circle, with empty desks removed and wide spaces between desks eliminated. The teacher should sit at a student's desk as part of the circle, to dispel the impression that he is the focal point of the discussion. In small classrooms in which a circle is simply not possible, a double semicircle or horseshoe is an alternative. If a semicircle is used, the teacher should avoid the temptation to sit or stand in the open side, but instead should join the group as participant rather than authority figure.

When the class divides into small groups, each group should pull their desks into a small circle. They should be encouraged to sit as close to one another as possible, so that they do not have to talk loudly and thus disturb other groups. Small groups should be spaced in the class-room in such a way as to maximize the distance between them. Parti-tions between small groups are useful in reducing distractions, but are certainly not necessary.

Assigning the Task

In the typical teacher-led discussion, it is not necessary for students to know what direction the discussion is expected to take or what goal they are supposed to reach. The goal is the teacher's responsibility, and students need only to follow along and they get there. However, in a group-centered discussion it is extremely important for the members to know precisely what they are expected to accomplish. Otherwise, the ambiguity of the situation produces confusion and hostility which se-verely limits the possibility of productive interaction. The teacher, then, must make very clear to the groups what task they are to work on and how long they have to accomplish it.

This implies, of course, that the teacher have a clear idea of what he wants students to do in a discussion. Too often a teacher may jot in his lesson plans something like: "Discuss *Lord of the Flies* in small groups." If students are given an assignment like this one, they are likely to accomplish little beyond becoming angry with one another and with the teacher. A better assignment would be: "Decide as a group which character in *Lord of the Flies* the author intends for you to see as admirable" (problem solving), or, "Share with the members of your group the way you feel about the way the boys treat one another in *Lord of the Flies*" (open-ended).

In most cases the assignment will be of the problem-solving type. That is, the teacher will give the students a specific description of the product he wants them to create by the end of the discussion:

I'd like you to take about twenty minutes to decide as a group three or four feasible means of controlling population growth.

Please use the next two class periods to come up with an answer to the following question that all members of your group can support: What was the chief cause of the Second World War?

By noon I'd like each group to arrive at a solution to the geometry problem on page 54.

Each of your groups is to plan a menu for a buffet supper that will serve ten persons for not more than $1.50 each. I'd like your final decisions by the end of the period tomorrow.

As a group, write a paragraph with details arranged in chronological order. You have fifteen minutes to finish it.

Let's see which of our small groups can come up with the largest list of things made from rubber.

If sharing ideas and feelings is the teacher's goal for a discussion, he should make this clear to the students. For more open-ended discussions, an assignment might be made thus:

For the next fifteen minutes or so, I'd like you to tell the other members of your group how you feel about the way the American Indians were treated during the period of westward expansion that we've been studying. It isn't important for you to all agree. The purpose is for you to express your own personal feelings.

Tell the other members of your small group about a time when you felt proud of yourself, like the boy in the story I read you.

Take a few moments to share with your group an experience you had when you were a child that made you feel much the same way as Claude in *The Two of Us*.

What is the most important thing you've learned about child care during this unit? Tell your group about it. I'll call time in a half-hour.

All of the examples given thus far of both problem-solving and open-ended assignments have been concerned with subject matter that is *external* to the group. That is, the discussion topics have been based almost exclusively on, or at least indirectly linked to, the subject matter of the course. There will be times, however (as we will describe in more detail in the following chapter), when the teacher will wish to focus the group discussion on *internal* topics, that is, the process of their work together and their ways of relating to one another. Despite the change of focus—from external to internal subject matter—the teacher must give the assignment clearly and explicitly. He should know exactly what purposes the discussion is to serve and give the students appropriate instructions. Here are examples of good assignments for problem-solving discussions with an *internal* focus:

> Decide as a group what the three most serious obstacles to good discussion in your group are and how you can best overcome them. Please take no more than thirty minutes to come up with your answer.

> I would like each group to devise a plan that will enable us to share the limited amount of lab equipment that we have. Take about fifteen minutes to arrive at a suggestion, and then we'll come together with the total class to decide which group's plan we can all support.

> I'd like you to evaluate the discussions you've been having by arriving at answers to the following questions. Please turn in your group's answer by the end of the period: 1) Who most often gets things started in the group? 2) Who rarely contributes to the discussion? 3) Why don't they? 4) Whose opinions seem to be most highly respected? 5) Who normally gives in and agrees with the rest of the group?

Like discussions with an external focus, a discussion with an internal focus can also have an open-ended structure:

> For the next ten minutes share with your group the way you have felt toward them during today's discussion.

> Let's spend the entire period today talking over with our small groups the difficulties we feel we have in communicating with them. It's not important today for you to arrive at any answers—just share the feelings of frustration that many of you have been voicing to me privately.

Most teachers find it helpful to make the assignment of group discussion topics while the class is still in the total group. He is then more likely to have the class's close attention and less likely to be interrupted by the noise of moving chairs and students warming themselves up for work. It is also helpful to write assignments on the blackboard or give a copy to each group, so that the members can refer to it if any aspect of the assignment becomes unclear during the course of the discussion.

The Teacher's Role

Having made the assignment and asked the students to divide themselves into groups, the teacher changes his role from leader to observer.
In a group-centered discussion, as we have emphasized before, the
leadership emerges from the group members themselves. The teacher
may aid this process by clarifying what is happening, by calling the
group's attention to its behavior and by asking questions. But he does
not attempt to lead the group in a predetermined direction. For one
thing, if there are several small groups working at once, it would be
physically impossible for the teacher to function as leader in more than
one at a time. But even when the total class is meeting in a large group,
the teacher will probably want to withdraw after giving the assignment
and to allow the group to move in its own way toward fulfilling the
assignment.

Imagine a classroom with three groups of nine students each engaged in group-centered discussions of the question, "Should the United
States have joined the League of Nations?" As soon as he makes the
assignment, Mr. Robertson begins to circulate among the tenth-graders,
watching them get started on their work. To one group that is still
fidgeting and chattering about last night's game he says rather firmly,
"You have only twenty minutes; better not waste time." To another
group that is working enthusiastically but not quite on the subject, he
says, "Let me interrupt a moment. Jim, what is the issue that your group
is discussing right now? *(Jim answers.)* Tod, do you agree with that? Is
that what you thought you were discussing? *(Tod answers.)* Well, I'd
urge you to look again at the assignment on the board and make sure
you're on the right track." As he approaches the third group, he is
accosted by Sara, who demands, "Mr. Robertson, the kids in this group
don't know what they're talking about. They've been saying that President Wilson . . ." Mr. Robertson smiles and touches Sara on the shoul-
der to show that he sympathizes with her frustration, then suggests that
Sara continue to work out the conflict with the other members of her
group.

When the twenty minutes are up, Mr. Robertson calls time. He may
feel that all of the groups have adequately considered the various aspects
of the issue and can move on to a new task. Or, he may wish to return
the students to the total classroom group in order to share their conclusions with the other members of the class, thus exposing them to points
of view they may have not considered. He may even wish to shift for a

moment to a teacher-led discussion, in order to raise questions that were not brought up in the small groups. His decision will depend on what he considers to be the purpose of the group-centered discussion and what he observed happening during the discussion. Sharing with the total group, we should emphasize again, is not something that needs to take place routinely. If the small group discussions have accomplished their purpose, asking someone from each group to report its findings to the total class is not necessary. Only if the small groups have uncovered or produced information that the total group would be interested in or would need in order to accomplish its goals, should the teacher plan a period of reporting back to the class.

Once a classroom group has developed the ability to work effectively together on a task, the teacher may change his role from observer to group member. That is, he may join a group with relatively the same status as any other member, contributing his ideas when they are appropriate and taking his share of the responsibility. As participant, the teacher does not dominate the group, he does not determine the direction in which the group is to move, he does not insist on special recognition. But he is free to share his ideas, to voice his opinions, to suggest dwelling longer on a particular question, to initiate new topics—just as is every other group member. However, we must emphasize forcefully that the teacher cannot hope to join a group as member until he has first withdrawn from leadership and demonstrated by his behavior that the group must take responsibility for themselves. He must realize that if he joins the group before they have developed their own competence at group work, they will almost invariably expect him to assume leadership of their group. And the average teacher is usually unable to resist the temptation to assume this role. Therefore, he must patiently function as observer until the group has learned to work without him (that is, until they have reached stage four in their development). Only then are they ready to receive him as a member.

LAYING THE GROUNDWORK: DEVELOPING SKILLS FOR GROUP DISCUSSION

From our glowing descriptions of group-centered discussion, it would be easy for the reader to assume that all that is needed for such a discussion to be productive and exciting is for the teacher to arrange the desks in a circle, write an assignment on the board and mill around watching the students interact joyfully. We only wish that it were that simple. The truth is that group-centered discussion requires much more than just the good intentions of the teacher. It is necessary for the students to have a number of basic skills in working together. If the group members do not have these skills, the group-centered discussion is likely to be unrewarding. In fact, a group-centered discussion has perhaps a greater probability of ending in disaster than a teacher-led discussion, since in the latter the teacher can use his leadership skills to compensate for the students' lack of discussion ability.

For example, in group-centered discussion all members have to take responsibility to contribute, or else the task doesn't get completed. In a teacher-led discussion, lack of this sense of responsibility can be somewhat overcome by the teacher's calling on various students to contribute. Likewise, in a group-centered discussion the members must consciously link their contributions to others in order to build a group product. If this does not happen naturally in a teacher-led discussion, the teacher can easily point out the relationships between contributions and assist the group in putting them together. The temptation is great for the teacher to continue to compensate for the lack of skills in the students by doing most of the work in the discussion himself, thus increasing the likelihood of a "good" discussion. As a result, students miss the benefits that come from interacting directly with one another and they may never develop the skills necessary for working with others.

An alternative to either a teacher-dominated discussion or a disastrous group-centered discussion is to assure that students develop the necessary discussion skills. It is possible for the teacher to perceive weaknesses in the group's ability to work together and to intervene with activities and suggestions for improvement. Thus, the success of a group-centered discussion need not be left to chance. The teacher can provide specific guidance in the development of a particular skill when he sees evidence in the group's work that they need help. Or, he can plan a training sequence of activities for the entire class that will develop the skills needed before the groups start to work on subject-matter tasks.

The fundamental skills and conditions for effective group discussion fall into nine categories, ranging from establishing trust to arriving at consensus. In the discussion that follows, the skills and conditions are presented in the order of their complexity; thus, the teacher who wishes to devise a skill-building sequence should use these activities in the order they are presented here, since each builds on those developed previously.

Getting Acquainted and Establishing Trust

In the early stages of any group, as we pointed out in Chapter Three, the participants usually "play their hands close to their chests" and risk very little. The implications for subject-matter discussions are obvious: if students are uncertain of the reactions of other members of their group, they are less likely to share their ideas freely, and the discussion will thus lack substance and commitment.

To avoid classroom discussions in which students never really get involved, the teacher must structure activities that will quickly get the members of groups well-acquainted with one another and reasonably trusting of the reactions of others. Getting acquainted and developing trust depend on knowledge of the other members of the group so that one knows what to expect from them. Hopefully, group members discover that they have a number of things in common with one another and that they do not have to be afraid of being hurt by others. Of course, the amount of trust in a group is relative, and only sharing a large number of experiences and being supported by the group over a length of time is likely to produce a truly trusting group. Nevertheless, the teacher—by encouraging students to share information about themselves—can facilitate the trust-development process and get a group interacting more freely from the beginning of its life together. Some or all of the following activities can be utilized in the early stages of group development:

* Ask students to go around the circle, each introducing himself to the group and telling something about himself that he thinks the others should know in order to be well-acquainted with him. Repeat this activity on successive days, instructing the students to share different information each time: hobbies, a description of their family, an adjective that describes themselves, one thing they particularly like, something they dislike or a principle they are strongly committed to.

* Play games such as "Going to Jerusalem" that will help students learn each others' names quickly: the first person gives his own name, the second person gives his name and the name of the first person, the third person gives his name plus the name of the second person plus the name of the first person, and so forth (See the example on pages 74-75). Repeat the procedure, starting at the other end of the circle. During another class period you might ask for volunteers to name each member of the group or require each person to name every other member correctly.

* Let students ask one another questions in order to learn as much as possible about the others in the group. A particularly interesting way to structure this process is to arrange a format such as "Meet the Press" or other TV shows in which a visiting celebrity is interviewed by reporters. Ask for a volunteer to be the visiting celebrity (or take each student in order around the circle), and instruct the other members of the group to ask him questions that will help them get to know what kind of person he is. Make it clear that the "celebrity" may decline to answer any questions he wishes.

* If you do not have time to utilize such a formal structure for the questioning, or in order to extend and supplement it, merely ask various students questions yourself during the final moments of a period or at some other "dead" time during the day. Direct one question per student and move quickly through the group: "What's your favorite kind of pie?" "Whom would you have voted for in the last election?" "If you could be any animal, what would it be?" "What's your favorite color?" "How many siblings do you have?" "If you could be anywhere else but here right now, where would it be?" The questions should not be deathly serious or probing, but should be asked in a friendly, lighthearted way in order to give students practice in talking about themselves and their opinions in front of the class and to provide other members of the group with information about them.

* Give each student a sheet of paper at the top of which is printed I AM . . . , followed by spaces about two lines in length numbered from one to ten. Ask students to fill in the blanks and then share their answers with the group. A student can be asked to read his entire list, or the group can go around the circle reading one item at a time. Other students can ask clarifying questions if they wish to.

* Divide the class into dyads. Instruct each pair to find out as much as possible about each other in, say, fifteen minutes. Then, reconvene the class and have each person introduce his partner to the group.

* Divide the class into dyads by instructing students to find someone in the group whom they do not already know. Tell them to spend ten minutes finding out as much about the other person as they can. Then, instruct each pair to find another pair (whom they do not already know, if possible) and spend fifteen minutes getting acquainted with the other pair. Then, combine the quartets into octets and repeat the getting-acquainted procedure. After the octets have gotten acquainted, combine each of them with another octet (or whatever the size of the class makes necessary) and continue until the class is back into the total group.

* Divide the group into an inner circle and an outer circle. Have one circle move around so that each person spends a few minutes getting acquainted with each person in the other circle. Give students a particular assignment,

such as, "Tell your partner about a time when you were happy," or, "Tell your partner how you'd spend $50."

* To give the class an opportunity to see quickly where various people stand on different kinds of issues (whether related to the subject matter or not), use a values continuum: Mark on the board a line, labeling one end "yes" and the other "no." State an issue ("The federal government should require couples to limit themselves to two children," or, "Smoking marijuana," or, "Stealing small change from your mother's purse") and have each member of the group mark where his own values fall on the continuum. Or, indicate the ends of the continuum with chairs and have each member of the group stand where he thinks his views fall on the continuum. It is important to provide the group with many different kinds of issues that would divide the class along many different lines (Adapted from Raths, Harmin and Simon, 1966).

* After students have experienced a number of getting-acquainted activities, ask them to tell what they now know about each of the other members of their group. You might wish to have them first summarize what the other person has told them about himself, and then ask for the person's inferences based on the other member's nonverbal cues and behavior in the group.

After the class has become fairly well-acquainted, there is value in beginning to call their attention to the process of developing trust, to help them become conscious of the factors that cause them to trust the group and that cause others to trust them:

* At the beginning of a class period, without any preliminary explanation, tell the class that you need three volunteers to perform a task in front of the group. Do not describe the task, but exert pressure until three volunteers have come forward. When you have obtained three volunteers, tell the class: "I had no special task in mind for these volunteers. I just wanted you to have the experience of being called on to volunteer, so that we could talk about the feelings that you have at times like that." Ask the volunteers to return to their seats and begin a discussion of the reasons why students are reluctant to volunteer to perform in front of the group or why they might be willing to:

"How did you feel while I was waiting for volunteers—what thoughts went through your mind? What made you wish to volunteer and what held you back? If you were somewhat afraid to volunteer, what were you afraid of? What kind of risks are involved in volunteering to perform in front of the group? What do other people do to make you afraid? Are your fears unfounded? What previous experiences have you had in volunteering? How did you feel then? How have your previous experiences influenced your present decision? What are some other times when you might feel the way you did while I was waiting for you to volunteer?" (Adapted from Mill, 1971).

* Ask students to imagine that they are going to tell their deepest, darkest, innermost secret to the members of their group. Make it clear that they are not going to be asked to reveal the secret in any way, but that you want them to imagine that they had just told it to the group. Then, ask each student to tell the other members of the group (either one at a time or taking the group as a whole) how he imagines they would react to hearing the secret. Would they be horrified? Would they laugh? Would they be understanding? Would they be sad? Would they dislike him?

* Ask members of the group to discuss among themselves what each person in the group could do to be more trustworthy: "What kind of behavior on the part of each person here would cause you to trust him more? What could he do to make you feel more free to talk in front of him about things that are important to you?"

Taking Responsibility

The next skill that group members must have if a discussion is to be successful is a willingness to take responsibility for the work of the group. Having experienced years of teacher-centered discussion, most students expect the group's leader to worry about whether the task gets done or not. Indeed, in most classrooms it is considered unfashionable to be concerned about the outcome of a learning activity, and any student who shows interest in getting the job done is likely to be ridiculed.

The teacher will therefore have to take deliberate steps to establish new norms in the classroom. He must demonstrate by his behavior as well as his words that when a task is assigned to a discussion group the group *as a whole* is responsible for completing the task. Therefore, he will probably wish to:

* remove himself from the group, so that they do not look to him for leadership;

* refrain from appointing a leader or chairman of the discussion group on whom the other members can place all responsibility; natural leadership should be allowed to emerge, or the groups themselves should decide they want a chairman and who they wish it to be;

* give the same grade to all members of the group if the quality of their

group product is to be graded at all; thus, cooperation rather than competition becomes the norm;

* give students instruction in the types of helpful roles they might wish to assume in a group. The most important membership roles in small-group discussion are the following:

INITIATOR—gets the discussion underway, helps the group organize itself, keeps the group moving steadily toward its goal;

CONTRIBUTOR—offers facts, opinions and experiences which might aid the group in solving the problem;

CLARIFIER—raises questions about contributions that are unclear, asks for definitions of vague or ambiguous terms, requests additional information;

SUMMARIZER—points out the relationships between contributions, summarizes where the group stands on an issue (then checks with the group to make sure he is accurate);

EVALUATOR—shows the group how well they are moving toward accomplishing their goal, points out problems they are having in working together;

RECORDER—keeps a record of the main points of the discussion, writes down the group product if it is to be submitted to the teacher, helps refresh the group's memory about what has been covered in a discussion;

ENCOURAGER—tries to get all members of the group to contribute by showing interest in what they say, praising their contributions, being friendly;

HARMONIZER—helps to relieve tension and settle disputes between other members, helps the group work out its disagreements, suggests compromises.

Write the roles on the board and explain them, or give each student the list on a sheet of paper. (For younger students the roles can be condensed into Starter, Contributor, Encourager, Responder.) Give examples of the sorts of things a person playing each role might say during a discussion and ask the students to suggest other examples. Point out that any person in the group can play any of the roles whenever he feels that it is appropriate and that he does not have to play the same role throughout the discussion. Then, to give students practice in playing helpful membership roles, secretly assign each member a role to play while discussing a controversial issue or some subject-matter question. Instruct the students not to tell anyone what role they've been assigned but to see if other members can perceive it through their behavior during the discussion. Call time after twenty or thirty minutes, and see if the group can guess what roles the various members were playing. If anyone had difficulty playing his role, ask him to explain why. Ask members of the group to suggest how one another could have played their roles more effectively. Reemphasize that any member of the group can play any of the roles when he feels he should during the course of a classroom discussion.

* To encourage all members to take an active part in the discussion, assign the group a simple topic—one which every member will know something about—and require every member to have contributed at least once (or twice) before time is called. A structure such as this encourages quieter members to join in by both exerting subtle pressure on them to contribute and putting the same expectations on all members of the group. As one rather shy student wrote after experiencing this exercise, "It's made it easier for me to talk without being self-conscious. Everyone feels the same, because we're all under the same pressure."

* Assign each member of a small group a specific responsibility—to make sure all members contribute, to keep a record of the group's decisions, to secure all resource material the group needs, to observe the group's process and point out to other members how the group can improve its functioning. These responsibilities can be exchanged from time to time so that all members have a chance to play all roles. What is important is that every member of the group feels that he has an essential contribution to make to the progress.

* Structure activities that require the group to evaluate their own performance and take responsibility for improving it, rather than informing them of your evaluation of their work. (See the section on Seeing the Problem (pp. 121-124) for suggested activities.)

Encouraging Others to Contribute

In addition to taking responsibility for the work of the group by contributing actively to the discussion, each member also must feel a sense of responsibility to encourage other members—particularly the less vocal ones—to share their ideas. Without this sense of responsibility, the more competent students ignore other members of the group, assuming that they can get the job done faster and more easily by doing all of the work themselves. These students usually meet with very little resistance from the quieter members of the group whom they ignore, since the less confident students are frequently all too glad to let someone else do the work.

Students need to be convinced of the value of the contributions of all members of their group. They must realize that the more information and opinions they can bring to bear on a problem the more likely they will be to arrive at a valid conclusion. In order to obtain the information that can be supplied by all members of the group, some members may have to directly encourage others to contribute it.

> * Perhaps the best way to demonstrate to students the need for encouraging others and to give them practice in doing so is to assign them a task which demands that every student's contribution be considered. Devise a puzzle or mystery and give each person in the group an essential clue. Then, set the group to work solving it. If the group is not skilled in eliciting contributions from all its members, they will not be able to solve the puzzle or mystery. It may be necessary to help them think through the problems they're having in working together by asking questions such as the following: Why wasn't the group able to arrive at an answer more quickly? Did the group have trouble getting organized and keeping order? What responsibility did each member have? What happened when some members did not present their clues? What could the other members have done in order to obtain the clues from quieter members? For examples of this type of activity, see *Learning Discussion Skills Through Games* by Gene Stanford and Barbara Dodds Stanford, listed under Additional Resources at the end of this chapter.

Students may also need to be taught specific ways to elicit contributions from others rather than discouraging them, particularly if they have the misconception that "discussion" means heated argument. Many students may assume that they are expected to challenge a speaker and question his ideas rather than accept them and encourage him to contribute more. To dispel this misconception, the teacher may need to give students specific examples of helpful responses and provide occasions for them to practice the new responses.

> * Write on the board or distribute to students examples of the listener behavior that helps to draw out a speaker:
>
> Asking clarifying questions;
> Expressing support and understanding;
> Reflecting what the speaker says or feels;
> Looking directly at the speaker and nodding to show you are listening.

Give examples of these behaviors and ask students to suggest other examples. Ask students how these behaviors differ from the way listeners in a group normally act. Ask why arguing or disagreeing with a person tends to discourage him from talking more. Then, divide students into triads to practice the drawing-out behavior. Instruct one member of each triad to be the focus of the conversation and to describe some principle he is committed to or some value he considers very important to him personally. Or, have him talk about a personal problem or something that has happened to him recently that bothers him. Instruct another member of the triad to respond in ways that will encourage the speaker to continue explaining his ideas. The third member acts as a referee to assure that the other two follow the directions carefully. Allow the speakers ten minutes, and then instruct the triads to exchange roles until all three students have had a chance to play all three roles. Then, reconvene the groups and have students practice encouraging responses during a group discussion.

Careful Listening

Almost every classroom discussion group suffers from a lack of listening ability. The typical group member views the periods when others are talking as at worst an annoying interruption in his own chance to talk, or at best an opportunity to think through what he is going to say next. As a result, he either fails to hear the other person entirely or he responds—usually by disagreeing—to something that he *thinks* the other person meant. If a discussion group is to succeed in building a group solution to a problem or in arriving at a decision the entire group can support, it is imperative that they be able to listen in depth to one another—both to understand accurately what the other person said and to perceive empathically the entire message behind the spoken contribution.

* Most groups can benefit from training in "reflective listening." Divide the group into triads. Assign one student the role of observer and instruct the other two to discuss a controversial topic that they disagree on—this can be some social issue or a question related to the subject matter of the course. Explain that the two students discussing the topic must abide by the following rule and that the observer is to monitor them to make sure they do so:

Before replying to the other person's remarks, you must first summarize them to his satisfaction. Only then may you point out how you disagree with him.

Instruct the observers to interrupt the speakers whenever they fail to follow the rule and to make sure that the first speaker is satisfied with the paraphrase of his remarks before allowing the second speaker to begin. The interaction that will result from this format will of course be awkward, but it will encourage students to listen closely to the speaker before deciding how they are going to respond.

* After students have had ample practice with this procedure in triads, return them to the group and begin a group discussion with the same rule in effect. Appoint one student to monitor the contributions and interrupt anyone who does not satisfactorily summarize the previous contribution before adding his own.

* Once students have developed the ability to paraphrase accurately the previous contribution, it may be useful to give them practice in perceiving and reflecting not only the words of the speaker but also the feelings behind his words. Divide students in dyads and give the following instructions: "Choose one member of your dyad to be the speaker and one to be the listener. You will be switching roles, so it doesn't matter whom you choose to start, since you will both take each of the roles before we've finished. The speaker is to describe to the listener something that is very meaningful to him personally." (If students need more specific instructions, suggest one of the following: something that you really like about yourself, something that you'd like to change about yourself, something that recently happened which upset you, a personal problem, something about you that the listener doesn't know.) "The listener will periodically stop the speaker and summarize what he has just heard. The listener, however, must do more than just repeat the words of the speaker or rephrase them slightly. He must try to understand what meaning the idea has for the speaker and how he feels about it, and to communicate this back to the speaker. For example, a listener might say, 'You had this argument with your best friend and now you're feeling really bad about it. You'd like to apologize to him but you kinda hate to back down. But being on bad terms with him has you so upset that you would really like to do what it takes to clear things up. Is that it?' The listener must be careful not to argue with the speaker or take the 'focus' off him in any way. All he does is to occasionally summarize what messages are being communicated to him by the speaker—both the verbal message and the feelings included in the message." (If you suspect the listeners will find it hard to avoid arguing or interjecting their own ideas, use triads instead of dyads and have the third member act as monitor.) Call time after ten minutes. Give the speaker a few moments to tell the listener how well he seemed to understand him. Then, have the students switch roles and proceed as above for ten more minutes, followed by a few moments for the new speaker to tell his listener how well he felt he was being understood.

Responding to Other Contributions

The "skyrocket" phenomenon is a familiar characteristic of a poorly skilled discussion group. Each member contributes by "firing up a skyrocket," that is, by introducing a new, unrelated idea for the group to marvel at. Everyone feels pleased with himself for taking such an active part in the discussion, but no one shows much interest in establishing connections between the ideas and no one troubles to link his contribution to the previous one. The result is a brilliant display of individual cleverness, but one which does not contribute to either a coherent discussion or a decision. Sensitivity to how his ideas fit with the direction of the discussion is an essential attribute of the skilled group member. This sensitivity is reflected in his ability to perceive to what extent his ideas agree or disagree with those of the previous speaker, to perceive whether his idea is appropriate to the direction of the discussion and to indicate to the group when he is making a contribution that will move the discussion in a different direction.

> * Give a group a question to be discussed—either a controversial social issue or a subject-matter problem. Instruct the members that they can contribute only by responding to the previous speaker—that is, telling him in what ways and to what extent they agree or disagree with his contribution. Rather than simply stating their own position on the question, they must comment on or add to the previous contribution. At first you may wish to give the discussion more structure by calling on the students to speak:
>
> 1. Call on a student to give his views on the question;
> 2. Ask for a volunteer to respond to him; this student must look directly at speaker 1 and comment on or reply to his remarks, adding any new ideas that he has;
> 3. When he has finished, call on a third student to respond to speaker 2 by looking directly at him and commenting on his remarks;
> 4. Continue until every group member has contributed in this fashion.

In groups that are somewhat more skilled, it might be possible to allow members to choose when they wish to contribute, but with the interaction governed by the understanding that they will look at and respond to the previous speaker before adding their own ideas. A student observer should be appointed to make sure everyone follows the rule.

* Ask three students to present their views on a controversial issue. Then, instruct another member of the group to summarize the differences between the positions expressed.

* During a discussion of a controversial issue or subject-matter question, stop the group occasionally and ask a student to summarize the similarities and differences between the positions expressed by various members of the group.

* During a group discussion, appoint a student observer (or several) to watch for instances in which a contribution does not seem appropriate to the direction of the discussion. Instruct them to interrupt the speaker and tell him why they do not think his contribution is relevant at that time. If he continues to think it is appropriate, the observers should instruct him to make this clear by prefacing his contribution with an explanation that will provide the proper transition. You might wish to give the group examples of these transitions before the discussion begins: "I would like to suggest a different reason that we haven't considered yet . . .," or, "I'd like to bring up again an idea that we discussed earlier but didn't seem to finish . . .," or, "We don't seem to be able to agree on this part of the problem; perhaps we should leave it for a while and come back to it later . . ."

* Assign a discussion topic that is likely to elicit a strong reaction from the group members. Call on one student to express his views. Then, call on a second student to respond to the first speaker. Instruct him to first summarize the remarks of the first speaker and then to tell all the ways in which he agrees with the first speaker. He is not to express any disagreement until he has both summarized the previous position and indicated all areas of agreement with it. Then, he becomes the speaker and can express his own views, including any disagreement with the first speaker. When he has finished, call on a third student to summarize speaker 2's remarks and state to what extent he agrees with him. Proceed until all students have contributed. Some groups may be able to do this exercise without direct supervision of the teacher. If so, appoint a student observer to monitor the interaction to make sure it follows the procedure outlined above.

Setting Clear Goals

Many times when group members make contributions that are not appropriate to the direction of the discussion, the reason is either that they were not aware of the goal of the discussion or that the group did not explicitly formulate a goal before they began. For a discussion to be successful, all members must know at all times what the goal of their interaction is. If the topic has been assigned by the teacher, and if it is narrow in scope and phrased in precise language, the group may be able to set to work without needing to formulate a clear statement of its goal. But if the teacher has left the question somewhat open, the group will need to spend time at the beginning of the discussion establishing exactly what the issue is. In either case, all members should know at all times throughout a discussion what issue the group hopes to resolve or what task they hope to accomplish. Only then can they decide how best to contribute.

* Interrupt the group at intervals during a discussion and ask various members to state precisely what issue the group is discussing and how it relates to the goal of the group.

* Without any mention of the purpose of this activity, ask each of the small groups to send a member to receive instructions and act as observer. Give each observer a copy of the form described below, on which to record their observations of the performance of their groups during work on two different tasks. Warn them not to make any suggestions to the group, but to sit outside the circle and make notes on the form of the group's behavior.

Observation Form

1. How often did members of the group ask for clarification of the goals or attempt to clarify the goals?

   Task 1:   *Task 2:*

2. What was the overall atmosphere of the group? Was it pleasant, hostile, friendly, excited, bored, encouraging, etc.? Did the atmosphere change during the discussion?

   Task 1:   *Task 2:*

3. How did members of the group act during the discussion? What things did they say besides contributing to the discussion? What things did they do during the discussion?

Task 1:   *Task 2:*

4. How far did the group get toward completing the task?

Task 1:	*Task 2:*
__Got nothing done	__Got nothing done
__Got very little done	__Got very little done
__Got an average amount done	__Got an average amount done
__Got much done	__Got much done
__Finished the task	__Finished the task

After the observers have returned to their groups, tell the class that you have two different tasks for them to do during that period, each of which will take ten minutes—and that you will warn them when nine minutes are up. Write the first assignment on the board or distribute it on sheets of paper to the students. This assignment should be worded in a very vague, abstract, ambiguous language. It can be either a subject-matter question or some topic of general interest to the students. An example might be, "What are the primary reasons why schools fail to adequately contribute to the social development of the average student?" The words should all be familiar to the students; but the exact goal of the discussion should be clouded by vague wording. Set the groups to work. After nine minutes have elapsed, warn the groups that they have only one minute left. When time is up, ask each group to submit its answer in writing.

Then, write the second assignment on the board and tell the group they have ten minutes to complete it. The second task should be extremely clear, such as, "List as many as you can of the ways in which students in this class spend their time after school." Warn the groups after nine minutes, and call time after ten. Then, tell the groups that you would like them to hear from the observers and to discuss the difference in their performance on the first and second tasks. The following questions can be used to guide the follow-up discussion: "How did we go about clarifying the goals of the assignment (especially task 1)? What were the consequences of not setting clear goals? Did having clear goals make the job easier? How did people act when the goals were unclear? Were they as happy in the group? Were they as interested in the task? Did they participate as much?" Then, ask each group to return to the first assignment and to attempt to clarify the goals of the task. They need not repeat their discussion, but should merely decide what the intended outcome of the discussion was. (Adapted from Mill, 1971).

Learning to Cooperate

The norm in most classrooms is competition. Competition is fostered by encouraging students, subtly if not explicitly, to make the highest grade in the class, even at the expense of their classmates; to please the teacher and thus get more attention from him than do the others; and to win "first place" in contests ranging from Homecoming Queen to Best Bathroom Monitor. Yet, for most tasks, cooperation yields more productive and valid outcomes than does competition, besides promoting an atmosphere in which students feel confortable and accepted. Members of classroom groups need to be encouraged to work *with* one another instead of *against* one another in accomplishing their goals.

> * Therefore, if students' work in group discussions is to be graded at all, the entire group should be given the same grade as a measure of how well the group accomplished its task. Thus, the brighter, more confident students will attempt to encourage the slower ones, rather than ignoring them in a quest for high grades; and slower students will be encouraged by group norms to do their best.

In group discussion cooperation takes many of the forms we have discussed earlier: encouraging others to contribute rather than ignoring them, drawing others out instead of arguing with them, sharing information and assembling all contributions into a group product that all members can support. Those groups who have mastered these subskills may benefit from an experience which requires that they use their best skills to help one another toward mutual goals rather than placing obstacles in one another's way:

> * For each group that will be assigned this task, prepare a set of squares of cardboard or plastic according to the following specifications:
>
> A set consists of five envelopes containing pieces of cardboard which have been cut into different patterns and which, when properly arranged, will form five squares of equal size. One set should be provided for each group of five persons.
>
> To prepare a set, cut out five cardboard squares of equal size, approximately six-by-six inches. Place the squares in a row and mark them as below, penciling the letters *a, b, c,* etc., lightly, so that they can later be erased.
>
> The lines should be so drawn that, when cut out, all pieces marked *a*

will be of exactly the same size, all pieces marked *c* of the same size, etc. By using multiples of three inches, several combinations will be possible that will enable participants to form one or two squares, but only one combination is possible that will form five squares six-by-six inches.

After drawing the lines on the six-by-six inch squares and labeling them with lowercase letters, cut each square as marked into smaller pieces to make the parts of the puzzle.

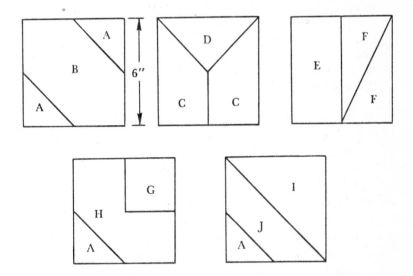

Mark the five envelopes A, B, C, D and E. Distribute the cardboard pieces in the five envelopes as follows:

Envelope A has pieces i, h, e
        B   a, a, a, c
        C   a, j
        D   d, f
        E   g, b, f, c

Erase the penciled letter from each piece and write, instead, the appropriate envelope letter. This will make it easy to return the pieces to the proper envelope for subsequent use when a group has completed the task.[1]

For groups with more than five members, have the groups decide which five will actually do the task, with the others acting as observers. Give the following instructions:

1. Reprinted from Pfeiffer and Jones (1969), pp. 26-27, with permission of University Associates, Publishers and Consultants.

"Today we are going to work a puzzle—a very special kind of puzzle—in a very special way. It will take five members of your group to work the puzzle. The others will sit outside as observers. Would the five working members please move your desks into a tight circle, and the observers please sit outside the circle.

"I am handing you an envelope that contains puzzle pieces. Take the puzzle pieces out of the envelope and set the envelope aside. Leave the pieces lying on your desk in front of you. Do not pick them up until I tell you to begin work.

"Distributed among the five of you are puzzle pieces that will form five complete squares of equal dimensions—one in front of each member. Your task is to assemble a complete square in front of each person. However, you must observe the following rules while assembling the squares:

a. Each person must construct a square directly in front of him on his desk;

b. You may not ask for a piece from any other member; this includes asking verbally or taking physically, as well as signalling, gesturing, motioning or in any other way trying to get a piece from the other members;

c. The only way you can get a piece from another person is for him to give it to you;

d. You may give any of the pieces you have to any other group member;

e. The only time you can talk is when you are giving a piece to someone else (This rule may be changed to, "You may not talk at any time during the exercise," thus limiting the group to nonverbal communication and thus making the task more difficult. Such a limitation may increase frustration unnecessarily, and we recommend it only in rare instances. However, if talking is allowed, it should be limited to helping the other members assemble their puzzles and the rule prohibiting asking for a piece should be strictly enforced.).

Observers will interrupt to enforce these rules. Are there any questions? If not, start to work."

After the groups have finished, discuss the experience. Allow students to talk about the difficulties they encountered and the strategies they used to overcome them. Then, ask them to summarize what they have discovered about cooperation—what attitudes and behaviors cooperation requires that are different from competition.

You may wish to repeat the experience, perhaps with the observers trading places with some of the group members, so that the group can utilize what it has learned from the first trial (Adapted from Bavelas, 1950).

* Other cooperation exercises can be found on pp. 66-70, Vol. II, and pp. 60-62, Vol. III, of Pfeiffer and Jones's *Handbook of Structured Experiences for Human Relations Training* and pp. 55-57 in Hunter's *Encounter in the Classroom*, both listed under Additional Resources.

Coming to Consensus

We have repeatedly emphasized in previous activities the need for discussion groups to pool their contributions and produce a product that reflects the best that all the members can contribute. For this to be accomplished, group members need to feel that by working together they can come up with more valid results than through individual effort. They also must realize that altering one's own views in order to further the group's goals is not always a sign of weakness and may in the long run lead to a better solution. Conversely, the individual must know that by not giving in to group pressure, even if he is in the minority, he can sometimes help the group avoid a mistake. Members need to learn that their individual contributions to the discussion are valuable for more than just enhancing their own self-esteem; the ideas they contribute are the substance from which a group product is built. Members also need to learn that a decision-making process that ignores dissenters and alienates a portion of the group, even if they are a minority, can be harmful in the long run even though it may lead to a quicker decision initially.

For these reasons, the teacher may wish to discuss with students the various forms of decision making and point out the advantages of each—contrasting their efficiency and effectiveness. A dictatorship, it might be noted, is highly efficient, but by not allowing for the input of diverse opinions an authoritarian structure runs the risk of making grave errors based on lack of information or of creating opposition or lack of commitment to the decision. Voting on issues and letting the majority rule is superior to dictatorship, in that it allows for various opinions to be aired and for various points of view to be discussed. But it has distinct disadvantages, primarily the polarizing effect it has on the group. When the majority (often as few as one-half plus one) are declared the winners in any voting, it is probable that the minority will be antagonistic and alienated. The relative efficiency of majority rule is achieved at the expense of a part of the group who are forced to accept a decision they do not agree with. The minority may then expend much of their energy trying to "get back at" the group that alienated them or in winning allies, rather than cooperating in achieving the group's goals.

The alternative is consensus. A consensus is achieved when the group arrives at a decision that all members of the group agree with or can support. To do so requires patience, a free exchange of information, willingness to compromise as well as a willingness to stand firm on important issues, and highly sophisticated skills of group interaction. The process may not be as efficient as either dictatorship or majority rule, but the advantages are many: the solution is more likely to be valid, since many different points of view have been carefully considered, and the possibility of resentment or alienation is reduced.

Consensus is not easily achieved (one reason why it is not utilized more often in decision making), and therefore most classroom groups will need help in developing the skills they need to use this approach. Primarily, they must learn to become aware of those persons who disagree with the majority and to assure that the minority opinions are listened to closely. As a group nears decision, they must ask more frequently, "Who does not agree with this?" and be accepting of the responses. Observers of the group process must be specifically alert for dissenters who are ignored, especially the quieter members who disagree but do not state their opposition vociferously.

* Most of the activities suggested previously help develop the skills necessary for decision making by consensus. However, you may wish to give some specific attention to the specific process of arriving at consensus. Write a statement on the board that reflects a highly controversial point of view, such as, "Abortions should be available to any woman on request," or, "Students caught cheating should immediately be expelled from school." Divide the group into dyads and instruct them to come to agreement on a position that either agrees with, disagrees with or changes the wording of the statement on the board. When a dyad reaches consensus, instruct them to form a quartet with another dyad that has reached consensus and to arrive at a new position that all four members can agree with and support. Continue to combine the groups until the total group comes to consensus.

* Utilize the activities on pp. 71-77 in Vol. III, and pp. 22-24 in Vol. II at Pfeiffer and Jones's *A Handbook of Structured Experiences for Human Relations Training,* and pp. 57-59 in Hunter's *Encounter in the Classroom,* both listed under Additional Resources.

* As we have suggested before, try to frame subject-matter assignments in a form that encourages groups to come to consensus ("Arrive at an answer that all members of your group agree with and can support"). This will give

the groups continual practice in arriving at consensus. When a group submits its product, check to see whether any members do not agree with it. If so, suggest that the group continue to work until they can come to agreement. Help them pinpoint the reason why they cannot reach agreement: Is it because they lack factual information that could be secured by outside reading or research? Is it that they have not clearly defined the problem or their goal? Is it that they are reacting to the persons holding the opinion, rather than disagreeing with the idea itself? Is the group polarized and hostile because they mistakenly assume that issues can be only black or white?

* In addition to giving groups practice in decision making by consensus, the following exercise provides a graphic means of comparing the relative effectiveness of individual effort, majority rule and consensus. Give each participant a sheet of paper on which the following instructions have been reproduced:

Imagine that a friend stops by your house on a Saturday morning in October and suggests that you go with him for a day-long drive in the mountains to try out his new Jeep. You quickly pull on jeans, a sweatshirt and sneakers to go along. By late afternoon you are on a trail in a remote part of the Rockies, when suddenly a snow storm blows up. The trail soon becomes almost impassable and you can hardly see where you are going. Suddenly the Jeep starts to skid and you plunge several hundred feet down a steep mountainside. Your friend is killed instantly and the Jeep is completely wrecked, but fortunately you have only a few scratches. By your best estimate you are thirty to forty miles from the nearest source of help. Luckily you discover a summer cabin nearby. Although it has no heat except a wood burning fireplace and no telephone, it does offer shelter and about a week's supply of food. You soon realize that you cannot hope to stay in the cabin until you are rescued, for no one has any idea where to start looking for you. Therefore, when the storm starts to abate, leaving almost three feet of dry powder snow, you decide to try to follow the trail back to civilization. You are fortunate that the cabin is well stocked with camping equipment and other supplies and you can take almost anything you want, but you know that your survival over the three days it will probably take you to reach help will depend partly on how carefully you select what equipment to take. Below is a list of some of the materials the cabin contains and their weight. Decide which of the following items you will wear or carry, not exceeding a total of 50 pounds.

A. _____wool hat (1 lb.)
B. _____heavy wool mittens (2 lb.)
C. _____axe (8 lb.)
D. _____50 feet of 1/8″ rope (1 lb.)
E. _____saucepan for melting snow for drinking (3 lb.)
F. _____folding camping saw (1 lb.)
G. _____rock-climbing gear, including rock hammer, pitons, etc. (10 lb.)
H. _____150 feet of 7/16″ rope (8 lb.)
I. _____gasoline camp stove and fuel (10 lb.)
J. _____plastic canteen filled with water (2 lb.)
K. _____one large can of beef stew (10 lb.)
L. _____fire-starting kit, including matches (1/2 lb.)
M. _____heavy wool jacket with hood (10 lb.)
N. _____pack frame and bag (6 lb.)
O. _____five two-pound cans of soup and vegetables (10 lb.)
P. _____sleeping bag (5 lb.)
Q. _____downhill skis, bindings, poles (10 lb.)
R. _____air mattress (3 lb.)
S. _____down-filled jacket without hood (3 lb.)
T. _____high-top hunting boots (6 lb.)
U. _____snowshoes (5 lb.)
V. _____canvas tent (15 lb.)
W. _____plastic tarp (2 lb.)
X. _____eight boxes of high protein dry cereal (4 lb. total)
Y. _____first-aid kit with splints and other equipment for setting bones (4 lb.)
Z. _____first-aid kit without splints, etc. (1 lb.)
AA. _____heavy wool pants (4 lb.)
BB. _____knife with can opener (1/2 lb.)

First, ask each student to mark the items that he would choose to take—not to exceed 50 pounds—according to his individual judgment, without consulting with other members of the group. (This can be done in class or can be assigned as homework.) When he has finished, ask him to write his name on his paper and turn it in for scoring. Do not let individuals score their own papers. After all students have finished working independently, give them each a fresh copy of the problem sheet and have them either form small groups of, say, ten students each, or meet as a total class. Instruct them to do the task again, but this time to record the items that the majority of their group thinks they should take (adjusting the list to keep it under 50 pounds). Suggest that they vote after a minimum of discussion, and point out that they do not have to vote the same way they did on their independent answers. While they are working as a group, score their individual answers according to the key below. (The correct answers were supplied by Bill May, author of *Mountain Search and Rescue* and member of the Rocky Mountain Rescue Group, and Bob Bruce, Merchandise Manager of Holubar Mountaineering, Ltd. and a member of the Certification Committee of the United States Ski Association.)

wool hat (1 lb.)
heavy wool mittens (2 lb.)
50 feet of 1/8″rope (1 lb.)
saucepan for melting snow for drinking (3 lb.)
folding camping saw (1 lb.)
plastic canteen filled with water (2 lb.)
fire-starting kit, including matches (1/2 lb.)
pack frame and bag (6 lb.)
sleeping bag (5 lb.)
air mattress (3 lb.)
down-filled jacket without hood (3 lb.)
high-top hunting boots (6 lb.)
snowshoes (5 lb.)
plastic tarp (2 lb.)
eight boxes of high protein dry cereal (4 lb. total)
first-aid kit without splints, etc. (1 lb.)
heavy wool pants (4 lb.)
knife with can opener (1/2 lb.)

To score individual answer sheets, penalize the student one point for each item on his list that does not appear in the key and one point for each item in the key which does not appear in his list. Total these points; this gives an overall score of the individual's performance. (The lower the score, the more accurate the student's answer.) If students are now working in several small groups, separate their answer sheets according to the groups they are working in. Locate the answer sheet of the individual in each group who has the best (lowest) score.

After the group(s) have finished voting, ask them to turn in their results on one sheet labeled with a number indicating their group. Then give each student a third copy of the problem sheet and instruct the group(s) to come to agreement (consensus) on which items to take. Include the following explanation in your instructions: "In trying to arrive at your answers, be sure to use reasoning and factual information instead of simply trying to get the group to see things your way. You should neither refuse to compromise nor give in just to make things easier. Try hard to understand the suggestions of other members, even when they disagree with your own choices. But don't change your mind just to avoid conflict; make sure that you can support any decision the group comes to. Do not use majority rule to decide on an answer; strive for complete agreement by all members of the group."

While the group(s) are trying to arrive at consensus, score the choices made by the voting, following the same procedure as described above for the individual answers. Prepare a summary sheet for each group that includes 1. the score of its most accurate individual, 2. the score resulting from majority rule and 3. the score resulting from decision by consensus. After the group(s) have arrived at consensus (a process that could require several class periods if you don't set a time limit), score their answers and add these to the group summary sheets. Then tell the students the choices that the experts made and let them compare their individual scores with their three group scores: the best individual score in the group, the score with majority rule and the score with consensus.

Follow-up discussion should center on questions such as these: Which method of decision making was most effective for the group—relying on the best individual, voting or consensus? How can the differences between the three scores be explained? Why was consensus harder than voting? What problems did you have in coming to consensus? What ways of working together did you develop while trying to come to consensus? Which method made you *feel* best about the decision? (Based on an activity originally devised by Jay Hall. A similar activity appears in Pfeiffer and Jones, 1969, and can be used for additional practice in arriving at consensus.)

COPING WITH OBSTACLES

A group that has developed the skills outlined previously should be able to handle group-centered discussions profitably and enjoyably. However, every group is likely to encounter some special kinds of problems from tim to time. The teacher needs to be alert for these and prepared to suggest pproaches and activities to help groups correct the problems.

Seeing the Problem: Feedback

The first thing that a group must have before it can correct a problem is awareness of the problem's existence. In many cases, particularly with groups that are already functioning well, merely becoming aware of a problem is all that they need to remedy it. Therefore, the teacher needs to have a number of ways of revealing a group to itself and helping them to analyze their own process.

We have previously described the initial role of the teacher in a group-centered discussion as being that of observer, and have suggested that he stop the group whenever they need to become aware of the process. This is a logical role for the teacher, since he is likely to have more knowledge of and experience with the ways groups work. However, as soon as possible the group itself should take over responsibility for monitoring its pro ess and diagnosing its problems. As the members become more skilled at group-centered discussion, the teacher can use means other than his own interruptions to help groups look at their ways of working together. They are more likely to correct problems they themselves have discovered than those pointed out by an outsider, particularly if the outsider is an adult in authority.

STUDENT OBSERVERS. A group member, either appointed by the teacher or—preferably—chosen by the group, sits outside the circle and observes the group's interaction, giving particular attention to how well they work together.

* Until they gain experience, student observers may need a list of questions to keep in mind while watching the group, with space provided for jotting down notes. The teacher can draw up an "observation form" containing questions such as the following:

1. How effectively is the group working toward its goals?
2. What problems does it seem to be having?
3. Who is talking the most?
4. Who is talking the least?
5. What attempts are being made to include all members?
6. How does the group seem to feel about the task? About each other?
7. What might the group do to improve its effectiveness?

* Or, give the observer a piece of paper with a circle drawn on it and tell

him to jot down the group members' names around the circle in the order in which they are sitting. Instruct the observer to draw an arrow from the member's name to the person to whom he speaks each time. If the member speaks to the group as a whole, the arrow is drawn to the center of the circle. After ten or fifteen minutes, the observer can stop the group and show them the diagram he has constructed. The amount of participation of each member will be clearly revealed and the number of remarks directed toward specific individuals will also be apparent. The group can then discuss what conclusions they draw from the observer's diagram, what problems it reveals and what can be done to correct these problems.

* Have observers use adaptations of the various interaction analysis scales described in detail in Chapter Nine.

* The "fishbowl" design for feedback utilizes one group sitting in a circle inside a larger circle of observers. Divide a group in half, and instruct one half to serve as observers while the other half conducts a discussion as usual. Or, if the group is small, pair two groups and have one serve as observers of the other group. Each observer can be assigned a specific thing to look for: one can watch for monopolizers, another can watch for students who are ignored by the group, another can try to determine what helpful roles the members are playing and so on. Or, assign each member of the observer circle a specific member of the discussion group to observe. After the discussion, the observers meet in dyads with whomever they were watching and give their suggestions for improvement. After the feedback period, the observers move to the inside circle and conduct a discussion that is observed by those who did the discussing in the first round. A similar period of feedback follows the second round.

* Student observers may benefit from a few suggestions on how best to give feedback to group members:

1. Point out the good things as well as the bad.

2. Try to report observations rather than make judgments. For example, it's better to say, "Three people seemed to do about 75% of the talking," than, "Three of you ruined the discussion because you took over."

3. Choose the three or four more important observations or problems rather than flood the group with more information than they can deal with.

4. If reporting to an individual (e.g., after the "fishbowl"), ask him to evaluate his own performance before reporting your observations. He is more likely to accept something if he thought of it himself.

See p. 152 for a more complete discussion of how to give feedback.

GROUP SELF-ANALYSIS. Ultimately, a group should become so skilled in group-centered discussion that the individual members will take responsibility to raise questions about process problems whenever they are appropriate. The ultimate goal should be for a member, when he identifies a potential problem, to interject a question such as, "Aren't we failing to hear the opinions of everyone in the group?" Thus, the group builds in its own maintenance mechanism and comes to correct and control its own process. Until groups reach this level of maturity, however, the teacher may wish to make deliberate provisions for the group to look at their own progress.

* Interrupt the group—either when a specific problem appears or at random intervals—and ask them to consider a question such as, "How are we doing?" "Are we working effectively?" "How far along are we toward attaining our goal?" "How are we feeling about the way the discussion is going?" "Do we understand exactly what we are supposed to be doing?" "Are we all equally interested in this task?" "Are all the contributions relevant to the purpose of the discussion?" "Have we been listening carefully to one another?" "Have we been trying to build on what the rest have been contributing?" Do not *tell* the group what you sense is the problem, but let them discover it on their own. Do not take more than a few minutes for this kind of in-progress evaluation. Then, ask the group to resume work.

* After a group has finished a discussion, have them consider questions similar to those above. Or, stop them a few minutes before the end of a class period (if the discussion does not have strict time limits) and have them evaluate their work.

* Administer a questionnaire to the group, summarize the results and report them to the group (or post them in the classroom). Use questions such as the following (which are also useful to stimulate a discussion of the group's effectiveness, as in the activity described above):

1. Did you have a chance to talk as much as you wanted to?
2. Were you happy during the discussion? If not, why?
3. What could members of the group do to make you happier during discussions?
4. Who seemed to do most of the work of the group?
5. Who in the group listens to you? Who does not?
6. Who did not seem to contribute toward the work of the group?
7. Did anything "bug" you during the discussion? If so, what?
8. What member is most important to the work of the group?

9. What should the group do to improve its functioning?

* Tape-record or videotape a discussion and play it back for the group. Ask them to point out the strengths and weaknesses they observed and to suggest ways to overcome the difficulties.

* Ask students to role-play one another during a discussion as a means of revealing to problem members what effect they have on others. Instruct students to "continue your discussion as usual, except each of you pretend that you are the person on your right. Act the way he usually behaves during a discussion." Or, allow each student to secretly choose another member of the group to play, and after the discussion let the group guess each person's identity.

Overcoming Apathy and Nonparticipation

For most teachers the silent group is far more unnerving than the overly aggressive group. At least the latter is *doing* something, whereas the silent group just sits. Apathy can take the form of indifference to the task as well as sullen withdrawal. Members may be, on the one hand, afraid to contribute, or they may be restless and determined to get the task over with as quickly as possible. The teacher will need to try to pinpoint the causes of the apathy and then choose an appropriate remedy:

* Make sure the task assigned is intrinsically interesting to the group or that adequate extrinsic rewards (grades, free time, etc.) are provided. The chief cause of apathy in group discussion is a task that the teacher thinks would be good for the group rather than one which the group themselves have chosen to undertake.

* Many groups accustomed to teacher-led discussions will wait to see how much of the actual discussion they are responsible for and how much the teacher intends to do himself. These students may need the teacher to demonstrate explicitly that he expects them to do the job themselves. The best procedure is to assign the task clearly, announce the time limit and then withdraw and wait for the group to take responsibility for themselves. It may be frustrating to have to stand by and watch a group muddle through a task, but in the long run only by sitting it out can you demonstrate that the outcome of the discussion is the group's responsibility, not yours.

* The activities on pp. 102-104 which demonstrate the importance of taking

responsibility for the discussion may also help the apathetic group who have been used to teachers dominating classroom discussion.

* If the group is inhibited by fear that their contributions are going to be judged and evaluated, they may benefit from the "brainstorming" technique developed by Alex Osborn (1957). Assign the group a task (such as, "How can we make newcomers to our school feel more comfortable?") and give the following instructions: "Today we are interested in the quantity of ideas you can produce and not so much in the quality. The object is to generate as many different ideas as possible for the group to consider. In order to do this, you should contribute every idea that occurs to you, no matter how good you think it might be or how you think other people will respond to it. Try not to judge your own idea before contributing it, and above all do not evaluate in any way the contributions of others. There is no need to agree or disagree with previous contributions in this exercise, but you may build on a previous idea (called 'piggybacking') if you think of a variation of it or if it reminds you of another possibility." Have the group choose a recorder to keep a list of all the ideas. After students become comfortable with the increased interaction that results from brainstorming, start instructing them to go back over their list when they have finished and choose the two or three ideas that the group agrees are best. Note that in the early stages, no evaluation of the ideas takes place; only as the group becomes less inhibited should you begin suggesting that they go back over the list they have generated and decide which suggestions are most feasible.

* If the group's lack of participation seems to be the result of their not feeling at ease with one another, utilize the get-acquainted activities described on pp. 99-101.

* The quieter members of the group may have difficulty making themselves participate even when they want to, and thus may feel more comfortable if the interaction is structured in such a way that every person is expected to contribute in order. "Going around the circle," with each person giving his views on an issue, will give the shy student practice in hearing the sound of his own voice and a chance to discover that the sky doesn't fall when he speaks to the group. If he does not have to compete with noisy members for a chance to talk, he may be more willing to share his ideas. However, "going around the circle" is most useful in the early stages of group development and should not be allowed to get in the group's way when they have become less inhibited.

* The shy member may also be encouraged to participate by having a chance to prepare for the discussion in advance. Give either the entire group or the shy member individually an explanation of what the discussion topic will be on the next day, and suggest how they might prepare themselves to contribute.

Keeping It under Control

Traditionally the way to deal with discussion participants who all talked at once was to appoint a strong leader and to require group members to raise their hands when they wanted to speak. In the group-centered discussion, where the goal is that leadership be shared by all participants, one is reluctant to impose autocratic leadership just to keep control, and it seems ludicrous to require members of a small group of five to raise their hands when they want to contribute. Yet, no one can deny that discussions do become so heated and the participants so enthusiastic that nothing gets accomplis d because no one is hearing anyone else. When this happens, the teac r who does not wish to resort to autocratic leadership too quickly has several alternatives:

* Use a feedback device (see pp. 121-124) to help the group see their problem. The feedback may be unnecessary if the group has realized its problem because it never seems to get tasks accomplished on time. Once the group identifies the problem, ask them to generate possible solutions. They may wish to elect a chairman to call on members to contribute and otherwise keep order. If so, let them experiment with it; this may be an entirely satisfactory solution to their difficulties. The important thing to remember, however, is not to impose the leader, but to let the group decide *they* want one and to select who it will be.

* Suggest—as a temporary intervention if a discussion gets momentarily out of control—that the group allow ten seconds of silence between contributions as a chance for people to think about what has been said before responding. Keep time for the group, signalling when the ten seconds is up and the next person may speak.

* Require that the group pattern their discussion after the listening exercise described on pp. 106-107: appoint an observer to enforce the rule (Before replying to the other person's remarks, you must first summarize them to his satisfaction. Only then may you point out how you disagree with him), instructing him to interrupt any speaker who does not abide by it.

* Have the group solve a mystery or puzzle, as suggested on page 105, which requires that all contributions be carefully heard and understood.

* Instruct an observer to watch for which member talks the most during a ten-minute segment of the discussion period. The observer "taps out" that person by informing him that he cannot speak during the next ten-minute segment, but can only respond briefly when others talk to him. After the second ten-minute segment, the observer "taps out" a new monopolizer and

the first person may then return to full participation (Adapted from Lang-meyer, Schmuck and Runkel, 1970).

Handling Hostility

Somewhat akin to the overly enthusiastic, aggressive, out-of-control group is the group which is hostile and polarized. Often this is caused by the presence of members who think that for a discussion to be interesting it must become a heated argument. They attack the contributions of others rather than accept them, and hold tenaciously to their own ideas and refuse to compromise. Often the group divides into two or more factions, and members start viewing one another as the "enemy" rather than collaborators in achieving a goal. Personal attacks on one another are not uncommon, and the teacher may be tempted to reassign the members to other groups if not expel them from the classroom completely. Fortunately, there are alternative ways to cope with this problem, and removing the students to different groups should be seen only as a last resort.

* To show the group that issues are not simply black and white, and that the persons with whom they disagree on one issue may be the same ones with whom they agree on another, use the values continuum described on p. 101.

* Make sure the cause of the frustration and anger is not that the group has been given an impossible task or one that is unclear or otherwise disturbing. Often members will become angry and impatient if they do not understand what they are to do or if they feel they cannot do it. Especially if a group has a large number of slower students, you may need to explain or alter the assignment.

* Instruct the group members to each take a position opposite from his own views and argue in favor of it as the discussion continues. Appoint an observer to make sure they do not slip back into their earlier position.

* Consider the possibility that students are suspicious of one another because they have not become adequately acquainted and trustful. Utilize the activities on pp. 92-102.

* Require each member to state the extent to which he can agree with the previous contribution before he states his disagreement. See the exercise on p. 109.

* Form dyads comprising members with opposing views. Instruct them to

spend fifteen minutes discovering all the things they agree on and to submit the list to you in writing.

* In cases of extreme hostility, the following procedure may be helpful. Form triads composed of two students who are extremely hostile toward one another plus a somewhat neutral member to serve as moderator (or the teacher or an outside resource such as a counselor may take the role of moderator). The moderator gives the instructions and keeps time:

1. Each of the hostile parties is to spend five minutes trying to find out as much as he can about the other person. He does so by asking any questions he wishes, and he must look directly into the face of the other student. At the end of his five minutes, he is told to summarize what he has learned about the other. Then, the other student repeats the procedure.

2. Then, each student spends five minutes describing what he dislikes about the other. He should be reminded to use the second person ("you"), rather than turning to the moderator and using the third person ("he").

3. Next, each student is instructed to name all the things about the other which he can like or admire. They should be encouraged to name at least two or three things, however trivial.

4. Finally, each student outlines his "demands" of the other. He should be asked, "What would you have him *do* in order for you to feel less hostile toward him?" It is not necessary to get the other student to agree to do these things; in fact, he need not respond at all. Or, alternately, the two parties may wish to spend some time negotiating a way in which they will each try to meet some of the other's demands.

* Utilize the activities designed to foster cooperation (see pp. 112-115).

Managing the Monopolizer

Hopefully, by the time a group has practiced the skills outlined in the previous section, members will have learned that the group-centered discussion simply cannot succeed if it is dominated by the views of only one or two members. Yet, monopolizing is a persistent problem, not easily cured because the behavior is usually directly linked to the emotional needs of the monopolizer. It may be that the teacher will wish to explore, perhaps with the help of the counseling staff, what may be causing an individual to insist on dominating classroom discussion and then devise alternate ways of meeting these needs. In the meantime, the monopolizer must be controlled and the teacher may need to draw on some of the following approaches to help the group cope with him:

* Use feedback mechanisms to show the individual what his behavior looks like from the outside. He may quite honestly be totally unaware of what he is doing, and may quickly put an end to his monopolizing as soon as he becomes aware of it. Any of the techniques suggested on pp. 121-124 can be useful.

* Make it clear to the group that you do not intend to move a monopolizer to another group and that you expect them to deal with his behavior as a group problem. This may encourage them to be more open in expressing directly their annoyance with him and thus use the pressure of group norms to bring about his cooperation.

* Give every member of the group an equal number of "time tokens" (poker chips are ideal) which they can redeem for, say, 30 seconds of "air time" each. When a member runs out of tokens he must remain silent, unless other members give him some of their tokens so he can continue to contribute (Adapted from Langmeyer, Schmuck, and Runkel, 1970).

* Utilize the "tap out" procedure described on page 126.

References   4

BAVELAS, A. Communication patterns in task-oriented groups. *Journal of the Acoustical Society of America*, 1950, **22,** 725-730.

LANGMEYER, DANIEL, SCHMUCK, RICHARD A., AND RUNKEL, PHILIP, J. *Technology for organizational training in schools.* Eugene, Ore.: Center for the Advanced Study of Educational Administration, 1970.

MILL, CYRIL R. *Twenty exercises for trainers.* Washington, D.C.: NTL Learning Resources Corp., 1971.

OSBORN, ALEX F. *Applied imagination.* (3rd ed.) New York: Scribner's, 1957.

PFEIFFER, J. WILLIAM, AND JONES, JOHN E., *A handbook of structured experiences for human relations training,* Vol. I. Iowa City, Iowa: University Associates Press, 1969.

RATHS, LOUIS E., HARMIN, MERRILL, AND SIMON, SIDNEY B. *Values and teaching.* Columbus: Merrill, 1966.

Additional Resources   *4*

HUNTER, ELIZABETH. *Encounter in the classroom.* A recent, though not very thorough work containing some excellent communication activities. $3.95. Holt, Rinehart and Winston, 383 Madison Ave., New York, N.Y. 10017.

Institute for Development of Educational Activities. *Learning in the small group.* Defines the principles and techniques teachers need in order to use the small group process as a learning vehicle. $2.00. /I/D/E/A/, Mail Orders, P.O. Box 628, Far Hills Branch, Dayton, Ohio 45419.

MILES, MATTHEW B. *Learning to work in groups.* An older, but comprehensive introduction to the need to train members in effective group behavior. $3.95. Teachers College Press, 1234 Amsterdam Ave., New York, N.Y. 10027.

MILL, CYRIL R. *Twenty exercises for trainers.* A set of basic group activities easily implemented by teachers. $3.75. NTL Learning Resources Corp., 1812 K St. N.W., Suite 305, Washington, D.C. 20006.

PFEIFFER, J. WILLIAM, AND JONES, JOHN E. *A handbook of structured experiences for human relations training,* Vols. I, II, III, and IV. Collections of useful activities, described in detail. $3.00 per volume. University Associates, P.O. Box 615, Iowa City, Iowa 52240.

PFEIFFER, J. WILLIAM, AND JONES, JOHN E. *The 1972 annual handbook for group facilitators.* See also the 1973 and 1974 volumes in this series: $10.00 each. University Associates, P.O. Box 615, Iowa City, Iowa 52240.

SCHMUCK, R.A., AND SCHMUCK, P.A. *Group processes in the classroom.* $2.50. William C. Brown, 135 S. Locust St., Dubuque, Iowa 52001.

STANFORD, GENE, AND STANFORD, BARBARA DODDS. *Learning discussion skills through games.* A handbook for teachers outlining activities for improvement of students' ability to participate effectively in class discussions. $1.65. Citation Press, 904 Sylvan Ave., Englewood Cliffs, N.J. 07632.

5

PERSONAL DIMENSIONS IN DISCUSSION

In the previous chapter we examined the use of discussion as an instructional mode—the ways discussion can be used to teach the traditional subject matter of the school. But this is only the first step in utilizing discussion. If, as we have postulated previously, education must include self-knowledge and self-understanding and if the goals of education should include producing humane, effective persons, then we will want to look at how discussion can also be used to enhance the personal development of the student.

This chapter, then, focuses on discussion methods that involve the student personally—that is, both cognitively and affectively in subject matter that is directly related to his own life and the life of the classroom group. This personal involvement can enhance the learning of external subject matter, but it also directly promotes the social and emotional development of the student himself. To achieve the kind of personal involvement that we are advocating in this chapter, the members of the class must possess basic skills in communication and be both trusting and trustworthy. Therefore, we will devote a section of this chapter to activities which prepare the group for personal involvement.

We have conceptualized personal involvement as having three primary foci: 1. personal ideas and feelings, 2. present experiences within the group itself and 3. reactions to the other persons present. We will be the first to grant that these categories are somewhat arbitrary, but we have chosen them as a convenient way of looking at the question of personal involvement, primarily because they fit closely into the scheme for describing group interaction—"Dimensions of Psychological Distance"—that we present in Chapter Nine. For each of the foci, we have given examples of approaches to traditional subject matter as well as a set of activities that can be used to promote that type of personal interaction.

PURPOSES OF PERSONAL FOCUS IN DISCUSSION

There was a time when about the worst thing a teacher could do was to "get personal" in the classroom. The student's own thoughts and feelings were considered none of the teacher's affair, and the average teacher probably saw personal involvement in discussion as asking students to reveal the skeletons in their families' closets or discuss their most vivid sexual fantasies. Such a teacher saw the goals of the school only in terms of traditional subject matter, and felt that classroom activities should focus only on topics that were theoretical, abstract and as far removed from the students' personal lives as possible. Fortunately, those days are drawing to a close. Modern educators are concerning themselves with ways of relating subject matter to the personal concerns of students, and are even seeing affective development as a valid subject matter in its own right.

Enhancing Traditional Subject-Matter Learning

Until the learner can perceive a relationship between the subject matter (be it multiplication tables, geography or diagramming sentences) and his own self-concept, what he "learns" will make little difference in his life and is not likely to be retained for any length of time. Hence, the teacher must give the student countless opportunities to relate the new information to his own concerns and personal needs. As we have pointed out in Chapter Two, the only real meaning there is in subject matter is *personal* meaning. It is through activities of the sort that we will describe in this chapter that personal meaning is discovered.

In addition to helping students relate subject matter to their own lives, personal discussion can also enhance subject-matter learning by removing the affective barriers that prevent the student from receiving new information. Often the contents of a book, movie or class presentation have such a high emotional impact or constitute such a great emotional threat to the student that they may interfere seriously with his perceptions of the new information. Only by focusing on the students' personal feelings toward the subject matter can the teacher free the students to receive the new data. Ignoring the emotional reaction with the excuse that, "I wouldn't want to ask students to talk about something as personal as their feelings," only assures that the students will be closed to the new information the teacher is presenting.[1]

Promoting Social and Emotional Development

Until only recently schools have taken no responsibility for helping students grow emotionally and socially, except for feeble attempts at providing guidance services (almost totally crisis-oriented rather than preventative) and extracurricular activities with the ostensible, but rarely achieved goal of helping students "get along with others better." We feel, by contrast, that one of the primary goals of education should be teaching toward self-understanding and personal effectiveness (see Chapter One). Activities of the sort proposed in this chapter can be used to help students better understand themselves and other people, learn more effective responses to other people, form more mature relationships with their peers and adults, and learn to identify and manage their emotions.

1. See R. M. Jones (1968) for a fuller explanation of affective blocks to subject-matter learning, and G. Stanford (1970b) for a more complete discussion of the relationship between emotional concerns and the traditional curriculum.

ACHIEVING PERSONAL INVOLVEMENT

Getting students personally involved in discussions is not the simple task it may seem. Merely throwing out a question such as, "How does that make you feel?" rarely achieves the desired results. The average class is not ready to plunge into highly personal discussions on the first day of the term, as we have explained in Chapter Three. For such discussions to be effective, the group must be prepared for them through classroom activities that develop basic communication skills and create an atmosphere of trust.

Developing Basic Communication Skills

Before students can manage a personally involving topic of discussion, they need to know *how* to discuss. Hence, the teacher will probably wish to utilize the sequence of skill-building activities which we outlined in Chapter Four, to assure that the class is proficient in discussion methods. To introduce highly personal topics before students have learned to listen to one another and to work together cooperatively on external subject matter may in some cases be seriously detrimental to the group's development. Therefore, we recommend that every group be trained in discussion skills as early in the term as possible, so that they can then turn their attention to productive discussions with a personal focus.

Establishing Trustworthiness

It is unlikely that any student will get personally involved in a discussion if he feels that he is likely to be hurt in some way by the other members of the group. As we have pointed out previously, threat hinders communication by narrowing perception; on the other hand, security breeds openness. Hence, in order for personally involving discussion to succeed, each participant must feel that he can trust the other members not to laugh at him, ridicule him, ignore him or otherwise hurt him when he shares ideas that are personally meaningful. It is imperative, therefore, that the teacher help group members become both trusting and trustworthy. Activities such as the following can be of help in achieving this atmosphere.

* Get-acquainted activities of the sort described on pp. 99-101 and pp. 178-183 should be emphasized and extended. *Never* assume that students are well acquainted, even though they seem to spend a lot of time together or even though they have grown up together in the same community.

* Teach group members to listen to one another supportively. The listening-in-depth exercises on pp. 106-108 can be repeated and extended. See also pp. 52-54 and 173-177 in Elizabeth Hunter's *Encounter in the Classroom*, listed under Additional Resources at the end of this chapter, for other training exercises in careful listening.

* Ask the group to think of a serious problem or worry that they are currently experiencing but which they would not wish to talk about to this group. Emphasize that you will not ask them to reveal the problem but that you merely want them to think about it to themselves: "When you have thought of a secret problem, raise your hand so that I can see you are ready to go on." When the class seem ready, instruct them to become aware of how they feel about the problem: "Does it worry you? Does it scare you? Does it make you sad?" Then, ask them to imagine how the other members of their group would react if they were told the secret problem. Go around the circle, asking each member to 1. tell how his secret problem makes him feel, and 2. how he imagines the group would react to hearing about the problem. If there is enough time, it is helpful to allow the student to tell *each* member of the group how he imagines he would react. Otherwise, he can just describe how the group might respond in general.

* Have each student look at each other group member, one at a time, and complete the sentence, "I think I can (or cannot) trust you because. . . ."

* Have each student look at each other group member, one at a time, and complete the sentence, "In order for me to be more comfortable in this group, you should. . . ."

* Certain nonverbal activities can be of help in developing or testing trust in the other group members. All should be done with *no* talking.

1. Have students form pairs. Blindfold one person in each pair, and instruct the other partner to lead his "blind" partner around the room (or, even better, outside) without giving him any verbal instructions.

2. Have students form triads. One person stands with his eyes closed and his back turned toward the other two. He lets himself fall backward until he is caught by the other two.

3. One member of the group lies on his back on the floor and closes his eyes. The other members of the group lift him gently, hold him waist-high and then return him gently to the floor. With more mature groups, they can lift him over their heads before returning him to the floor.

4. A group of six or eight students sits in a tight circle, with another student standing in the middle. They press their feet tightly against the standing member's feet. He closes his eyes and slowly falls, and the others catch him and roll him around the circle, supporting him with their hands and feet. After any of these experiences, the students should be given an opportunity to verbalize their reactions: "How did you feel when you had to trust the other members of the group? Did you worry that they would let you get hurt?"

* Establish group unity through activities that help the group discover their special identity as a group.

1. After the group has experienced activities such as those described above, ask them to choose a sound that "fits" their group and to repeat it until it becomes comfortable. Then, instruct them to discover a rhythmic group movement that fits their group. Finally, have them combine a group movement with a group sound and repeat it—first quietly, then louder, then quietly again.
2. Ask the group to construct a collage, bulletin board display or collection of artifacts that describes their unique group characteristics. Instruct them to put together some means of explaining to other classes what they are like and how they are special as a group. See the description of the "Time Capsule" technique on pp. 151-161 in Weinstein and Fantini's *Toward Humanistic Education,* listed under References at the end of this chapter, for a more complete explanation of this procedure.

FOCUS ON PERSONAL IDEAS AND FEELINGS

Once the class has developed basic skills in communication and have achieved an atmosphere of trust, it is possible to begin to structure experiences that will allow students to share their personal ideas and feelings and to relate the subject matter to these concerns.

Finding Personal Meaning in Subject Matter

Stated simply, the way to help students find personal meaning in subject matter is to add "you" questions to the lesson plan. "You" questions, according to Harmin, Kirschenbaum and Simon (1973), can be distinguished from "fact" questions and "concept" questions. On page 139 are examples, drawn from their work, of how "you" questions can be related

Subject-matter Topic	"Fact" questions	"Concept" questions	"You" questions
American government	What resolutions did the Constitutional Convention pass on the issue of slavery?	If the Constitutional Convention had declared slavery illegal, how might the course of American history have been different?	If you were at the Constitutional Convention, how would you have voted on the question of slavery?
War	Name the wars in which the U. S. has been directly involved since 1776.	What are the major causes of war?	Under what circumstances would you kill? Have you ever been involved in a physical fight? What caused it? What were the results? Would you respond in the same way again?
Newton's Laws of Motion	What are Newton's Laws? Learn the formulae derived from the laws.	Describe the application of these laws in certain simple machines and devices used in the moon shot last summer.	Seat belts in cars stem from one of these laws. Do you use them? Why or why not?
Geology	What precious gems are found among the minerals in the earth?	Discuss the similarities and differences between precious and semiprecious stones from a scientific point of view.	When you get engaged, do you think you will give an expensive ring to your fiancé, or if you are a girl, do you think you will want one? Why? Can you think of any alternative ways a man might show affection for his fiancé?
Arithmetic	Examine a mail-order catalogue and then figure out the shipping charges and insurance costs for the things you would like to buy. Consider differences between express and parcel post, and between shipping many things together and separately.		How important are material things to you? How do you decide what you want to buy? Do you usually want the things your friends have?
Poetry	What choice did the speaker in "The Road Not Taken" make?	What does the poem seem to be suggesting that the reader choose?	What was the most important choice in your life that you have had to make? In what way has it made a difference in your life? Are you proud of your choice?

to almost any subject matter.

Virtually any topic in traditional subject matter can be given personal meaning through the use of "you" questions. If it cannot, it is not worth learning. The "you" approach can be used at the beginning of the lesson to concretize the situation, progressing then to the subject-matter facts and concepts to which it relates. For example, a language arts lesson could begin with the direction, "Remember a time when you felt very lonely and tell us about it." After students have shared their personal experiences, they could read a short story about a boy who has no friends and discuss the events in the story. Or, conversely, they could read the story and discuss it and then, finally, move into the process of linking it to their own experiences: "Did you ever feel like the boy in this story? Could you tell us about it?"[2]

Facilitating Self-Disclosure

Implicit in the process of discussing the personal meaning of subject matter is the revealing of personally significant information to others. This has been called "self-disclosure" by Jourard (1964) and we have adopted his term for use here. Self-disclosure also comes into play when the goals of a personally involving discussion are to promote the students' social and emotional growth, for self-understanding is almost directly a result of discussing one's self with others. (Someone has said that "I understand myself to the extent to which I reveal myself to others.") The teacher can facilitate the process of self-disclosure among members of the classroom group with activities such as those on page 141.

> * The get-acquainted exercises described elsewhere (pp. 99-101 and 178-183) are all relatively nonthreatening experiences in self-disclosure. They should be used before moving into any of the more threatening exercises listed below.
>
> * Let students express their opinions on various questions through voting by show of hands rather than discussing them. The teacher might give

2. The senior author has prepared a high school literature program with each lesson linked to a personally involving activity and an accompanying composition program based on students' personal concerns. See the *Teacher's Book* for *Changes* and *Mix* and *Journal 3* and *Journal 4* in the *New World Issues* series, listed under Additional Resources at the end of this chapter.

instructions such as the following: "I am going to ask you a series of questions and you are to answer by raising your hand. For example, if I ask, 'How many are hungry?' you would raise your hand high if you are very hungry, you would raise it only about halfway if you aren't sure whether you're hungry or not, and you would leave your hand in your lap if you aren't hungry at all." Questions that might be adapted for use in the activity are endless. Here are some examples: "Have you ever been lonely?" "Have you ever been afraid?" "Is there something you'd like to change about yourself?" "Do you ever worry about dying?" "How many of you sometimes get angry with your parents?" "How many of you are sometimes afraid to talk in class?" (Adapted from Raths, Harmin and Simon, 1966).

* Designate one wall of the classroom as representing one extreme opinion on an issue, personal characteristic or point of view and the opposite wall as representing the opposite extreme. Then, have the students arrange themselves in a line to indicate where along the continuum they fit personally. For example, one wall could represent "Always Happy" and the other could represent "Always Sad." Ask students to stand in such a spot as to indicate how happy they usually are. Or, you could ask the students to line up from "most" to "least" according to dimensions such as "how cooperative I am," or "how good I feel about myself." As a variation, let *one* group member indicate where he thinks each member of the group should stand.

* Have the students draw a picture of themselves and explain it to a small group.

* Have students make a collage titled "This Is Me" by pasting pictures and words cut from magazines onto a piece of poster board. These could be mounted in the classroom for other students to look at.

* Younger students can make life-size outlines of themselves by lying on a piece of butcher paper while a partner draws around them. The outlines can be cut out and mounted on the classroom walls as a place for students to post pictures and other information about themselves.

* Have students keep an "All About Me" folder filled with anything that might help the rest of the class understand them.

* Have students write a short autobiography to be reproduced and distributed to other members of the group.

* Let students take turns preparing a bulletin board display of photographs and other artifacts that will help others in the class know them better. The bulletin board could be titled "Meet Don Leonard" (or whatever student was being featured that week), and might include photographs of his family, postcards from trips they've taken, and other interesting data.

* Instruct students: "Draw a line on a sheet of paper about six inches in length. Imagine that this line represents your life up to now. Now, divide the line into four or five segments that represent the major periods in your

life as you perceive them. Over each segment, write a word that describes that period in your life. Now, find a partner and explain your time line to him."

* Have students think of something that they would like to do but are afraid to do. Then, have them role-play the action in front of the class. (Before undertaking any role-playing activities, see Chapter Six.)

* Have students role-play the person they would like to be. This can be a real person or an imaginary ideal person.

* Pretend that you are the proprietor of a Magic Shop where students can exchange a personal characteristic they don't like for one that they would rather have: "Today I want you to imagine that you are visiting a Magic Shop. This is not like any store you have ever visited before. It is filled with personal characteristics like courage, confidence, modesty, humility, strength, intelligence and so on. In fact, just about any personal quality that you would want is available here. But in order to 'buy' any characteristic in the Magic Shop, you must leave behind a characteristic you already have that you don't want any more." Tim, for example, might ask for "the ability to control my temper" and be willing to leave behind his "tendency not to listen when other people are talking."

* Give each student a sheet of paper and pencil. It is best that all papers and writing instruments be identical. Instruct the class to write down a problem or worry that bothers them. Suggest that they camouflage their handwriting to protect their identities. Ask them to explain the problem in as much detail as possible, but not to mention any names or places that might identify them. When all have finished, have them fold their papers the same way and put them in a bowl or box. Scramble the papers up and redistribute them at random. Warn students that if they get their own paper they are not to say anything that would let others know, but to proceed as though it were somebody else's. Then, have each student read the problem described on the sheet of paper he has received. After each reads the problem, ask him, "How would it feel to have that problem?"

* Conduct the following lesson in absolute silence. Enter the classroom and write on the board, "I'm Mr. _____ and I like apricots." Then, hand the chalk to one of the students and nod toward the board. When he gets up, sit in his place. Hopefully he will write a response similar to yours and will pass the chalk on to someone else. See "Silence Makes the Heart Grow Louder" by Bud Church, *Media and Methods,* October, 1970, for more explanation of this and other silent activities.

* Ask students to stand up and walk around the room without talking, looking at the other students carefully. After a few minutes, tell them to divide themselves into groups of four or five (or whatever number divides the class evenly) without any talking at all. Tell them to choose the others

on the basis of those with whom they feel most comfortable. Do not allow any talking and do not let them have more or fewer than the required number in each group. When the groups have formed, say, "When the four of you are satisfied that this is the group you feel most comfortable with, sit down together. If you think you are in a wrong group, try to move to a different group." After all groups are settled, ask students to look around at the other groups. "Ask yourself, why did you choose this group? How did you feel during the activity? Did you feel nervous about choosing other people? Were you afraid that you would not be chosen? How is your group different from the other groups? Now, discuss these questions with your group and share some of the feelings that you had during the exercise."

* Have students imagine that they are countries: "Today we are going to study the geography of the self. Imagine that you are a country. Ask yourself: If you were a country, what would your major imports and exports be? Where is your capital city?" and other pertinent questions. See a more complete explanation of this activity, devised by Gerald Weinstein, in Harold C. Lyon, Jr.'s *Learning to Feel—Feeling to Learn*, pp. 142-145, listed under Additional Resources at the end of this chapter.

* Questions such as the following can be used in a variety of ways to facilitate self-disclosure. In the early stages of a group, some of the questions could be combined into a questionnaire, to be filled out anonymously by the students, with the results compiled and posted in the classroom. Or, answers could be shared verbally with a single partner, a small group or the entire class, depending on the teacher's purposes and the trust level in the group. One of the authors (Stanford, 1970a, 1972) has described elsewhere his use of questions such as these, having each student in the class answer in turn around the circle.

1. Make a list of five things that other people like about you or should like about you and share them with the group.
2. Make up a new name for yourself. Why do you like this name? Do you like it better than your old name?
3. What do you need/want from this group? Who can supply it?
4. What is one thing you have done that you are proud of?
5. What do you like best about yourself? What do you like least?
6. What would you buy with $50?
7. Describe a time when your feelings were hurt.
8. Tell about a time when you were angry; when you were afraid; when you were worried; when you were happy.
9. What is something that makes you happy? that makes you sad? that makes you angry? that makes you afraid?

10. How do you feel when you enter a new group?

11. What do people feel about you when they first meet you?

12. What is your greatest strength?

13. When you are in a new group, when do you feel most comfortable?

14. What do you want to be like when you get out of school?

15. Tell the group something about you which they don't know.

16. Tell the group one thing you like about yourself; one thing you don't like.

17. What is something that worries you?

18. How are you different from most people your age?

19. What misconceptions do people in this group have of you?

20. What impression have you tried to give this group, or how have you tried to fool this group about yourself?

21. What does it take courage for you to do?

22. What is one thing that you are often afraid to talk about?

23. What do you value most?

24. Who is your hero and why?

25. When do you feel most confident? most insecure?

26. What will you be like ten years from now?

27. How have you changed most in the past year?

* A carefully structured program on self-disclosure for elementary grades is built into the *Human Development Program* by Harold Bessell and Uvaldo Palomares. See the list of Additional Resources at the end of this chapter.

FOCUS ON PRESENT EXPERIENCES

For some reason most educators have overlooked the events that take place naturally in the classroom as a source of learning, preferring instead to look to the world outside the school for subject matter. Indeed, use of the expression "the real world" (as opposed to the world of the school) indicates how totally separated from life the everyday events in the classroom are thought to be.

Educators who overlook the value of naturally occurring events would do well to look into the work of Maxwell Jones, the British psychiatrist who developed the concept of therapeutic community as an approach to treating the socially maladjusted (1953, 1962, 1968a, 1968b).

Dr. Jones has used the terms "social learning" and "living learning situation" to describe events that occur naturally, from which the participants can learn about themselves and how better to relate to other people. He suggests that as conflicts arise they be confronted and examined by the participants to see what can be learned from them. Indeed, the process of the group should be continually examined and learned from.

Because of their immediacy, naturally occurring events and present experiences are ideal vehicles for both subject-matter and social learning. The details of the experiences are not clouded by bad memory, and information is perceived first-hand rather than read about. In fact, there is probably no better way to learn social skills than by looking at what happens as part of the everyday life of the classroom. Democracy can be experienced directly, rather than being read about in a textbook. Sharing can be learned through actual practice, rather than as a result of a teacher's nagging. Ways of managing one's emotions can be developed by examining the consequences of various forms of behavior.

Relating Present Experiences to Subject Matter

In looking for ways to relate the goals of a subject-matter lesson to naturally occurring events in the classroom, the teacher should ask himself, "What has happened or is happening right here in this group that illustrates the point of the lesson?" He will find, for example, that the themes of literary works have parallels in situations in the classroom. Principles of social studies can be demonstrated as similar to ways the students in the class relate to one another. Here is how one teacher, the wife of the senior author, related the concept of de facto segregation to her high school class:

> "Look around you at the way you are sitting," I asked my all-white Black literature class a couple of weeks ago. "How have your seating patterns changed since the beginning of school?"
>
> "I don't know. I came in late," George answered quickly, to rid himself of any responsibility for dealing with this rather threatening question.
>
> "Well, I just sat down here because I like this chair," Winkie, who was sitting near the back, said very defensively. "Is there anything wrong with this seat?"

"Did I say there was anything wrong with it?" I replied, trying my best not to get defensive and angry in return.

"We're kind of spread out now," Pam finally observed.

"Some people get together in little groups and talk among themselves," Nancy added, getting bolder.

After the observation was clearly established, I suggested the relevance to the subject matter: "It seems to me that the way this class started out, with everyone mixed together in one circle, and has gradually broken up into separate groups of people with similar ideas, is comparable to the way our cities have broken up into the inner city and suburbs, with blacks, whites, Chicanos, Jews and every level of social class having their own separate area."

"Naw. It doesn't have a thing to do with it. I don't know what point you're trying to get across," Winkie said quite hostilely.

I struggled hard to maintain my composure, violating the theories of those who suggest that the teacher should freely express his or her emotions, and continued, "Well, I think there is a similarity, and I think that by exploring the reasons why we separate in this class, we will get an idea of why blacks and whites separate in our cities. Can any of you explain why you have chosen the seats you have today?"

After a rather long pause, Janice confided, "Well, I usually try to sit by either Lynn or Michelle whenever I can because I am new this semester and they have both gone out of their way to be friendly to me."

"We were the first ones here," Gail volunteered, "and when everyone else came in, they sat on the other side of the room."

"I usually get here late," Julie said sheepishly, "so I tend to sit at the back."

"How do you feel about the patterns you have developed?" I asked next. "Do you think it is better for people to sit with those who are similar to them, or is mixing with all different kinds of people a good goal?"

"Well, I learn a lot from discussing with people who disagree with me," Nancy said quickly.

"I'm kind of afraid to talk when people disagree too much," Polly added rather timidly.

"Why can't everyone do his own thing?" Winkie demanded.

Dave ignored her and agreed with Polly. "I can express myself much more freely when I am with people who understand me."

"But you don't learn anything when everyone just agrees with you," Nancy countered.

The discussion continued heatedly for the rest of the period, and the class left without deciding whether they felt they wanted to work all together or separately. I saw thoughtful, slightly disturbed looks on their faces as they moved on to their fourth period classes. Michelle summed up their feelings:

"This class has kind of scared me. I had always assumed that integration was a goal that it would just take us a little time to reach. Now I'm beginning to wonder if it is really hopeless. If the people in this class who are really pretty similar can't work together, I wonder if there really is any hope for our country."

In addition to using events that occur naturally as examples to illustrate subject-matter principles, the teacher can contrive events to give students direct experience with some aspect of the subject matter. Aaron Hillman (Brown, 1971) gives this lesson plan for introducing students to *Lord of the Flies:*

Circle of students. In the middle a table with a rubber mallet. Set the problem: "You are a group on an airplane flight who have crash-landed on a remote and uncharted island in the vast Pacific. Your pilot is dead; your radio is dead. No one knows you are missing. This group, as you are now, is there. You are alone on the island. It is your problem." The teacher remains completely silent and assumes the attitude that these students are in that situation. It will take days, but eventually the students will form a government of their own in the same manner as the boys in *Lord of the Flies* (pp. 62-63).

This activity bears resemblance to simulations and simulation games, as discussed in our Chapter Seven. Like a simulation, it provides students with an immediate experience to which they can link understanding of a subject-matter issue.

Facilitating Social Learning

Aside from their relationship to traditional subject-matter goals, present experiences of the class can be used to help students develop social awareness and improve skills of relating to others. The classroom can be seen as a microcosm of society or even a society in its own right. By learning how to function more effectively with one another in the classroom, students learn better ways of relating in the larger world outside the classroom.

Events that we might call "teachable moments" occur continuously in any class. A student comes in from the playground complaining that he was treated unfairly by the others playing four-square ball. A third-grader tells of being made the butt of jokes by fifth-graders before school. A group of high school juniors accuses the teacher of discriminating against them. Two students argue over who gets to use the classroom dictionary first. And on and on. Of course, there isn't always time to stop and examine each of these events with the class. Sometimes they must be handled immediately by the teacher. But more often than you might imagine it is possible for the teacher to stop and turn to the class and let them examine the problem with questions such as, "How could _____ have handled this situation? What are we going to do about this problem? What is the best solution to this difficulty?" Students begin to see that they can have some control over the problems in their lives, rather than always assuming that the teacher will make the decision.

In addition to using the teachable moments as they occur, the teacher may wish to schedule regular sessions in which the members of the class examine what is happening in their group. The book by Elizabeth Hunter listed under Additional Resources at the end of this chapter contains several excellent examples of classroom meetings on pp. 177-181 and 183-194. Approaches such as the following can be used to structure such sessions:

* Seat the class in a circle. Introduce a question such as, "What problems do we seem to be having as a group?" or, "How do you think we could improve our work together in this class?" or, "What would you like to change about this class?" The teacher must sit in the circle with the students, to emphasize that he acknowledges that he is a part of the social process in the room. He must be willing to let his own actions come under scrutiny by the group and to share his own feelings honestly. If this is difficult, it is sometimes helpful to have an outsider—the school counselor or perhaps another teacher—to serve as chairman of these 'classroom meetings,' so that the teacher can feel more free to respond as any other group member.

* In large classes where it is difficult for the whole group to talk together at the same time, use the "fishbowl" approach: Arrange an inner circle of six or seven chairs, and arrange the remaining desks in an outer circle around

it. Choose five students to constitute the inner circle (leaving one or two chairs vacant) and to discuss a question such as those given above. Students in the outer group are told that if they have an idea to share they may join the inner group by taking one of the empty chairs in the inner circle, but that they may stay there only long enough to provide the inner group with their new idea. Under no circumstances can members of the outer circle become members of the inner circle.

* Administer one of the many questionnaires on group process or other feedback devices (see pp. 121-124), and process them in a classroom meeting. Three good instruments are included in the activity titled "Personal Instrumented Feedback" in Pfeiffer and Jones's *A Handbook of Structured Experiences for Human Relations Training,* Vol. III, pp. 40-47, listed under Additional Resources at the end of this chapter.

* When students identify a particular classroom problem, the following procedure is useful for solving it: Ask them to specify the goal they want to achieve—that is, the solution they hope to come to (e.g., "to encourage more people to participate in discussion"). Write this goal on the board where all students can see it. Then, make a chart on the board with two columns. Label one column, "Helping Forces" and the other, "Hindering Forces." Explain to the students that a helping force is one that would help move the group toward the goal, and a hindering force is one that would prevent them from getting to the goal. In the example of "more participation in discussion" given above, a helping force might be "asking questions directed at shy members," and a hindering force might be "confident people rushing in to do all the work and not giving others a chance."

After the class has generated as many helping and hindering forces as possible, go back and examine each one in detail. Ask the class to indicate which ones they could do something about. For each of these, have the class generate the steps they could implement to strengthen it—if it is a helping force—or decrease it—if it is a hindering force. Keep these action steps as practical as possible and continually check to see if the class is willing to commit themselves to following through with them. Finally, make a list of what steps the class agrees to undertake to solve the problem. At a later classroom meeting, review the progress they have made toward the goal (Adapted from Mill, 1971).

FOCUS ON PERSONS PRESENT

As the pressure for individualized instruction mounts, teachers are more and more putting students to work on study packets which require them to work on their own, or seating students in study carrels where they work in isolation from the others in the class. As much as we support the idea of tailoring learning goals to the needs of the individual, we deplore the movement toward separating students from one another and reducing the interaction that should be the source of significant learning.

If students are ever to learn to understand other people and to empathize with them (and what educator would deny that this is an ultimate goal of education?), they should be given frequent opportunities to focus their discussion on the persons present in the classroom environment and their relationships to these persons.

Keeping the interaction centered on the persons present can be synonymous with saying that current experiences should be emphasized, but often it is quite different. For example, let us assume that an altercation has just taken place in a fifth grade class. The teacher may choose to handle the situation by having the students analyze their behavior and therefore learn from it. Let us imagine the following exchange:

> JOHN: "I don't care what you say. Mr. Bishop gave *me* permission to do it, and I don't think anyone else should."
>
> DAVID: "That's not right. Mr. Bishop said anyone could work on it who wanted to."
>
> TEACHER: "Let's clear up exactly what Mr. Bishop did say."

Discussion is then centered on resolving the conflict before the class can progress. This may provide an appropriate and helpful experience, but it is *not* the same as centering on the persons present.

If the interaction had centered on those present, the dialogue might have been as follows:

> JOHN: "I don't care what you say. Mr. Bishop gave *me* the permission to do it and I don't think anyone else should."
>
> DAVID: "That's not right. Mr. Bishop said anyone could work on it who wanted to."
>
> TEACHER: "You both feel that you have a right to work on it, is that right?"

Discussion then follows about the feelings of the two boys. This is quite different than discussing what Mr. Bishop said, although both are pertinent to the current situation. By focusing on the two boys (persons present) the conversation is more relevant and has greater impact and learning potential. If indeed it becomes important to learn exactly what Mr. Bishop had in mind, then he should be asked to enter into the discussion even if the discussion has to be postponed.

Relating Subject Matter to Other Persons Present

The focus on persons present tends to overlap the focus on present experiences which we discussed in the preceding section. We therefore refer the reader to that section and encourage him to reread it, keeping in mind the ways in which the activities suggested can facilitate an understanding of the subject matter by pointing out its relationship to the other persons in the class.

Facilitating Feedback

Discussion of one's perceptions of, and relationship with, other persons present in the classroom environment almost always constitutes what has become known as "feedback" in the jargon of behavioral scientists. It refers to information which tells a system (whether it be a missile guidance system or a human being) what the result of its behavior has been. Only by processing feedback can the system know what adjustments must be made in order to ensure reaching its goal. If, for example, a person has as his goal being perceived by others as a warm person, he never knows whether or not he is "on target" unless he receives feedback (in either verbal or nonverbal form) that he is, indeed, being perceived as a warm person. If he overhears two of his acquaintances discussing how aloof he often is, then this piece of feedback can help him analyze his behavior to see how he is failing to give the desired impression.

Most of the feedback which we receive during our lives occurs naturally—we overhear a remark, we perceive nonverbal cues such as a facial expression or a change in posture, we notice a shift in tone of voice—and we process these cues almost automatically, often unconsciously. However, because the feedback is often covert rather than explicit, we are in danger of interpreting it incorrectly. More explicit feedback—that is, having persons tell us directly how they are reacting to our behavior—is sometimes useful.

The activities suggested below provide structured opportunities for students to share with one another the ways they are reacting to each other's behavior. Both giving feedback and receiving feedback can be highly threatening experiences, and we therefore caution the teacher not to undertake these activities until the group has developed a high level of trust and trustworthiness and has learned how to give descriptive feedback.

* Begin by explaining the concept of feedback to the class. Then, teach them the Do's and Don'ts of Giving Feedback outlined below:

1. DO invite the person to describe his own behavior before you give him feedback about it. If he says it himself, he's more likely to believe it than if you tell him about it. Ask, for example, "Why don't you tell me how you see yourself behaving around strangers, and then I'll tell you how I reacted to you when we first met?" Sometimes writing down a self-description is easier and less threatening than talking about it.

2. DO describe the behavior. Tell him how it looks, sounds and feels. Example: "You sometimes pull away from the group and seem to be daydreaming."

3. DON'T evaluate the behavior. Avoid words that imply a judgment. Let him decide whether the behavior is good or bad.

4. DON'T use general terms such as "hostile," "arrogant," or "modest." These imply that you've made an interpretation. Instead, describe the specific behavior which leads you to that interpretation. Let the person make the interpretation for himself.

5. DO describe behavior that the person can do something about. It does nothing but discourage and frustrate the receiver if feedback focuses on a problem, such as a physical handicap, over which he has no control.

6. DO ask the receiver to repeat and rephrase what he has heard you say to make sure you have communicated clearly.

7. DO give the receiver an opportunity to check the accuracy of your perceptions by determining whether others in the group see his behavior the same way you do.

* Give students practice with the Do's and Don'ts of Giving Feedback with the following exercise. Divide the class into groups of eight (or any other even number). Instruct each student to choose a partner within his group. Half the group form an inner circle, and their partners sit in an outer circle around them in such a way as to be able to observe their partners in the inner circle closely. The students in the inner circle discuss a question such

as, "What was the most embarrassing thing that ever happened to you?" for ten minutes. Then, the partners in the outer circle take five minutes to give feedback based on what they have observed during the discussion. Next, the partners can reverse roles and repeat the procedure. Finally, lead the class in a discussion of how well they followed the Do's and Don'ts of Giving Feedback.

* Have students describe, in positive terms only, a person in their class—without mentioning his name. Other students try to guess who has been described.

* Have students choose a partner: "Tell him what you think he feels about you (or what he thinks you're like), then ask him to tell you if that is correct."

* Have each student choose another member of the class, but not indicate whom he has chosen. He then describes the person by telling what a) animal, b) piece of furniture, c) color, d) kind of music, e) food and f) automobile the person reminds him of. Then, the other members try to guess whom he has described metaphorically.

* Early in the term—preferably during the first week of class—have the students write down their first impressions of each of the other students: "What kind of person do you think he is?" These first impressions can be used in different ways, depending on the trust level of the group: They can be signed by the writer, collected by the teacher and stored in a safe place until later in the term, when they are returned to the writer. He can then either share them with the group or use them for his own information about how his perceptions have changed. Or, the first impressions can be shared with the group as soon as they are written. Or, they can be written anonymously and read aloud by the teacher. As a feedback device, the latter procedure is probably the most effective. First, have students write their first impression of each member of the group. Do *not* have them sign their papers. Collect the papers and read all the impressions that members have written about each participant. Then, give each one in turn a chance to react to what he has heard about himself—what he felt, what surprised him or how he disagrees. Then, repeat the procedure for the second participant, and so on. Or, to save time, compile the various impressions into a written list for each member and give it to him privately.

* Ask for a volunteer or use a device such as "choose a number" to select one student at random. Have him stand in front of the group and listen without reacting verbally as members of the group tell him what his strengths are. Instruct the group to contribute only positive things about the target person and to say only things that they sincerely mean.

* Instruct students to divide a sheet of paper into three vertical columns and to label the columns as follows: l. Others think I am . . . 2. I really am

... 3. How do *you* see me? Have them fill in the first two columns—one at a time—with five to ten items each. Then, instruct them to fold back the third column so that a person writing in it cannot see what has been written in the other two columns. Have the students choose a partner to fill in the third column. When the partners have listed five to ten items in the third column, they return the papers to the original owners, who compare the three columns. Suggest that the students consider questions such as the following: "Do others know what kind of person I really am?" "Do I think others recognize qualities that I have?" "What things about myself do I get across to others?" "What are some things about myself that others don't see in me?" (You may wish to limit students to listing only strengths or positive things when filling out the three columns, making the activity less threatening.)

* Ask members of the group to list the names of the other members in rank order from most similar to least similar to himself. That is, the person he lists as no. 1 is the other group member he thinks is most nearly like him, and so on until he reaches the last person, who is the one he feels is most different from him. Next to each name, have the students write the characteristics of the other person which he had in mind when ranking that person. Then, have the members read their lists aloud to the group and allow the group to react to what they have heard.

* Have students choose a member of the group and tell what literary character or historical figure he reminds them of.

* Have students give an imaginary award to another member of the group. For example, Helen might present Joe—who helps relieve tension in the group with his witty remarks—the "Comedian of the Year Award."

* Choose one member of the group to leave the room for a few minutes. While he is gone, the other members of the group decide who in the group is to be "It." (Even the person who has left the room can be "It.") When he returns, he tries to discover who is "It" by asking members of the group to perform certain acts (either physical or verbal) in the way that the person who is "It" would perform them. In other words, they are to imitate the person who is "It" in order to give clues to the person who was out of the room. He can request that they sing, dance, tell a joke, argue with someone or walk around the room—and they must do so in the way they think "It" would perform the act. (For a more complete explanation of this activity, devised by Gerald Weinstein, see Lyon's *Learning to Feel—Feeling to Learn*, 1971, pp. 140-141, listed under Additional Resources at the end of this chapter.)

* As a way for students to examine their behavior and its impact on the functioning of the group, the following procedure is suggested. It often fits

naturally into a classroom meeting in which some students have been complaining about the behavior of the class.

Ask the students to list on the board the ways people differ in their behavior during a discussion. Arrange their answers into two columns: column one contains a form of behavior (e.g., "talk too much"), and column two contains its opposite (e.g., "don't share their ideas"). After several pairs of opposites have been listed, choose one of the pairs and ask the students to decide which way they usually behave in a discussion (e.g., whether they are more likely to talk too much or to be quiet and not share their ideas). Have them divide themselves into two groups according to the way they have classified themselves. Have one group form an inner circle and the other group form an outer circle around them. Ask the students in the inner circle to anwer these three questions: "Why did you classify yourself into this group?" "Why do you behave the way you do in a discussion?" "What do you think about people who act the opposite way (i.e., members of the other group)?" After all students in the inner circle have answered the three questions, have the groups exchange places and the second group answer the three questions. The procedure can be repeated with each of the pairs of opposites which the group listed (Adapted from Mill, 1971).

* Use the following questions in any variety of ways:

a. If you could be anyone else in the group, who would it be?
b. Who here is happier than you?
c. Whose attitude toward you or behavior toward you would you change? How would you want it to be different?
d. Who in the group seems to be most liked?
e. Who in the group do you like best?
f. Who in the group would you choose:
   to be the leader of a class project?
   to be stuck with on a desert island?
   to play a game with?
   to ask for help if you were in trouble?
   to trust with a secret?
   to look after your girlfriend while you were away on a trip?
g. Who in the group makes you nervous (uncomfortable)?
h. Whom in the group would you like to know better? What would you like to know about him?
i. Who in the group likes you the most?
j. Who in the group listens to your ideas most closely?

* The exercises on pp. 66-69 and 82-84 of Pfeiffer and Jones's *A Handbook of Structured Experiences for Human Relations Training,* Vol. I, listed under Additional Resources at the end of this chapter, are useful—particularly with more mature students.

HANDLING SPECIAL PROBLEMS

Opponents of humanistic education often predict that letting students express their personal feelings will lead to all kinds of catastrophes ranging from suicide and psychotic breaks to communism and juvenile delinquency. Of course, the countries where communism has been most successful have never been noted for their humanistic schooling practices, and psychological breakdowns began occurring long before there were any schools at all. Humanistic educators will have quite a challenge if they hope to surpass the psychological damage which traditional schools have done to the average child.

However, there are some problems which are more likely to emerge in a class that is examining significant personal issues than in a traditional class, and dealing with these problems effectively can be a useful learning experience for students. These same problems are likely to occur in a traditional classroom, but they are traditionally dealt with as discipline problems, instead of as symptoms of psychological conflict.

Anxiety and Resistance

Horseplay, giggles and withdrawal may sometimes be legitimate symptoms of boredom, but they are also frequently signs that the subject matter has become too threatening for students to deal with and may serve the same function that comic relief serves in a tragedy. They allow a quick release of tension and an escape from the threatening ideas being discussed. They also serve as a safety-valve to keep things from becoming too hot. Healthy human beings know when a concept is becoming too frightening for them to handle, and will usually find a way to escape from it—often by some sort of disruption that brings an end to the discussion. This is the major reason why the common fears about personal discussions in the classroom are groundless. Most healthy people will not allow themselves to get into a discussion more deeply than they can handle. The dangers arise when the teacher refuses to accept the students' signals about their limits and resorts to ridicule, group pressure or authoritarian techniques to force students to talk about things that are too threatening for them.

It can be a helpful learning experience for a teacher to respond to a group of giggling girls by explaining that giggles are sometimes a useful escape-valve for a deep topic, allowing the class to relax a few minutes with jokes and laughter, and then discussing why the subject matter became so threatening. Sometimes it may be necessary to spend the remainder of the period in a less threatening discussion, and return to the threatening discussion at a later time if desirable.

Much harder to deal with is hostility, but it too is frequently a symptom of the same problem. A comment like, "This is a boring discussion. Why don't we ever talk about anything important!" or, "You're just a dirty-minded old man who's trying to snoop into our heads," or, "When are we going to study *real* social studies like the other classes instead of talking about ourselves?" can cause the teacher's blood pressure to rise and can make a calm, rational response difficult to come up with. It is a rare teacher who can respond to hostility as a symptom of threat instead of counterattacking.

Try to keep in mind that the student is expressing his own need to defend himself psychologically, instead of seeing his words as an attack on your competence as a teacher (easier said than done). Attempt to show understanding of his feelings by a response such as, "You seem to be very angry at me for asking you to talk about yourself." Encourage him to express his feelings of hostility and try to accept them nonjudgmentally. Always focus first on the student's feelings rather than on the content of the statement itself.

A good way to respond to hostility is to check out the rest of the class: "How do the rest of you feel?" If a large number of students also express hostility or discontent, they probably need less threatening activities. If most of the group want to continue the discussion, allow some time for the hostile members to vent their anxiety, and if the activity allows it, assign them a less threatening role such as observer or recorder for the remainder of that activity. Under no circumstances should you become locked in combat with the hostile student, trying to force him into an activity that is too threatening for him to handle. No student should ever be *forced* to participate in a personally involving discussion.

Usually a teacher should be quite careful about trying to push students to talk about things they obviously do not want to talk about.

However, some teachers overreact to symptoms of anxiety and give up on an activity if the class does not grab it up enthusiastically in the first two minutes. Initial inertia is not unusual. It take a few minutes for students to get their minds out of the old groove and onto the new ideas the teacher is suggesting. Like inmates of any institution, students have learned how to cope with the pressure of daily expectations—and that is usually by not getting involved in anything.

Therefore, the teacher who asks a questions such as, "What misconceptions does this group have about you?" and then changes the subject because hands do not fly up immediately is expecting too much from the students. Willingness to wait until the class is ready to respond sometimes is useful, since most students will be sitting there mumbling to themselves something like, "Maybe if we don't say anything she'll give up and go on to something that takes less effort." It is also useful to structure an activity in such a way as to subtly encourage students to participate. "Going around the circle" has the advantage of letting every student know he is expected to participate, and thus of reducing some of the anxiety associated with volunteering.

Uncontrolled Expression of Feelings

Many teachers who might like to deal with feelings in the classroom are terrified that one of their students might have an hysterical fit and run from the classroom crying. Such occurrences are about as rare as other classroom emergencies such as epileptic seizures and vomiting, and the teacher's response should be approximately the same. He should remain calm, indicate that the behavior is acceptable and do what is necessary to meet the needs of the suffering student and the rest of the class.

If a student in the class begins crying quietly, the teacher will probably want to recognize what is happening with a comment like, "Would you like to tell us what you are feeling, Jim?" If the student does not want to talk about the problem, do not try to force him. It is quite possible that the problem is the result of something very upsetting which has happened outside of class, and the student may not be ready to talk about it at all. One of the authors recalls a time when he was conducting a feedback exercise with a high school class and noticed a girl near the rear of the room crying openly. Sure that the feedback exercise had upset her, he was ready to bring the activity to an abrupt close, only to discover that she had recently broken up with her steady boyfriend and had been crying off and on throughout the day—regardless of the topic of class discussion.

If the upset student is willing to talk about his feelings, he should be encouraged to do so. But don't overlook the needs of the other students in the class. They are probably also experiencing strong feelings as a result of seeing him upset, and they should be allowed to vent those feelings in response to a question such as, "How are the rest of you feeling?"

On very rare occasions, a student may become very upset and leave the classroom abruptly. In this case, it may be helpful for a close friend to go after him—with instructions to stay with him if necessary and bring him back at the end of the period, or whenever he is ready to return. Under no circumstances should the person who may have caused the upset—through expression of hostility or some other comment—go out to "patch things up." The upset student left the classroom because he or she couldn't deal with the issue; it does more harm than good to continue confronting him or her with the source of the distress. In most cases the teacher should remain with the class and deal with their feelings about the episode: "How do you feel about Mary's leaving?" "What do you think upset her?" "Are any of the rest of you upset about that?" "How do the rest of you feel?"

If possible, the teacher will want to check back with the student who left the class (almost immediately with younger children, at the end of the period with high school students). If the schedule permits, the teacher might offer the student a chance to talk over the problem before proceeding to his next class. If the problem seems severe, the teacher might go with the student to the school counselor or another trained person whom the student trusts.

Strong hostility between members of the group is more likely to occur in a traditional class where discussion is often equated with heated argument, than in a class that examines their current feelings toward one another. However, it does occasionally occur in a class that is dealing with feelings, and it is perhaps more likely to be expressed openly than in a traditional class. Several suggestions for handling hostility come to mind: Encourage the hostile parties to be descriptive rather than evaluative in their comments about one another (see the section on feedback earlier in this chapter). Ask questions such as, "What is he doing that specifically irritates you?" rather than letting the student continue calling someone a bastard.

Several of the activities introduced in Chapter Four (see pp. 127-128) can be helpful in dealing with hostility, particularly the structured confrontation described on p. 128. In using any of these approaches, however, the teacher should not expect the hostile students to become friends. The anger and resentment is likely to be deep-seated, and turning the warring parties into bosom buddies may be too much to hope for.

Cultural Differences

When the teacher is from a different cultural background from the students, or when the students are from very mixed backgrounds, humanistic approaches are more important than ever, but there may be some special problems unique to the situation.

Building trust is much more difficult in a group of people who do not have very much in common. In fact, almost all groups in our society are subtly taught to distrust and make fun of people who are different from them. Students quickly learn to hide or disguise these feelings while they are in the classroom, but when the teacher asks for honesty and openness in a personally involving discussion, these feelings are likely to become more apparent. Therefore, a white teacher who has appeared to have a fairly good relationship with his black students while focusing only on math may discover a big gap between himself and them if he begins to introduce more personal topics of discussion. While his students probably trust his knowledge of math and are willing to learn from him, they may be unlikely to trust his acceptance of their more personally significant ideas.

Therefore, in a class where the teacher or a large percentage of the students are from a different cultural background, trust-building activities are considerably more important and will probably occupy much more time than in a class where everyone belongs to the same social subgroup. The teacher should be aware that in a group such as this the threat level is tremendously higher for almost all activities dealing with self-revelation. Students who are all of the same social group will probably be fairly willing to talk about their families, but it might be a tremendous challenge for a child who does not know who his father is to talk freely about his family to a child from a very strict, "proper" middle-class family. But the rewards of this kind of interaction are also much greater, for the classroom may be the only place where these people will ever have the opportunity to learn to understand and trust each other, and if our multicultural society is ever to succeed, such intercultural contacts are essential.

On the other hand, personal interaction in a culturally mixed class may not succeed. The hostilities between many groups in our country are so deep that it will take far more than a semester or a year of personally involving discussion to even begin to break down the barriers. If a group of white middle-class students simply come to understand the depth of resentment that blacks, Chicanos or Indian students may feel toward them, and the degree of misunderstanding between the groups, the teacher has probably accomplished as much as can be expected.

Even if a class of culturally different students does overcome the trust barrier, the teacher is still likely to encounter problems in communication. As they begin to talk about more personal topics, students will tend to slip into the vernacular, which may annoy administrators who "do not like that kind of talk in the school," but may also frustrate the teacher—and other students—who may not understand what is being said. Admitting ignorance may be embarrassing, but it is probably most effective—particularly if the teacher really believes in honesty and openness in communication.

Differences in values may also cause problems when dealing with a culturally different class. For example, a middle-class teacher we know displayed great sympathy when a girl in his class told of having to drop out of school for a year to have a baby. However, the girl was delighted with her child and felt that a baby was worth far more than a year of school; hence, she interpreted the teacher's display of sympathy as a lack of understanding. In another case we are familiar with, a white teacher in an all-black school instituted a discussion about attitudes toward the police, but was not at all prepared for the extreme hostility which the students expressed. Eventually the black teacher from next door had to come in to conclude the discussion.

One of the most effective ways the culturally different teacher can deal with lack of communication and differences in values is to find a person in the culture who is willing to communicate with him and act as "informant" about the different culture. Often there will even be several students in the class who are willing to give the teacher feedback, if he is willing to ask for an explanation of his own errors, not for tattling about other members of the class. A teacher from the same background as the students can be of invaluable help to the culturally different teacher, but he should keep in mind that just because two people have black skin or speak Spanish does not necessarily mean that they are from the same cultural background.

Inquiries from Administrators and Parents

One of the authors recalls the first semester that he was experimenting with personally involving activities with his high school classes. One day a note appeared in his mailbox instructing him to report to an administrator. "Tell me, Gene," the administrator said, after some preliminary chatter about the weather and sports events, "in these experimental classes of yours—are you having the students hold one another's hands?"

No matter how "humanized" our schools, most of us will still have enough authority-consciousness left to worry about the reactions of parents, administrators and fellow teachers to what we are doing in our classes. In most cases, these fears are relatively groundless. Chances are that the principal or department head will be delighted to see new life being pumped into classes through personally involving discussions.

Nevertheless, there has been in many communities a lot of worry about "encounter groups," "sensitivity training" or other humanistic approaches. Frequently these complaints come from protest groups who have heard that sensitivity training is "communistic" or "encourages people to take off their clothes and do anything they want," but who have very little idea what is really going on. In these cases, the teacher may have nothing more to do than state sympathetically—and perhaps a bit self-righteously—"Of course we're not doing sensitivity training. We're conducting democratic discussion!"

On the other hand, many complaints about "sensitivity training" have been well-founded. When the movement was new, too many teachers went to a single weekend encounter group and returned full of ecstasy, eager to turn on their classes with the same activities, with no thought at all to the differences between the two situations or of the relevance of the encounter activities to the goals of the class. In some communities, the serious humanistic teacher may have to work patiently to overcome the thoughtless acts of other colleagues, or even his own earlier indiscretions.

Careful thought and planning in terms of well-defined goals and an intelligent rationale are the teacher's best defenses against criticism, as well as the best guarantee of a successful class. The teacher who chooses activities because they will help fulfill the goals of his class, instead of because they are freaky or fun or unusual, will not have to worry about how he is going to justify these activities to the principal.

Being open about class activities all the way through is essential. A brief, but honest explanation to the students of the purpose of an activity will usually assuage their anxiety and preclude their complaining to their parents about the classroom activities. Explaining to the principal at the beginning of the term that you would like to experiment with a new approach—and substantiating your decision with sound reasoning—can assure you of his support. For example, in arranging for the experimental classes mentioned earlier, one of the authors drew up a written proposal for an "Experiment in Integrating the Cognitive and Affective Domains" and submitted it to the administration. Included were a complete rationale, sample activities and an offer to attend training workshops during the summer. The proposal was approved, with the only stipulations being that the district's research specialist design a means for testing the outcomes of the experiment and that the faculty be kept informed of the progress of the experiment so they could benefit from it too.

A casual but sincere invitation to the principal to observe a particularly interesting activity—or even to "drop by any time and see how things are going"—will help allay his worries about what you are doing. However, going out of the way to get written parental permission for activities is likely to create suspicion rather than allay it. It doesn't hurt, though, to keep parents *informed* about the exciting new approaches you are using with their children.

No matter what we do to preclude it, people will often be threatened by and suspicious of what we are doing. It is a temptation to attack or discredit their concerns and questions, but that is a route which contradicts the principles of human relations on which interactive education is based. Humaneness and healthy personal relationships cannot be promoted in one setting and contradicted in another. Therefore, if a teacher is to be effective he must show evidence of a humanistic attitude in all spheres of his life. This means that relationships with administrators, parents and peers must stress the person and not the role he plays. It means we must recognize that these persons have opinions and concerns that are valid from their frame of reference, and that we need to recognize our part in contributing to those opinions and concerns. It does not mean that we need to submit automatically to their concerns and fears. But we must treat them with respect and provide the data necessary for a valid judgment of us and our teaching methods, so that their place in the entire school process can be adequately and accurately ascertained.

A teacher cannot survive without the support of fellow teachers, the administration and the community. It is essential to have the support of all three. The support of the administration and peers will depend primarily on the clarity, openness and directness with which one's teaching methods are presented and with the consideration shown to others in the process. When dealing with the community, the same principles hold. However, the additional problems of infrequent contact and different frames of references and difficulties in communication with parents place a heavier burden on the teacher. The teacher needs to initiate contacts and open channels of communication with all persons in the community, but especially with the parents of the students involved. Actually, the implications are greater than this. If the experiential aspects of learning are going to involve the community (as we suggest in Chapter Eight), the community needs to be helped to understand the process and their role in it. If their role is to be effective, it must be a participatory one in which they understand what is being attempted and what is required of them.

It would be a serious mistake to assume that the community could not support an open approach to interactive education, and to therefore attempt to implement it by subterfuge. If, indeed, we believe that people have the capacity to make their own decisions about matters that affect their lives, this would be an untenable assumption—that we know better what is good for them than they do. Also, it would likely increase their suspicion and raise doubts in their minds about the competencies and motives of teachers. Therefore, we strongly urge that in implementing interactive approaches, one not sell the community short, but instead attempt to relate to all community members using the same principles advocated for all interpersonal interaction throughout the educational process.

But let us not be overly idealistic. You can try as carefully as possible to keep communication open and still get in trouble. There are some parents and administrators who are basically irrational and who can cause you trouble even though you have been circumspect in your planning and have a flawless rationale for what you are doing. In that case, be happy you are a martyr for humanistic education (and think of the Jon Kozols who have gone before you). After all, if they didn't get you for having the kids introduce themselves to the class they probably would have gotten you for teaching evolution, or the new math, or quoting from the Bible!

The Problem of Terminating

Once the teacher has managed to establish a high level of trust and has facilitated the personal involvement of students in discussion of significant personal concerns, the problems are not over. The teacher who has helped a group develop cohesiveness, a sense of identity and a caring atmosphere may dream that the students will leave the classroom on the last day singing his praises, thanking him for a beautiful experience and lamenting that the year is over. Unless he knows how to handle the process of terminating, however, he may be in for a rude awakening and his dream may turn into a nightmare of hostility, resentment and bewilderment.

Psychotherapists have known for some time that near the end of a successful period of treatment the patient may develop all sorts of symptoms related to the fact that his satisfying relationship with the therapist is coming to an end. He may actually regress emotionally and old symptoms may reappear temporarily, as though to say, "Look, I'm no better than I was before I started treatment with you." Or, he may turn in anger on the therapist and declare something to the effect that, "If you really cared about me you wouldn't make me leave." Or, again, he may attempt to assuage his pain by denying that the experience was a good one: "I really don't mind leaving, since nothing very good happened here anyway."

Interestingly enough, a class that has dealt successfully with personal concerns may manifest some of the same "termination anxiety" and may react in many of the same ways. Some of the reactions are inevitable, but if the teacher can identify and deal with the termination anxiety, the end of the term is likely to be much more pleasant for both teacher and students.

The first step is to acknowledge and verbalize the feelings associated with ending a good experience. Be alert near the end of the term (for the final several weeks, in fact) for remarks—usually made in a wistful tone of voice, but sometimes sarcastically—that may be messages of regret. Respond to these by expressing your own feelings of regret: "Yes, I feel sorry that the year is almost over, too. It seems like I've just gotten to know you." The more you, the teacher, express your feelings of regret openly, the less likely that the class will feel it necessary to hide their feelings in hostility.

But when confronted with expressions of hostility, accept them and try to help the students understand how they might be related to the problems of leaving a good group. The senior author remembers a class that he worked with, who had became a tightly-knit, caring group. On the very last day of class, they all turned on him fiercely, accusing him of not teaching anything, of wasting their time, of making them do all sorts of things they didn't want to do. On a hunch, he asked them if their hostility toward him was really anger at having to leave what had been a very satisfying experience. No miracles occurred, but several students stayed after class to explore their feelings and finally acknowledged that what they were feeling was sadness and regret rather than anger at the teacher.

The pain of terminating can be lessened through activities such as the following:

* Suggest that each student tell what was the best thing that happened during the term. Encourage the students to enter into a "remember when" discussion.

* Go around the circle and have each student give an imaginary gift to another member of the group. For example, Evelyn might give Vic "a big bag of self-confidence," since he has mentioned several times during the class that he feels unsure of himself. Often this activity can continue with students contributing in no particular order, until they have given as many "gifts" as they like.

* Let students discuss how their first impressions of one another have been altered during the time they have spent together.

* Let students spend the last week constructing a "Time Capsule" (see page 138) describing their experiences together during the term.

The goals of any terminating activity are to let the group reminisce about the good times they experienced together, to express appreciation for the support they received from one another and for the teacher's facilitating of the experience, and to finish up anything that is still hanging from previous discussions. Given this opportunity, the group can deal with the distress of leaving and be free to move on to new experiences in the future.

References   5

BROWN, G.I. *Human teaching for human learning.* New York: Viking, 1971.

HARMIN, M., KIRSCHENBAUM, H., and SIMON, S.B. *Teaching subject matter with a focus on values.* Minneapolis: Winston Press, 1973.

JONES, M. *The therapeutic community.* New York: Basic Books, 1953.

JONES, M. *Social psychiatry in the community, in hospitals, and in prisons.* Springfield, Ill.: Charles C. Thomas, 1962.

JONES, M. *Beyond the therapeutic community.* New Haven: Yale University Press, 1968.

JONES, M. *Social psychiatry in practice.* New York: Penguin Books, 1968.

JONES, R.M. *Fantasy and feeling in education.* New York: Harper, 1968.

JOURARD, S. *The transparent self.* Princeton, N.J.: Van Nostrand, 1964.

MILL, C.R. *Twenty exercises for trainers.* Washington, D.C.: NTL Learning Resources Corp., 1971.

RATHS, L.E., HARMIN, M., and SIMON, S.B. *Values and teaching.* Columbus, Ohio: Merrill, 1966.

STANFORD, G. Human relations training in the classroom. *Human Relations Training News,* 1970, **14**, 4, 1-3.

STANFORD, G. Sensitivity education and the curriculum. *Educational Leadership,* 1970, **28** (3), 245-249.

STANFORD, G. Psychological education in the classroom. *Personnel and Guidance Journal,* 1972, **50** No. 7, 585-592.

WEINSTEIN, G., and FANTINI, M. D. *Toward humanistic education: A curriculum of affect.* New York: Praeger, 1970.

Additional Resources   5

ADIRONDACK MOUNTAIN HUMANISTIC EDUCATION CENTER, Upper Jay, N.Y. 12987. Write for free bibliography of materials.

BESSELL, HAROLD, and PALOMARES, UVALO. *Human development program.* Theory manual and lesson plans for structured program of self-disclosure and personal development for elementary grades. 1967. Approximately $10.00. Human Development Training Institute, 4455 Twain Ave., San Diego, Calif. 92120.

BORTON, TERRY. *Reach, touch and teach: Student concerns and process education.* Description of how a curriculum can be linked to the personal concerns of students. $2.95. McGraw-Hill Book Co., 330 W. 42nd St., New York, N.Y. 10036.

BROWN, G. *Human teaching for human learning.* A report of Brown's work with the Ford-Esalen Project, which adapted affective activities for use with the school curriculum. $2.45. Viking Press, 625 Madison Ave., New York, N.Y. 10022.

Concern. A series of booklets to stimulate discussion of topics ranging from poverty, race violence and revolution, to drugs, sex and love, marriage and the generation gap; Leader's Guide, by André Auw, provides questions and helpful hints. 1971. Students' books, 60¢ each. Leader's Guide, $1.50. Silver Burdett Co., Morristown, N.J. 07960.

DINKMEYER, DON. *DUSO: Developing understanding of self and others.* A comprehensive kit of puppets, role playing activities, songs and stories for grades K-2. Kit for 3-4 in preparation. 1970. $82.00. American Guidance Service, Publisher's Building, Circle Pines, Minn. 55014.

HUNTER, ELIZABETH. *Encounter in the classroom: New ways of teaching.* $3.95. Holt, Rinehart and Winston, 383 Madison Ave., New York, N.Y. 10017.

LEWIS, HOWARD R., and STREITFELD, HAROLD S. *Growth games.* A collection of verbal and nonverbal activities to increase self-awareness and improve interpersonal relationships, adaptable for classroom use. 1970. $1.50. Bantam Books, Inc., 666 Fifth Ave., New York, N.Y. 10019.

LYON, HAROLD C., JR. *Learning to feel—Feeling to learn.* A comprehensive view of many approaches to humanistic education, citing specific activities drawn from a variety of sources. 1971. $3.95. Charles E. Merrill, 1300 Alum Creek Drive, Columbus, Ohio 43216.

OTTO, HERBERT A. *Group methods to actualize human potential.* A handbook of activities adaptable to classroom use. 1970. $9.95. The Holistic Press, 329 El Camino Drive, Beverly Hills, Calif. 90212.

People watching: Curriculum and techniques for teaching the behavioral sciences. Magazine containing practical suggestions contributed by teachers, psychologists and counselors. $5.00 per year. Behavioral Publications, 2852 Broadway, Morningside Heights, New York, N.Y. 10025.

PFEIFFER, J. WILLIAM, and JONES, JOHN E. *A handbook of structured experiences for human relations training,* Vols. I, II, III, and IV. Four excellent books filled with activities adaptable to classroom use explained in detail. $3.00 each. University Associates, P.O. Box 615, Iowa City, Iowa 52240.

RATHS, LOUIS, HARMIN, MERRILL, and SIMON, SIDNEY B. *Values and teaching.* 1966. $3.95. Charles E. Merrill, 1300 Alum Creek Drive, Columbus, Ohio 42316.

REICHERT, RICHARDS. *Self awareness through group dynamics.* $1.50. Pflaum/Standard, 38 W. Fifth St., Dayton, Ohio 45402.

SCHRANK, JEFFREY. *Teaching human beings: 101 subversive activities for the classroom.* 1972. $3.45. Beacon Press, 25 Beacon St., Boston, Mass. 02108.

SIMON, SIDNEY B, HOWE, LELAND W., and KIRSCHENBAUM, HOWARD. *Values clarification: A handbook of practical strategies for teachers and students.* $3.95. Hart Publishing Co., 719 Broadway, New York, N.Y. 10003.

STANFORD, GENE, and STANFORD, BARBARA DODDS. *New world issues: Changes, Mix, Teacher's books, Journal 3* and *Journal 4.* Harcourt, Brace and Jovanovich, 757 Third Ave., New York, N.Y. 10017.

STEVENS, JOHN O. *Awareness: Exploring, experimenting, experiencing.* $3.50. Real People Press, P.O. Box 542, Lafayette, Calif. 94549.

6

ROLE PLAYING AND ACTION METHODS IN THE CLASSROOM

The "acting out" of ideas and social situations has historically been an important way for people to understand and cope with themselves and their environments. In his *Poetics,* Aristotle suggested that drama can have a therapeutic effect on the audience by cleansing them through arousal of the emotions of fear and pity. Historians and anthropologists report primitive tribes who rehearse for battle through dances which incorporate the actions that will be used in war, and cite other tribes who enact events as a means of reporting and explaining them to others in the group.

However, it was not until the pioneering work of J. L. Moreno in the twentieth century that the full implications of dramatic methods for education became apparent. Moreno demonstrated that by enacting ideas and situations an individual can understand them more deeply and can gain insight into his own feelings. He, like Aristotle, also pointed out

The authors acknowledge with gratitude the contributions to this chapter made by Frank Chew of the Academy Theater, Atlanta, Georgia.

that because of their identification with the actor, members of the audience also learn from the enactment. Many of Moreno's theories have been substantiated recently by research in social psychology, particularly that when a person is required to act "as if" he holds a certain belief, his attitudes are likely to change in the direction of accepting that belief.[1]

In addition to the development of *psychodrama,* a method of psychotherapy in which the troubled individual enacts his conflicts, Moreno's work gave rise to two approaches that have particular usefulness in education: *sociodrama* and *role playing.* The former has as its focus social problems and conflicts between groups, rather than problems of a troubled individual. The latter is usually less concerned with emotional conflicts than either psychodrama or sociodrama, and since it has come to be used as a collective label for many types of dramatic activities in education, we have chosen to use it throughout the discussion that follows. We will use the term *action methods* to refer to learning activities in which the students get physically and affectively involved, but which do not result in the enactment of scenes.

USEFULNESS OF ROLE PLAYING AND ACTION METHODS

In spite of the fact that almost every education methods text contains a brief section on the value of role playing as an instructional tool, the usefulness of this approach has not been fully understood by most educators. Role playing—like films, records, filmstrips and tapes—has most often been viewed as a means of adding variety to the curriculum, one more item in the teacher's repertoire of gimmicks to keep students from getting bored with the usual reading and reciting to which most classes are subjected.

But this sells role playing short. Role playing can make special contributions to the student's development that sit-and-talk approaches simply cannot accomplish. Through role playing and action methods the student can:

DEVELOP INCREASED SELF-UNDERSTANDING AND AWARENESS OF HIS OWN FEELINGS. Role-playing activities that focus on concerns of the student

---

1. See the writings by Culbertson (1957), Janis and King (1954) and Jansen and Stolurow (1962), listed in the References at the end of this chapter.

can bring into consciousness feelings and attitudes that the student may have been only vaguely aware of previously. Through reflecting on how he behaves spontaneously in certain enactments the student can obtain a clearer picture of his typical behavior in everyday situations.

RELEASE FEELINGS "SAFELY." Hostility, suspicion, anger, anxiety and other emotions that may not be appropriately vented under ordinary circumstances can be released through role playing. As Shaftel and Shaftel (1967) put it: "It is 'safe' to role-play an angry or bitter response, and then go on to explore other, more socially acceptable solutions. How much better to siphon off the anger in role-playing than to have it find expression in making a scapegoat of some vulnerable child on the playground" (p. 33).

DEVELOP EMPATHY FOR AND INSIGHT INTO OTHER PEOPLE. "You never really know a man until you stand in his shoes and walk around in them," states an old proverb. Until modern science develops a better way to exchange places with another person, role playing is the nearest we can come to *being* another person. In role playing a student can try to see things from amother person's point of view and to respond as he would respond. By consciously trying to *be* the other person, the student can gain an understanding of him and a deeper sensitivity to his feelings.

TRY OUT NEW BEHAVIOR AND EXPERIMENT WITH NEW ROLES. Role playing provides a safe situation in which the student can explore new ways of acting. The passive child can try on assertiveness without fear of ridicule. The class clown can be serious for once and test others' reactions to him. The prim, tightly controlled young woman has a chance to shout profanities without shocking those around her. Role playing gives students permission to experiment and thus helps them extend the range of their behavior.

LEARN AND PRACTICE NEW SOCIAL SKILLS. No more effective means of helping students learn new social skills exists than role playing. Whether it be asking a girl for a date, ordering in a restaurant, accepting a gift graciously or applying for a job—new skills can be practiced in the relative safety of a simulated situation before the student actually tries them out in the "real" world. He can receive suggestions from others in the class and can incorporate their suggestions as he practices.

DEVELOP SKILLS OF GROUP PROBLEM SOLVING. We have described in detail (Chapter Four) the skills needed for working together as a group to solve a problem or accomplish a task. Many of these skills can be learned and reinforced through dramatic activity as well as through discussion. Role-playing situations require, for example, that the individual take responsibility for contributing, that the group work together cooperatively, that they remain sensitive to each person's potential contribution and that leadership emerge spontaneously from the group.

IMPROVE PSYCHOMOTOR SKILLS. While classroom experiences in role playing can never be a substitute for carefully planned physical education programs, they can help the student gain control of his body and practice more effective movement.

FOSTER CREATIVITY AND IMAGINATION. As presented here, role playing relies almost totally on the individual's ability to react spontaneously to the demands of a situation and to exercise his own imagination in the creating of an enactment. Without the use of scripts and elaborate instructions from the teacher, the student has the freedom to express his own uniqueness and stretch his imagination to the fullest.

ENHANCE SUBJECT-MATTER LEARNING. Finally, role playing can give the student insight into the subject matter of the traditional academic disciplines. Science, history, mathematics, language arts—all present occasions when role playing and action methods are the best means through which the student can formulate concepts and arrive at new understandings. In these cases role playing is used for specific purposes within the context of the goals of the lesson, and is not seen as merely a gimmick for adding variety to the lesson.

ESTABLISHING THE PROPER ATMOSPHERE

We have had much to say previously about the type of classroom "climate" that allows students to explore and experiment, but there is value to seeing how these conditions apply specifically to role playing. First of all, it is essential that the atmosphere be free from threat; this is best accomplished by the teacher adopting a nonjudgmental attitude. A student's performance in role playing should *never* be graded or otherwise evaluated. There is simply no "best" way or "right" way for a role to be played. There are different ways, more productive ways, but no right way. Hence, the teacher must not make judgments, criticize or say, "No, that's not good." By withholding judgment, the teacher not only avoids being a source of threat himself, but also encourages the class to likewise withhold judgment, tolerate the experimentation of others and allow one another freedom from threat. Critical remarks and other forms of ridicule should be squelched immediately and firmly by the teacher: "Let's get one thing clear: we do not laugh at other people in this class." If students attempt to evaluate the performances of one another, they should be gently reminded by the teacher: "There are many different ways to play a role, but one way is not necessarily better than another—just different."

Perhaps the most essential aspect of setting a good atmosphere for role playing is for the teacher to participate fully in the activities. He must say to himself, "While using role playing I'm going to get down on the floor along with the kids, get my clothes dirty, do crazy things and even look foolish some of the time. I'm going to risk appearing silly to my students, because if I'm not willing to appear silly and do the kinds of things that I ask them to do, then how can I expect them to take the risk?" As soon as he explains an activity, the teacher should move right into it, modeling through his enthusiasm and willingness the attitude he wants the students to adopt. Of course, the teacher must also remain somewhat detached from the activity in order to give assistance when problems arise, to change the pace when needed or to make more detailed explanations if students seem confused. He therefore must play a dual role; on the one hand, he often participates along with the students, but he also remains objective and takes responsibility for the overall direction of the group.

Another important aspect of atmosphere is the setting in which the activities are to take place. It is very difficult for students' creativity to flower when there are all kinds of things around that they can't touch and can't use. Students must have the freedom to move unrestricted, without having to worry about breaking things or hurting themselves. Hence, a large, carpeted, uncluttered space is ideal. But when this ideal is not available and a typical classroom must be used, what the teacher can do is to remove any objects that are breakable and to try to cultivate an attitude of YES, THAT'S TERRIFIC, rather than DON'T. If the classroom contains all kinds of things that the teacher won't let kids pick up or throw around or use as something else, the teacher will be constantly having to say, "Don't break that. Don't pick that up. Don't use that. Don't write on the blackboard. Don't knock over the plant. No, you can't stand on that chair," and the students' spontaneity will be effectively destroyed. Either remove the forbidden objects, take the class to a different room or try to develop an attitude of permissiveness.

A word needs to be said about some special problems likely to be encountered in role playing with older students. By the time a student has reached junior high age he has developed inhibitions and self-consciousness that are not apparent in children in the lower grades. Whereas a second-grader will respond eagerly to the teacher's suggestion, "Let's all be trees in the forest," the older student is afraid that others will laugh at him and that he will appear silly. He has come to welcome the relative safety of lessons that require him only to sit at his desk and answer an occasional question. Role playing represents a considerable risk for the older student. It means putting himself on display, and that means the added chance of ridicule. Therefore, it is likely that the teacher who tries to introduce role playing into the average secondary school classroom will meet with resistance and reluctance. Students' anxiety will be evident in their almost continuous giggling and other forms of "messing around." They will refuse to take the activities seriously and will approach them half-heartedly, if at all. The only remedy is to recognize the students' self-consciousness and move slowly. The students will have to be eased into action exercises gradually, and the teacher should be as gentle and understanding of their inhibitions as possible. To force these students into role playing too quickly will only result in disaster.

Another problem that the teacher is likely to encounter when using role playing with older students is their fear of touching one another. Whereas second- and third-graders will gleefully tumble all over each other, unabashedly hugging each other and walking with arms slung over each other's shoulders, the older students will shrink from so much as a handshake and refuse even to maintain eye contact with one another. It is likely that the fear of touching which begins to appear about junior high age is linked not only to a growing awareness of our cultural norms that prohibit touching under most circumstances, but also to the student's confusion over coping with his own emerging sexuality. To the adolescent, touching almost always has sexual overtones. Since he is not yet comfortable with his sexual impulses and not sure that he can control them, he tries to avoid situations—such as holding hands, sitting close to another person, or touching the face or body of another—that have even muted sexual overtones. This is particularly true when the activity involves a member of the same sex, although—especially up to age sixteen—the reaction also occurs with members of the opposite sex.

Therefore, role-playing activities and action methods that involve physical contact are likely to be very anxiety-producing to older students. This is usually apparent in their nervous laughter, wisecracking and giggling, refusal to participate, lack of enthusiasm or lack of seriousness. The solution is to move students ever so slowly into situations that require physical contact, gradually desensitizing them to the anxiety through activities that become progressively more threatening. The teacher should observe the group carefully and use the giggling, non-cooperation and "messing around" as an index to the students' anxiety level. If it becomes too great, he is moving too fast into threatening activities, and there is nothing to do but back off and move more slowly.

PREPARING STUDENTS FOR PARTICIPATION

If there is a single reason for the frequent failures in the way role playing has been used traditionally by teachers, it is the myth that "Anyone can role play." Some well-meaning civics teacher calls on three students to "act out that story we read in the newspaper about the policeman and the two hippies." The teacher wants to prove a certain point, so he sets up a situation and the students plod through it mechanically. They know what the point is, the teacher knows what the point is, everyone knows what the point is, and everyone is bored.

For role playing to be successful the students must be free to respond with flexibility and to allow the enactment to evolve organically rather than mechanically. This requires more than just an atmosphere free of threat in which the students can take the enactment in whatever direction they please. It requires students who are comfortable with one another and free of inhibitions; it requires students who can respond to objects and other students as though they were different from what they were originally; and it requires students who are able to sense subtle changes in the behavior of others and to respond almost unconsciously to these changes.

Most of the time when students do role-playing activities, they are not really ready emotionally and physically. They are still too inhibited and tied up in knots, as well as embarrassed about doing things in front of a teacher and each other, to really make the role-playing activities worthwhile. Hence, the teacher's task is to prepare students for participation by getting them to the point where they can do something unusual, strange and weird without being cued and without having the rest of the students breaking up over it. The process of preparing students for role playing must be a deliberate one, much like the training in discussion skills we proposed in Chapter Four. Even though it may be seen as time-consuming and as a needless postponement of the "real stuff," careful preparation is essential, because unless the students are ready, whatever the teacher does will be useless.

The three-part sequence of activities suggested below constitutes the sort of preparation a group needs before attempting serious role playing. 1. It begins with getting the students acquainted with one another and comfortable working together. 2. This is followed by a series of exercises to promote students' ability to pretend, and 3. by another series of exercises that teach the skill of responding to subtle changes in the behavior of other actors or in the situation. We recommend that the teacher utilize these activities—in the order given here—before moving into serious role playing. With younger students (roughly grades one through five), the teacher may find he doesn't need to adhere too closely to the suggested sequence. The younger students, as we have pointed out earlier, are generally less inhibited and more willing to use their imaginations than older students. With students in grades six and up, however, the teacher is advised to follow the order closely, making sure students have developed each of the skills before moving on.

Getting Acquainted

We have seen countless classrooms in which the teacher wanted to use role playing, but where we were astounded to discover most of the students in the class didn't even know one another's names. Sometimes they didn't even know the name of the teacher! For the same reasons that students must be well acquainted with one another before attempting meaningful discussions, students must know one another well before beginning role playing.

1. If students have not already experienced the verbal get-acquainted activities suggested on pages 99-101, arrange for them to do so. The verbal activities can be used prior to the action exercises described below, or they can be interspersed between them.

2. Test the students' knowledge of one another's names by playing the game "Name Quickdraw." Tell students: "You are to imagine that you are Western gunmen. Walk slowly around the room, looking at the other 'gunmen.' As soon as you make eye contact with another person, quickly pantomime drawing a gun and 'shoot' the other person by calling out his name loudly. The one of you who calls the other's name correctly first wins the duel, and the other one must drop to the floor dead. The 'gunman' who stays up longest is the winner." (Or, the losers of each match can be allowed to come to life again in order to continue playing.)

3. Ask students to choose a partner, someone whom they do not know very well. Instruct them to tell the other person about themselves—but from the point of view of someone else who knows them, such as their mother, brother or girl friend. That is, they are to role play the other person describing them. For example, Lisa might say to Terry, "I'm Mrs. Sanders, Lisa's mother, and I'd like to tell you about my daughter Lisa. Well, for one thing, she's not too neat; her room is always a mess. But she's a good student and has four or five close friends."

4. Instruct students to choose a partner and either arm-wrestle or thumb-wrestle with him. (To arm-wrestle, the partners clasp right hands and, keeping their elbows on the desk or floor, attempt to force the other person's hand to the desk top or floor; to thumb-wrestle, partners grip fingers of right hands and attempt to pin down the other person's thumb for the count of three.) This activity has several purposes: a. it starts inhibited students interacting physically in a low-threat situation; b. it helps them get better acquainted; and c. it gives restless students an appropriate means of venting nervous energy.

5. Relaxation exercises are also useful with restless classes, especially during the early stages of training in role playing when their anxiety is likely to be high. Give the following instructions: "Lie flat on your back on the floor. Find a space that will allow you to stretch out fully and extend your arms without coming into contact with another student. Now, is everybody settled? Fine. I want you to start by relaxing as fully as you can. Close your eyes and imagine that you are in some pleasant place. Do not say a word; you are in your own private world." (If nervous giggling continues, quiet those students individually and then continue.) "First, without saying a word or making a sound, I want you to clench your fists as tightly as you can and hold it. Then, release your hands and relax those muscles completely. Now, do the same thing to your toes. Tighten them as much as you can, then relax them. Move up to the muscles in your calves. Tighten them

and release them. Now, your thigh muscles—tighten and release. Now, tighten your stomach muscles; hold it, then release them. Now, move up to your shoulders; tighten them, then release. Now, see if you can tighten the muscles of your neck and face. Can you tighten your face muscles? Okay, now release them. Now, I want you to open your eyes and quietly find a partner. I want you to see how completely your partner can relax. One of you in each pair is to lie down on the floor. The other is to test his relaxation by moving his arms, legs and head, by pushing him, rolling him over and trying to pull him gently off the floor, but during all this the person on the floor remains completely relaxed and doesn't use any muscles whatsoever. If you think your partner is not relaxing a certain set of muscles, tell him and see if he can relax them more."

Circulate among the pairs, checking to see that the person on the floor is completely relaxed and that the other partner is being gentle in his manipulations. After a few minutes, ask the partners to change places and continue the exercise. After both partners have been manipulated, instruct each pair to join with another pair, forming a group of four. Everyone is to manipulate one person on the floor until each of the four has been manipulated. Then, go to groups of eight. Finish the exercise with everyone in the group gently picking up one person at a time—still lying flat and completely relaxed. Have them hold him waist high and gently sway him, then slowly return him to the floor. The entire relaxation sequence should be done with a very minimum of talking, and students must be cautioned to take the exercise seriously and not joke around and risk hurting someone. (The second part of this exercise, beginning where the students form pairs, may be too threatening for some. If so, skip it and move on to exercise no. 6.)

6. Have students choose a partner for the "mirror" exercise. Have them stand, facing each other about three feet apart. Instruct the taller of each pair to assume he is facing a mirror. His partner is his reflection and, hence, must follow his movements exactly. Let the students spend a few moments doing the activity any way they wish. They will probably make fast, complex motions that are difficult for the "reflections" to follow. After they have begun to tire of this, introduce these specific instructions: "Look directly into the eyes of your partner, relying on peripheral vision to track the movements. Go very slowly, slowly enough so that you are actually working together and not trying to trick each other. You should get to the point where it is hard to know who is the leader and who is the reflection."

With practice they should be able to do this exercise so well that nobody is leading; both people are simply doing the same thing at the same time. You can turn the activity into a contest by trying to see if other students can tell who is leading and who is the reflection in each pair. After students have learned to do this activity well, have them exchange partners (several times perhaps). You might also wish to introduce background music, preferably something slow and graceful. The mirror exercise can also be undertaken by groups of three or five. At first the members can take turns serving as leader, with the others mirroring his movements; later they can attempt to stay together without any one person leading.

7. Have the students play as many different kinds of Tag as you can think up. Start with the well-known garden variety in which one person is "It" and must touch another person, who then becomes "It." The object of the game is to avoid becoming "It." Then, move fairly soon into the many variations. First, try Stoop Tag in which a person is "safe" from being tagged if he squats. Then, try Blind Tag in which everyone is blindfolded except the person who is "It." The others try to catch him; he signals his whereabouts by nudging people, making strange noises, blowing in their ears, et cetera. The point is to see how daring the person who is not blindfolded can become—how close he can get to the others without being detected.

Other children's games, such as Blind Man's Bluff and May I?, are useful to help older students loosen up and get in touch with their playfulness and spontaneity.

8. Place students in a circle and instruct them to take turns suggesting a weird sound and having the entire group imitate that sound. Emphasize that they are to make a strange, weird, abstract sound but no words. As soon as one person introduces a sound, the entire group is to echo it immediately. Then, the next person around the circle to his right makes a different sound, and the group imitates him. Then, the person on his right makes another sound and the group imitates it. Get a rhythm going so that there will be no joking around between turns, just sound and imitation, sound and imitation, sound and imitation, et cetera.

9. Instruct the group to break into pairs and carry on a conversation using only gibberish. (You may need to demonstrate this with a student to show the class what you mean.) After the pairs have experimented for a few minutes, give the exercise structure by suggesting a particular emotion that they might wish to express while talking in gibberish—joy, anger, suspicion, sorrow. Then, appoint one person in each pair to be Person A and the other to be Person B and suggest situations such as the following, to be enacted in gibberish: A is a husband watching TV and B is his wife who has just wrecked the car; A is a policeman and B is a man parked illegally who doesn't want a ticket; A is a young man who wants to go to a baseball game and B is his girl friend who would rather go to the ballet.

As a variation, try "translating gibberish." Students form small groups. One person speaks gibberish, then points to another person, who must "translate" what was said.

10. Tell the class they are going to construct a huge machine using only their own bodies. One person starts by making a repetitious movement,

such as moving an arm up and down rhythmically, making a distinctive sound in the same rhythm. One by one, others join him, attaching themselves to him and to one another in some way and adding their own movements and sounds. Continue until the entire group is interconnected and moving in many ways, making many sounds.

11. Instruct the group to stand and close their eyes. Tell them to use the tips of their fingers to tap, gently but firmly, the tops and sides of their heads. They should attempt to imitate hard rain falling on their heads. Tell them to move their hands around, tapping the top and sides of their heads, then their faces and the backs of their necks. Then, suggest they change from tapping to slapping, hitting only hard enough to cause a pleasant sting but not pain. Guide them in slapping around all sides of their heads, their faces and their necks.

Then, instruct the group to divide into pairs. Have one person in each pair bend over while his partner slaps his back and shoulders, with hands slightly cupped. Then, change positions. This exercise can also be done in groups of three or four, with several persons slapping on different parts of the back and shoulders of one member of the group. (You will probably need to demonstrate carefully the tapping and slapping technique before the students begin this exercise, to help them make it a pleasant, not painful, experience for one another.)

12. Divide the group into pairs or triads. Name an emotion and instruct them to form themselves into a sculpture conveying this emotion. Words you might use as stimuli are: timidity, sadness, fear, bravery, confusion, despair, relief.

As a variation, divide the group into pairs and appoint one person in each pair to be the sculptor and the other to be the clay. The "clay" is to be flexible, but must hold any position the sculptor puts him in. The sculptor molds the "clay" into a form which expresses some attitude suggested by the teacher, giving attention to every detail, including facial expression. Remind the sculptors that they are not to give verbal instructions to the "clay," but are to manipulate it physically.

13. Divide the group into pairs. Instruct the taller in each pair to pretend he is blind (provide the blind partners with blindfolds if at all possible). Tell the other person in each pair to guide his "blind" partner around the room (or preferably outside the room in as many different types of "environment" as possible) without saying a single word to him. He must guide the blind partner through touch alone, avoiding the temptation to say things like, "Lower your head," or, "Watch the stairs." Allow the pairs approximately fifteen minutes to do this, then instruct them to exchange roles, with the person who was formerly "blind" now leading his partner.

14. Have the group stand and close their eyes (or put on blindfolds).

Instruct them to arrange themselves in order from the shortest to the tallest, without talking.

15. Instruct the group to form pairs and to examine their partners carefully, without saying a word. Then, have them all put on blindfolds (or promise to keep their eyes closed) and move around the room until they've lost their partners completely. Then, instruct them to find their partners without making any sound whatsoever. They will have to feel each other's hair, shoulders, eyes, clothing, et cetera, to find the person they were paired with. When everyone has found a partner, have them open their eyes to see if they have found the right one. Then, have them change partners and try again. This time they know what they are looking for and should be a little better at it.

Then, have everyone close their eyes and *you* pair them up with their eyes already closed (or blindfolded) so that they never see that person. Tell them that they are going to have to identify this partner later, so they should get acquainted with him (still with eyes closed). Then, have the group mix themselves up and instruct them to find their new partner again.

(This is an excellent getting-acquainted device, but very anxiety producing for some groups. It should, therefore, be used with caution.)

Let's Pretend

The purpose of the second phase of this training sequence is to get the group to the point where they can pretend to be someone else, can imagine objects and situations to be something different from what they started out being and can imagine that other members of the group have changed in some way. With classes of younger children, who usually have no difficulty at all exercising their imaginations, these activities can be seen more as games than as learning experiences. With older students, however, the activities are training exercises to help them regain the ability to pretend and to react imaginatively without being embarrassed or inhibited.

1. Arrange the group in a circle. Give them an object, such as a rope, a piece of fabric or a chunk of wood. Tell the group: "Your job is to do something with this object to make it become something else and the rest of the group has to guess what it is. As soon as someone guesses correctly, you say, 'Yes' and pass the object to the person on your right. He then must make it become something different." For example, the piece of rope could be placed on the floor in a circle and the student come crawling out of it as though it were a manhole. Or, he could let someone else hold one end of it

and sit on it like a bird on a telephone line. The activity may move slowly at first, but give the group time to get started. Remind them *not to use words* but to indicate by only their actions what the object has become.

After the group has become proficient in this exercise, change the rules slightly. Now, instead of the rest of the group guessing what the object has become, they become part of the action revolving around the object. For instance, if someone makes the rope into a manhole, then everyone else becomes part of the work crew which is working around the manhole. Again, this is done entirely without words.

2. Instruct the group to walk quickly around the room, mingling with each other but not running into one another. Then, call out different ways in which they are to move: silly, tired, angry, graceful, reluctant, drunk, preoccupied, et cetera. Then, instead of calling out adjectives, describe situations and have them move as though they were in those situations: going home from school after getting all F's; to a party that you've been looking forward to; on a shopping trip with your mother; et cetera.

3. Have the group continue walking around the room, but call out changes that they are to imagine are taking place in the environment and which they must respond to: the floor has become sticky; the air has become very thick and it's difficult to breathe; the force of gravity has suddenly increased ten times; the force of gravity has suddenly disappeared; or there are all sorts of objects on the floor which have to be avoided. (With some groups a teacher has to work very hard here to spot those fakey, unreal kinds of reactions that reveal that students don't want to take the activity seriously, such as: "I'm going to step real high over every object even though every object isn't really big," or, "I'm going to be real cute and see how many people I can make laugh." This is something that the teacher must deal with firmly, to establish a norm that one is not to be cute, is not to entertain other people, but is to create for himself a belief in something that really isn't true. So, this is a very tricky kind of exercise. It is difficult to get older students to respond if they are still embarrassed and inhibited. If they are, more getting-acquainted exercises may be in order before going on with the Let's Pretend sequence. The ultimate goal is to get students to the point where they can pretend and make a situation real for themselves and for each other, and not for them to entertain each other.)

4. Instruct the students to curl up on the floor and make themselves as tiny as possible. Then, tell them to imagine that they are growing into one of the following (or something similar): a tree, a huge rock, an incredibly tall person, a fat person, a strong person, a skyscraper, et cetera. Encourage them to move slowly in coming up from the floor and expanding themselves into the specified person or object. After everyone has "grown," then have them "melt" back to the floor to start again: "The sun has come out. It is

very hot, hotter than it has ever been. You start to melt and ooze slowly back to the floor."

5. Have the group divide into smaller groups of five to ten persons each and engage in an imaginary tug of war with another group.

6. Have the group divide into pairs and engage in an imaginary pillow fight. The fight can enlarge to include everyone in the room.

7. Have the class take the various roles of baseball players on two opposing teams and play an imaginary game in slow motion.

8. Put the group in a circle and have them throw an imaginary ball back and forth across the circle. From time to time change the kind of ball: a ping pong ball, a beach ball, a volleyball, a baseball, et cetera.

9. Sitting at their desks or lying on the floor, each student is to imagine that each of his hands is a person. Instruct them to have their hands "discover" each other and react to each other in some way.

10. Divide the group into pairs and have them imagine that their right hands are people who are meeting for the first time. Give the students suggestions as to what emotions the hands might express: anger, affection, curiosity, shyness, boldness, et cetera. Emphasize that the students are not to talk at all during the exercise.

11. Tell the class to imagine that the room has been transformed into a jungle and they can be any animal they wish to be. Instruct them to wander around the "jungle" and discover each other. (You may have to watch carefully that they don't get into fights.) Call time after about ten minutes and let the group share what animals they were pretending to be.

12. Have students choose a partner. Tell them to imagine that they are complete strangers who are meeting for the first time. Using only nonverbal means of communication, they are to meet for the first time, discover that they like each other, go somewhere together (such as to a picnic, a dance or a movie) and have fun together, then become angry, then make up and then say goodbye. You will want to give one part of the instructions at a time, moving on to the next when the students seem to be ready.

13. Instruct the students to move slowly around the room without talking or running into each other. Call out each of the following characters and instruct the students to pretend they are that person as they walk. Encourage them to move their arms and other parts of their bodies appropriately for each character: a sad old man, a worried mother, an excited teenager, an airline stewardess, a shy child, an angry father, a school principal or their best friend.

14. Have the students seat themselves comfortably on the floor. Tell them to close their eyes and relax. "When I tell you to open your eyes you are to imagine that you are in a strange place and you want to get out. The first thing you see when you open your eyes you believe is a way out of this strange place, so you hurry to it. But as soon as you get there and come in

contact with it (whether it's a post or a desk or even an open door) you realize that it is not a way out after all, and that you are still trapped. You turn, and the next thing you see you think may be a way out. You hurry to that spot, but discover that it isn't a way out either. You keep going until you gradually become desperate." (Students may wish to add words to express their growing desperation.)

15. Have students choose a partner and designate one in each pair A and the other B. Allow the pairs five minutes to conduct one of the conversations suggested below, then call time and move on to a different situation: a. A is a mother who is angry with her daughter B for having such a messy room; b. A wants to watch TV but B wants it off so he can read in peace; c. A wants a date with B, but B isn't at all interested; d. A has just come home tired from work, but B has had an exciting day and wants to talk about it; e. A tries to ask the teacher B a question, but doesn't understand the teacher's answer.

16. Have the group mill around slowly. Point out one student and instruct the others to continue milling but to imagine that he has become a monster. Or, designate a student whom they suddenly are to start admiring or disliking or being suspicious of. Help the students to respond to the person as though he had really changed.

Transformations

The problem with too many role-playing situations (as role playing has been used traditionally in classrooms) is that the teacher sets up the situation very rigidly and students plod mechanically through the situation and remain totally insensitive to the behavior of others in the scene. But if students are familiar with the concept of transformations and know how to use it, they can break out of what has been set up and move in a more profitable direction. They can handle the times when things aren't working and do something about them. They can respond to the immediate behavior of others in the scene instead of struggling relentlessly on in one direction set up by the teacher in the beginning. Instead of limiting themselves only to what the teacher had in mind, they can let the scene evolve naturally.

The concept of transformations is closely akin to free association or stream of consciousness. Subtle stimuli in a scene can be used by the participants to move the scene in new directions. Characters can change; the time and place can change; a situation can change—not just on whim or because someone wants it to change, but because some sort of association clicks within someone's mind. To be effective, role playing must be spontaneous and scenes must develop organically rather than mechanically. This requires that students have developed the ability to work together as an organic whole, remaining sensitive to the behavior of others in the scene and responding to the subtle changes that take place both in others and in their own awareness.

The sequence described below is designed to develop in a group the ability to move from one situation to another, working together as a group. Most of the exercises are aimed at cooperative group action, hence they can be seen as an extension—in the physical dimension—of the exercises in Chapter Four. In fact, the best approach would be to use both verbal activities and action methods at the same time, since they focus on many of the same skills.

The sequence below should be followed very closely, since each skill builds very clearly on what was learned previously. Only a general explanation of each step has been given. Specific instructions will have to be devised by the teacher for whatever age level he is working with.

1. Begin by getting everyone into a circle. Have one student start clapping in a rhythm and everyone else pick up the rhythm and follow him. It should be a very definite kind of rhythm. Then, tell the group that you want different people in the group to change the rhythm slightly and for everyone else to pick up on the change so that everyone once again is in the same rhythm. Encourage them to stay with one rhythm until it is well established, that is, until everyone is together. Then, someone else changes the rhythm and everyone else follows him. (This exercise generates much data about who are leaders and who are followers. It is an excellent introduction into the problems of taking risk in introducing a new idea into the group and the fear of not having others respond to your idea.)

2. Once students have mastered step no. 1, introduce the idea of interlocking rhythms. Everyone doesn't have to be doing the same rhythm, but all rhythms should fit together in some kind of organic whole. Don't have ten different people doing ten different things, however. (You may need to demonstrate an example of interlocking rhythms.) Remind the group to make sure one pattern has been well established before trying to move the group into a new pattern.

3. To the sound of a pattern established in step no. 2, add movement of the hands and head, so that the person who is changing the rhythm should also change the way he is moving his hands and head, and everyone follows him. At first you may wish to have everyone in the group doing the same thing, then you can introduce the idea of variations on the pattern, so that finally everyone is fitting into the pattern but not doing exactly the same thing.

4. Change the hand clapping to rhythmic vocal sounds and repeat the steps outlined above. Emphasize that you want abstract sounds, not words.

5. Then, have the group stand up so that they can use other parts of the body in their rhythmic movements (not just head and hands as before). However, the same procedure is followed: someone starts a rhythmic sound with an accompanying movement of the body, and everyone else picks up on this and gets involved in it in some way. Once a rhythm has been well established, anyone else can introduce a change at any time.

6. When students have mastered the steps up to this point, instruct them to limit themselves to abstract body movements with no sound. The rhythm is to be established by movements of the body alone, and those movements are to be entirely abstract (so that anyone looking at them could see no purpose for the movement). The same procedure is followed: as soon as one movement is well established, then anyone can change it and everyone else must pick up on it in some way.

7. Then, add abstract sounds to the abstract body movements. Instruct the students to still avoid using words.

8. Introduce purposeful movements to replace the abstract rhythmic movements. Start the group off with a realistic movement such as picking flowers or putting on clothes in a certain rhythm. Everyone is to imitate the realistic movement. When it is well established, anyone can change the movement to another kind of realistic movement.

9. Then, add sounds (but not words) to the realistic movements.

10. Then, encourage students to lengthen each section somewhat. In this step, the group continues to combine abstract sounds with realistic movements, but instead of simply imitating each movement, the group will try to join in the action in some way. For example, if someone starts the action of picking flowers (accompanied by an abstract sound), everyone does not have to pick flowers, but one person could be carrying the basket the flowers go into, someone else could be mowing the lawn and someone else could be digging up a flower bed. The point is that they jump into the action with some kind of action which becomes part of what is going on in the group. After the scene has become well established, anyone can initiate a change by introducing a new movement and a new abstract sound. The rest of the group picks up the sound and joins in the action in some way.

11. Now comes the tricky part—adding words. It's tricky because at this point students are sometimes tempted to either start being "cute" or begin writing a play, and you have to stop and explain to them that the point is not to be cute, to be funny or to write a play but simply to let their mind float with what's happening. The principle to emphasize is this: If someone is doing something that reminds you of something else, start doing the thing it reminds you of. For example, everyone is picking flowers and you're pushing a gasoline lawn mower, which suddenly reminds you of an automo-

bile engine, so you start working on the engine. You are the initiator of the change in which the lawn mower is transformed into the automobile engine, and it becomes everyone else's job to fit themselves into "your thing," which is the automobile engine. That's the transformation. These changes should not be conscious attempts to be clever, but simply whatever comes into someone's head spontaneously. This is a difficult concept to convey to students, but until you do role playing will not tap the real associations that are in their heads because they're going to be thinking of what they're going to do next instead of just doing what comes automatically.

If the addition of words trips up the students or causes them to start entertaining each other rather than reacting spontaneously, go back to abstract sounds so that they can't use words. Point out the differences between the scenes with words and those without. Get the students back on the track of simple free association and responding physically to what happens when they are associating and not thinking about it consciously.

After completing the sequence described above, or as part of it, utilize the following activities that help students develop the skills necessary for working as a responsive unit in evolving a scene:

1. Seat the group in a circle. Have the first person begin a story but tell only the first sentence. The person on his right adds a second sentence, and so on, with each person around the circle adding one new sentence to the story. Encourage the group to follow the leads of previous members rather than disrupting the continuity of the story.
2. Remind students of the story of Noah and the Ark (or tell it carefully to younger students). Appoint one student to be Noah and tell the others that they are other persons on the Ark, watching as Noah releases the dove in hopes of finding dry land. Instruct them to watch (without saying a word or making a sound) as he lets the dove go and to follow its flight as he points. Then, repeat the action, but this time have the group follow the flight of the dove without Noah pointing and watch it until it returns to his hands. With practice, and perhaps some coaching, the group will develop the ability to follow the same imaginary stimulus and respond to it as a unit.
3. Place the students in a long corridor. Group them fairly close together but not touching. Instruct them to walk to the end of the corridor and return, but without communicating to one another verbally. They are to start together, to stop at the end of the hall at the same time, turn around together and return together. Of course they will require practice before they can manage this smoothly. Smaller groups can be used at first to make the task easier and can be gradually enlarged as the students become more proficient.
4. Group the class in a circle. Choose a volunteer to stand in the middle of

the group. Another volunteer enters the scene as any character he chooses and encounters the first person. The first person must respond to him appropriately and continue interacting with him. After a few moments a third person enters the scene and replaces the first person. The third person enters as a new character and the second person must switch characters to suit the new situation. The process continues indefinitely, with the scene changing as each new person enters.

5. As a variation of the above, a single character can set a scene. For example, a young man is waiting for his girl friend. A second character enters and the two begin to interact. A third person enters and joins them, and the first person remains (instead of bowing out, as above). Then, a fourth person enters and joins the interaction. In each case, the person must join whatever scene is underway rather than changing it abruptly.

APPLICATIONS OF ROLE PLAYING AND ACTION METHODS

Once the classroom group has been adequately trained in the use of dramatic methods, the teacher will be ready to utilize role playing and action methods as instructional tools to meet learning goals such as those outlined earlier.

Story Dramatization

The simplest and least emotionally involving approach is story dramatization. The teacher selects a story that the class is studying or one that he wants to read to them, and asks students to act it out, following the plot and characterization provided by the author. This application can be especially useful in helping students understand confusing plots in literary works such as *A Midsummer Night's Dream*. It also helps students understand the actions of the characters, even the minor ones. After acting out *Hansel and Gretel* for example, the children who played the mother, the father and the witch might be asked to try to explain why these characters acted the way they did.

The teacher can give students more freedom in story dramatization by suggesting that they make up their own dialogue rather than borrowing it from the text of the story. Of course, when dramatizing an episode from history, for which no written dialogue is available, the students would have to exercise their imaginations more fully. A civics class could dramatize the events of the trial of the Chicago Seven, and thus gain a better understanding of the reasons for the apparently irrational actions on both sides of the case. Or, a science class might enact the steps involved in the development of the atom bomb or Nobel's invention of dynamite, and thus come to understand the conflicts between the desire for scientific discovery and the fear that the discovery will be used wrongly.

Expanded Story Dramatization

Story dramatization can, of course, be carried beyond the written text of a story. The teacher can ask students to be characters in the story as they might act in a different situation or to imagine what happens after the story ends. What happened to Ellison's *Invisible Man* after he emerged from his hole? What did Telemachus do after Odysseus returned to Ithaca? Imagine Deborah from *I Never Promised You a Rose Garden* as she enters college at the end of the book. How would Thomas Jefferson have acted in the 1972 Presidential campaign? What if Chiang Kai-shek had won the war for China? A clever teacher can set up a specific situation that will enable students to explore these developments beyond the literary text or the historical event.

Students can further explore characters from history or stories by imagining characters from different episodes thrown together or a character placed in a new setting. Students in an English class, for example, might be asked to dramatize a scene in which Kate from *The Taming of the Shrew* marries Hamlet, or in which Albert Schweitzer sets up his hospital in Umuofia, the African village in *Things Fall Apart.* Younger children could be asked to enact a scene in which Winnie the Pooh joins Dorothy and her friends on their way to meet the Wizard of Oz.

Action Methods

Dramatic techniques can be utilized without the development of a full-fledged scene. For example, a student could be asked to take the role of a historical figure such as Mahatma Gandhi, a literary character such as Bigger Thomas in *Native Son* or a figure from science such as Gregor

Mendel. Then, other members of the class could interview the character, directing to him questions related to the subject matter as well as more personal ones. The student playing the role could be encouraged to improvise responses that are consistent with his view of the character, even though they might not be historically accurate. His deviations could then be the topic of class discussion.

Even mechanical systems or biological processes can be personified through action methods and thus in many cases be more easily understood by students. For example, the digestive system could be improvised, with a line of students representing the esophagus, a circle of students holding hands representing the stomach, and so forth. A student portraying a lump of food could come skipping down the esophagus and enter the stomach, only to be met by combative characters (stomach acids) who attempt to "break down" the food lumps. We leave the rest of the process to the reader's own imagination!

In studying poetry, suggest that the students consider what kind of person they visualize as the speaker or narrator of the poem and that they read the poem aloud as though they were that person. Choose a poem such as Robert Frost's "Stopping by Woods on a Snowy Evening." As a group activity (particularly with younger students) or as an individual assignment for more mature students, read the poem carefully and consider questions such as the following: What kind of person is the speaker in this poem (this is often different from the "chief character" in the poem)? How old do you think he is? How is he dressed? Where do you picture him standing or sitting as he speaks this poem? After the students have imagined the character they think of as the speaker, have them role-play this character reading the poem. When making their presentations, they should be asked to describe in detail the speaker and setting before they begin. In a group activity, several students can role-play the speaker according to the ways they see him. The different interpretations can be discussed to see how well they fit the actual text of the poem.

Translation into Modern Parallels

To make the situations and feelings more immediate, it is often possible to have students translate a piece of literature or an historical event into modern terms or into a version more closely parallel to their own experience. A class studying *Antigone* could improvise a scene in which a young woman hides her brother, a soldier who has gone AWOL after being given orders to Vietnam, because he does not believe in participating in an unjust war. As in *Antigone*, the protagonist must decide between obeying the law and living according to her convictions. The scene could focus on the brother asking her to hide him, or on a confrontation between the young woman and the authorities who come searching for her brother.

A situation can also be made more immediate if the students translate themselves into the historical or foreign situation. For example, students pretend that they themselves are living in Nazi Germany and members of the S.S. ask them about the whereabouts of their Jewish neighbors. Or, students might imagine they are faced with resolving the conflict between the Cherokee Indians and the whites who wanted them moved to Oklahoma. Or, they might play a panel of judges who must decide whether Galileo should be permitted to promote theories that are contrary to church teachings.

Simulation Games

A more structured approach to role playing can be found in many simulation games. For a detailed discussion of this topic, see Chapter Seven.

Personal Concerns in Subject Matter

In using subject matter as a vehicle for promoting the personal development of students, teachers often look for ideas in the subject matter that speak to the students' personal concerns. In Chapter Four, for example, we saw a teacher leading a discussion in a class that was studying the rise of technology and urbanization in America. He asked the students to imagine how their own lives would be different if they lived in a town than they would be if they lived in a city.

Role-playing situations can be used to explore these themes that have relationship to the personal problems and interest of the students. The situation is not as directly connected to the subject matter as the approaches we have described up to this point, but emerge instead from general themes in the subject matter. For example, suppose a class were studying *The Hunchback of Notre Dame.* The teacher might pose the following role-playing situation: "One of you is Dick, a boy who is pitifully unattractive. You recently saved Martha, an attractive, popular girl at school, from drowning while on a class picnic. Now you realize that you are falling in love with her and want to tell her so. Martha, you are grateful to Dick and want him to know it, but you cannot forget how ugly he is." Such an approach will give students indirect insight into the conflict of characters in the novel they are studying, but it will also give them an opportunity to work directly with a problem that many adolescents have to face.

Direct Exploration of Social Situations

Similarly, the personal development of students can be enhanced when role playing is used to help them understand events and problems that concern them, although these concerns may have little or no relationship to the subject matter of the course. Conflicts with parents, teachers, friends and members of other groups can be dramatized to give students more insight into the problem and a deeper understanding of the other people involved.

Assume, for example, that students come in off the playground complaining that the playground supervisor, a teacher aide employed for that purpose, has been dealing unfairly with some of the students. The teacher could ask for volunteers to play the roles of the various people in the situation: the supervisor, a student who complains to her that a boy has been breaking line and the boy she punishes for line breaking.

Or, imagine that a high school class gets into a heated discussion about the problems of cliques in the school and wonders what can be done about it. Role-playing situations, in which students take the roles of members of the different cliques engaged in some sort of confrontation, can increase their understanding of the conflicts as well as start the development of empathy for the other people involved.

Role Training

Role playing can be used as a sort of rehearsal for future behavior, an opportunity to learn and practice new social skills. This approach is often referred to as "role training." The emphasis is on practice, not insight or empathy. Its effectiveness is credited to the assumption that behavior can change by practice and reinforcement, whether or not the student experiences insight. Role training is an excellent means, therefore, of teaching skills such as those needed for improved communication, vocational success, social competence and mature interpersonal relations.

With younger children, role training can be used, for example, with the teaching of proper table manners ("Divide into groups of four and pretend that you are eating dinner in a restaurant"), with giving directions to strangers ("Choose a partner; one of you pretend to be a stranger in town and ask for directions"), or use of the telephone ("Who wants to show us how you might take a message if your mother isn't home?").

Students in vocational courses in high schools have frequent opportunities to learn from role playing. In fact, next to on-the-job learning experiences, role playing is the most effective way to develop necessary skills. Other students can use role playing to practice skills ranging from effective ways of expressing anger, techniques of interviewing and starting conversations with newcomers to turning down an invitation, making introductions and applying for a part-time job.

Other Uses

The applications we have suggested here should be seen only as examples of the wide range of possibilities. In fact, almost any learning goal lends itself to role playing or other action methods. The teacher simply needs to ask himself, "Is there something that students can learn more readily by acting it out rather than only talking about it? Can I help make this concept more concrete by getting students physically and emotionally involved in it? Can I provide practice in this skill by having students pretend to be in a situation that requires it?" Dramatic approaches will begin to suggest themselves for almost any subject matter and at every grade level.

STRUCTURING ROLE-PLAYING ACTIVITIES

Merely knowing what situation or conflict you wish to focus on in a role-playing activity is not enough to assure its success. Too many teachers in the past have failed to understand or plan carefully the proper procedure for role playing. This may explain why this technique has generally been limited to adding variety to lesson plans rather than being seen as a particularly valuable form of learning. The teacher who is serious about role playing sees the importance of each of the steps explained below and gives each the emphasis it requires, rather than merely calling a few students to the front of the room and telling them to begin acting out a scene.

Step One: Training the Group

Serious role playing should not be undertaken until the students are free of inhibitions, can exercise their imaginations and can react spontaneously to changes in the behavior of others in the scene. We strongly recommend use of the three-stage training sequence outlined earlier in this chapter before attempting to use role playing in the classroom.

Step Two: The Warm-Up

Even if a group has been properly prepared for role-playing activities through the training sequence, attempting to enact a scene without properly warming up is usually as unsatisfactory as plunging into a football game with no period of calisthenics. The warm-up helps to mobilize the students' spontaneity and focus their awareness on the themes of the role-playing situation.

Activities that put the participants in touch with their own present emotional and physical state and get them moving physically are especially useful as warm-up exercises. Each of the activities in the section "Preparing Students for Participation" earlier in this chapter is appropriate for a warm-up, especially those that include physical activity such as "Building a People Machine" (p. 181) and "Trapped" (p. 185). In addition, the following exercises are useful warm-up activities:

> 1. Begin with the relaxation exercise (no. 5) on page 179. After students have relaxed, continue with these instructions: "Focus your attention on your toes. Wiggle them and notice how they feel. Now, move your attention

to your legs. Relax them completely. Can you feel the floor pushing up on them? How does that feel?" (These questions are rhetorical only; if students attempt to answer them aloud, say quietly, "Just think about the questions I am asking you; do not answer them for the whole group to hear.") "Become aware of your hips. Tense them, then relax them. Feel the pressure of the floor on your hips. Now, feel your back. Stretch it out its full length, and then relax it. Try to feel the floor along your spine. Now, focus on your shoulders. Move them around and around. Now, relax them. Now, tense the muscles in your neck and relax them completely. Try to relax your entire body. If any part seems tense, focus on that part, tense it and relax it. Now, at your own speed and keeping your eyes closed, begin to stand up. Move slowly, as though you were a tree sprouting from a seed. When you are standing, become aware of the person on either side of you. Then, slowly open your eyes and look around the group."

2. In conjunction with the exercise above, or as a separate activity, have students focus on their breathing. Instruct them to lie on the floor with their eyes closed. Give the following instructions: "Without changing your breathing in any way, become aware of your breathing. Allow it to continue, but follow it. Focus on the way you breathe. Now, consciously start changing the way you breathe. Take a deep breath, deeper than you've ever taken before, and hold it. Now, release it and force the air all the way out. Do that again. Inhale deeply. Deeper. Keep going, fill your lungs all the way up. Now, exhale completely. Let your breathing return to normal. Once again follow it, pay attention to it, but do not attempt to change it. Let your body relax completely. Then, slowly rise and open your eyes."

3. Guide the students on a "fantasy trip." Use the relaxation exercise (no. 5) on page 179 to quiet the group. Then, continue with instructions such as the following: "Imagine that you are standing in a broad meadow. It is early morning, but the sun is shining down warmly. You can feel the sun on your skin and the gentle breeze that is causing the tall grass to rustle. You walk across the meadow to a low hill, from which you can see for miles in all directions. Try to picture the scene clearly in your mind. As you are standing on the hill, you look up and see a giant bird approach from out of the sky. He is huge, but you are not frightened by him. He is a friendly bird with soft feathers. The big bird lands near you and a strange little man steps off his back. The man approaches you and says that you may ride the bird to anywhere you please and stay there for one day. So you climb on the bird's back and whisper in his ear where you'd like to be taken. I am going to stop talking now and I will give you a few moments to imagine spending the day in the place of your choice. Where did you tell the bird to take you? What do you want to do when you get there? (Allow four or five minutes of silence.) Now the bird is ready to take you back to your meadow. You climb aboard and fly gracefully back. The little man is waiting for you right

where you left him. You step off the bird and say goodbye to the little man as he jumps onto the bird and flies away."

4. Help students vent their restlessness and begin to warm up verbally by giving them an opportunity to yell as loud as they can: "When I give the signal, I want you to all yell as loud as you possibly can. Really try to raise the roof. Okay? One, two three—yell! Fine, but I'm not sure you were trying to yell your very best. Let's try it again, and this time really put some power behind it! Now, that was much better." This same procedure can be used with laughing, particularly if students seem inclined to go into hysterics whenever a role-playing situation begins. Giving them deliberate instructions to laugh during the warm-up helps diminish their need to laugh during the enactment.

5. The warm-up need not be limited to formal exercises. Even the simple chore of moving back the furniture in the classroom can be turned into a warm-up procedure, as Brian Way (1967) has pointed out: "The following are a few of the many different manners in which we can suggest the furniture is moved: a. we (the class) are all members of a secret society; our task is to blow up the enemy headquarters; the classroom is the basement of those headquarters and we are going to pile up great crates of high explosives near the walls of the basement; we have to work with complete silence and secrecy as there are many guards about; we also have to work quickly as the high explosive is time-fused; the chairs and desks are the crates of high explosive; we can work either on our own, or help each other as a team; b. we are all simple shepherds carrying gifts (in the story of the Nativity); c. as in b, but we are the Wise Men; d. as above, but we are all kings; e. slaves building the pyramids (or anything else we may decide slaves should build); f. astronauts assembling a space platform in outer space (in slow motion); g. builders of some kind during a go-slow strike; h. miners working against time to reinforce a pit that is in danger of caving in; i. clumsy removal men getting a grand piano down a narrow staircase; j. a scene from a film: removal men are clearing a house but something has gone wrong with the camera so everything is happening at half-speed; k. as in j, only the fault in the camera makes everything go at twice normal speed; l. moving very precious and delicate ornaments; m. craftsmen putting their own work on display" (pp. 83-84). The teacher can easily think of dozens of other situations that will allow students to incorporate the rearranging of classroom furniture in preparation for role playing into a warm-up activity.

6. Divide the group into pairs. Instruct them to stand back-to-back and to hook their arms together at the elbows. Tell them to walk around the room without talking or breaking loose from one another.

7. Instruct students to divide into pairs and to face each other, placing the

palms of their hands together. Tell them to push against each other as hard as they can, attempting to push their partner through the opposite wall.

After giving the students an opportunity to mobilize their spontaneity through self-awareness and physical activity, the warm-up should continue with a brief period of introduction to the problem that the role playing will deal with. The teacher should help the students "tune in" to the theme of the approaching enactment and to see how they can identify with the situation.

The form that this introduction takes will depend on the purpose of the role playing. If the enactment is planned as a means for giving students insight into subject matter, the teacher may wish to introduce it something like this: "You will remember that we've been discussing for several days the ways in which slaves were transported to America. We have seen that slaves were taken from their homes, usually captured in a war, and were then dragged to the shores of the Atlantic, where they were kept until the ships arrived from America. These ships had been constructed carefully so that many slaves could be crammed into as small a space as possible. Let's try to get the feel of what it must have been like in one of those ships by pretending to be slaves being forced on board a slave ship."

If the role playing deals more directly with concerns of students, the teacher may wish to begin with a discussion of the problem rather than of the subject matter to which it relates. For example, in an English class that has been reading Richard Wright's *Black Boy,* students have been appalled by the extreme punishments that have been meted out to the chief character by his parents. To help them relate this to their own feelings about punishment in their own lives, the teacher plans to have the students role-play situations in which a child does something which the parents feel they cannot allow. He helps them warm up to the situation by an explanation such as this: "I'd like you to think back to when you were a child of, say, six or eight. Can you remember what kinds of punishments your parents used to control you? Who wants to tell us how he was punished? Jerry? (Jerry explains.) Thank you, Jerry. Can someone else remember how he was punished by his parents? Okay, Melinda. (Melinda contributes her example, and the teacher continues until several other students have given examples.) It seems that many of you remember vividly how you were punished by your parents. Let's look now at some specific situations in which a child gets into trouble and see how you think parents might handle them. Who'd like to play a six-year-old in the first scene?"

It is important to adequately introduce a role-playing activity in order to assure that all members of the group, not just the few who are chosen as players in the enactment, are emotionally involved in the situation. This issue of audience identification, although emphasized by Aristotle in the days of ancient Greece, has been overlooked by many teachers who attempt role playing. When the situation is one in which most of the group have an emotional stake, they benefit from it as much as the students doing the actual enactment, by identification with the players and by experiencing the situation vicariously through the players. Therefore, the teacher must be sure that he has the entire group "with him" before he moves into setting up the enactment.

Step Three: Choosing the Players

Having warmed up the group adequately, the teacher is ready to begin the enactment. He may wish to describe briefly what characters the scene will require: "Let's begin with a scene between the girl and her mother after her father has forbidden her to see her boy friend ever again. How old should the girl be? About sixteen? Okay, who wants to play the girl?"

In every case the teacher should rely on volunteers from the class and not call on students to participate. In addition to preventing embarrassment to a student who might feel threatened by playing the role, this procedure assures that the players chosen will be those students who are warmed up to the roles, who are ready to begin feeling the parts they are to play.

With younger children, it is important to allow everyone to get involved as actively as possible. They are less willing to content themselves with merely watching others perform, and are eager to join in the action themselves. Therefore, the teacher may wish to add a number of secondary characters (waiters in restaurants, secretaries in offices, et cetera) to allow as many students as possible to participate. The need to involve a large number of students can also be met by breaking up the group into several smaller groups and having each group prepare and present the scene as they think it should be enacted.

The role of the audience can be made more active by giving them explicit instructions for what to look for during the enactment. They should be told to be active observers, watching to see whether the enactment is realistic and thinking of alternate ways of enacting the scene.

Step Four: The Enactment

Once the players have been selected, the enactment per se begins. Begin by giving brief instructions to the players. The extent to which the teacher should predetermine the initial direction of an enactment depends on the purpose of the role-playing activity. In some cases it may be important to be very specific about the personal qualities of the various characters, the setting in which the scene takes place, the reactions that the characters will have to one another initially and the action that will take place in the scene. However, to the extent that the teacher leaves these details up to the players, the enactment will increase in spontaneity and the students will gain added experience in stretching their imaginations.

In any case, the players should be asked to describe themselves and set the scene as exactly as possible. This point cannot be stressed enough. It is essential that both the players and the audience have an opportunity to visualize the characters and the setting in detail before the action begins. The characters should describe to the audience the physical setting of the enactment: the location of furniture in a room, the decor, the location of doors and other rooms, the pictures on the walls, the color of the draperies, the scene outside the window. Important pieces of furniture or other essential parts of the scene can be represented by desks and chairs. These should be moved into place by the characters themselves, not by the teacher. The characters should also inform the audience of the time of day at which the scene is taking place, as well as the season of the year. The more specific the players can be, the more likely they and the audience are to feel that the scene has "come alive."

If the students have difficulty describing the scene from their imaginations, the teacher can assist by asking questions: "What time of day is it? What room of the house are you in? Can you describe this room? What color is the carpet? Are there pictures on the walls? Would you say the furniture is modern or more traditional in style? What are the pieces of furniture? Where are they? Where is the door? What is outside that door?"

The chief characters can then be asked to describe themselves in what may be called a *self-presentation*. Instruct each character to introduce himself to the audience, telling them what kind of person he is. If the student has a difficult time thinking what to say, the teacher can ask questions in a sort of interview: "How old are you? Are you married? Do you have any children? What sorts of things do you enjoy doing in your spare time? What kind of person are you? What do other people think about you?" Questions that are especially pertinent to the role-playing situation can also be introduced. The period of self-presentation should be very brief and should not be allowed to delay the enactment unnecessarily. But it should be included both as a warm-up for the student playing the role and as an aid for the audience in visualizing the character.

The students are now ready to start the enactment. They begin to "be" the characters they are playing and to interact in the ways they imagine the characters would. At this point the teacher should withdraw somewhat and allow the players to determine the direction the interaction will take. The following should be kept in mind by the teacher during the enactment:

1. From the time a student volunteers for a role, always address him by his *role name*, not his own name. This helps to warm him up to the role and to keep him in character during the enactment.
2. If a player drops out of character and turns to talk to you or to the audience, direct his attention back to the situation and the character he is playing: "Tell your *wife* that, not us. You're home, watching TV."
3. Do not allow scenes that seem to be getting nowhere to continue indefinitely. Cut the scene, and either begin again with different players or move on to a different scene.

A number of special techniques can be utilized during the enactment for specific purposes:

1. Perhaps the most useful technique is what is known as *role reversal*. This is particularly valuable as a means of giving a player insight into another character and developing empathy. Assume, for example, that Tim has come to class complaining about a run-in he has had with the principal that morning. Rather than *talking* about the episode, allow him to role-play the

situation, with another student playing the principal. From time to time, instruct Tim and the "principal" to reverse roles. Tim then plays the principal and is thus encouraged to view the incident from the principal's point of view.

A particularly good time to call for a role reversal is when one character has asked another character an important question. Imagine that Tim says to the principal, "Why are you always picking on me?" At that moment the teacher can quickly instruct the two players to reverse roles. Tim is now the principal and must answer the question. He is confronted with the need to understand why the principal is doing what he's doing. (*Important:* always instruct the players to repeat the last thing that was said before you called for role reversal. In the example above, the boy chosen to be principal, who has just been reversed into the role of Tim, would repeat, "Why are you always picking on me?" and then Tim, as the principal, would answer.)

Role reversal is also useful as a practical way of providing other players with information they may not have about a character or situation. This is usually needed when a role-playing situation deals with a real-life problem that a member of the class has experienced. For example, Dana wants to learn new ways of communicating with her mother. Another girl in the class volunteers to play her mother and they begin to enact a typical situation at home. At the very beginning of the enactment, a role reversal would allow the other girl, now playing Dana, to learn enough about Dana's mother by watching Dana play that part briefly, to play it satisfactorily. In situations such as this, the principal character (Dana, in our example) could also have been asked to reverse roles when it was time for a self-presentation of her mother before the enactment began. She would pretend to be her mother and introduce herself to the audience. This not only gives the girl who will play Dana's mother data about the role she is to take, but also helps Dana see things from her mother's perspective.

2. If students seem to be having difficulty with their roles, temporarily suspend the enactment and assign each character a *consultant* to confer with him briefly about the role and how best to play it.

3. Use action methods to make conflicts and relationships in the role playing more concrete:

a. If one character has a position of power or authority over another (or, if perhaps he simply has a pushy, powerful personality), instruct him to stand on a chair while enacting the scene, thus emphasizing his power. This technique might be a useful one, for example, in the Tim-and-the-principal situation discussed previously.

b. If a character is torn in two directions by a conflict, as was Martha in the *Hunchback* example suggested earlier, assign him a double (see 4 below) to represent each part of himself (in Martha's case, the part that wanted to show appreciation to Dick and the other part that was repelled by his unattractive physical appearance). Instruct each double to take one of the player's arms and to pull him in opposite directions to symbolize the conflict.

c. When a character seems to be constrained by certain forces or if some force is preventing him from doing something he wants, use a "wall" made of several members of the audience with arms linked to represent the force. Instruct the character to break through the wall that is restraining him.

d. To release and express anger, provide the player with a sturdy pillow to pound.

e. In cases in which a character does not listen to another, instruct him to turn his back on the speaker and cover his ears with his hands, repeating over and over, "I won't listen." Other similar techniques may suggest themselves to the teacher as an enactment unfolds. He should always be alert for ways of making the themes in a situation concrete by turning talk into action.

4. When characters seem to be thinking or feeling something that they are not expressing, the technique known as *doubling* can be useful. Ask for a volunteer, someone who feels he understands a character particularly well, to serve as that character's *double*. He sits or stands next to the character and acts as a sort of alter ego, imitating the body movements of the character and, more importantly, expressing the ideas and feelings that he imagines a character to have but is not expressing openly. For example, let's use the Tim-and-the-principal situation described above. In order to help both Tim and the audience understand more fully what may be going on inside Tim while he is interacting with the principal, the teacher may assign a double to Tim. When Tim asks, "Why are you always picking on me?" the double might interject, "This guy sure makes me mad!" to make Tim's feelings explicit. The double, of course, can only guess at the underlying thoughts and feelings and must, therefore, check them out with the character. The character should nod if the double's comments are on target, or can disagree by telling the double he's wrong. If the character does not signal his agreement or disagreement, the double can add a comment like, "Is that right?" or, "Huh?" to encourage a response. As a rule, the double cannot speak to or be spoken to by other characters.

Doubling is a highly sophisticated technique of role playing, and it is probably most useful with older students who are becoming aware of unconscious motivation and thoughts and feelings that go unexpressed. At no time should doubling be used if it confuses the students or otherwise gets in the way of the role playing.

5. Another, less complicated, means of making available to the audience the inner thoughts and feelings of a character is to ask him to perform a

soliloquy. Interrupt the enactment and instruct the character to turn his head to the audience and state openly what he is thinking but not saying.

Once a scene has been enacted, the teacher may wish to suggest other scenes that would follow logically or be appropriate extensions of the first scene. Tim, for example, might be asked to imagine going back to the principal and telling his side of the story.

Or, the first scene can be enacted again with different players, who would demonstrate other approaches to the problem. After the first enactment the audience is likely to be eager to share their ideas about what happened and to suggest other ways in which a role could have been played. Rather than talking about alternatives extensively, give the students an opportunity to enact a situation in a different way or from a different perspective. It is possible to change only the main character, keeping the subordinate characters the same for subsequent enactments. Or, to give more students a chance to participate, the entire cast can be changed each time.

Step Five: The Follow-Up Discussion

After the enactment has been completed, it should be followed by a period of discussion. This is an essential part of the role-playing process and should never be neglected. Its purposes include the following: to give students a chance to verbalize any insights they have derived from the experience; to give the players a chance to express any feelings generated by the experience; to help students generalize the insights they have derived to other aspects of their lives; and to give the audience a chance to express any feelings that might have been caused by their identifying with the characters in the role-playing situation.

The discussion period is *not*, however, a time for evaluating the performance of the players. Except for instances in which the praise is appropriate ("You know, Jim, you played Mr. Jones just the way he really is!"), students should not be allowed to comment on the performance of others. If they do not agree with the way a role is being played, the appropriate time for them to do something about it is when a scene is to be reenacted. They can then volunteer to play the role in a different way. But once the discussion period has begun, they should not judge the performance of other students. The teacher, also, should be very careful to avoid criticism at this time.

As soon as the enactment has ended, the teacher should gather the group, both players and audience, into a circle and begin the discussion with a question such as, "Has a situation like this ever happened to you?" or, "Was there anything in this situation that reminded you of something in your own life?" This focuses the discussion on the group, encouraging them to generalize the role playing to their own lives, rather than on the performance of the players.

If the role playing has been used to enhance subject-matter learning, the follow-up discussion will tend to focus more on the concepts and principles that can be drawn from it than on whether students have been involved in a similar situation. Nonetheless, whenever possible, students should be encouraged to make the connection between the role-playing situation and their own lives.

A FINAL WORD

We hope that two main principles have become clear to the reader of this chapter: a) that role playing is a powerful instructional tool which has generally been relegated to a minor role in education heretofore; and b) that for role playing to be effective it must be undertaken seriously by a group that has the requisite skills and by a teacher who understands both applications and procedures. The teacher who is willing to help his class develop role-playing skills through the use of a training sequence such as we have outlined in this chapter and to warm the group up adequately at the beginning of each session will find that dramatic methods can enhance almost any lesson dealing with almost any subject matter at almost any grade level.

References 6

The basic works of Aristotle. New York: Random House, 1941, pp. 1460, 1464-1465.

CULBERTSON, FRANCES M. Modification of an emotionally held attitude through role playing. *Journal of Abnormal and Social Psychology,* 1957, **54,** 230-233.

JANIS, IRVING L., and KING, BERT T. The influence of role playing on opinion change. *Journal of Abnormal and Social Psychology,* 1954, **49,** 211-218.

JANSEN, MATHILDA J., and STOLUROW, L. M. An experimental study of role playing. *Psychological Monographs,* 1962, **76,** No. 31.

MORENO, J. L. *Psychodrama,* Vol. I. New York: Beacon House, Inc., 1964.

SHAFTEL, FANNIE R., and SHAFTEL, GEORGE. *Role playing for social values.* Englewood Cliffs, N.J.: Prentice-Hall, Inc., 1967.

WAY, BRIAN. *Development through drama.* New York: Humanities Press, Inc., 1967.

Additional Resources 6

AESTHETIC EDUCATION PROGRAM. *Theatre game file.* A set of 210 cards, each presenting an action activity developing improvisational skills. $29.50. CEMPEL, Inc., 10646 St. Charles Rock Rd., St. Ann, Mo. 63074.

BLATNER, HOWARD A. *Acting-in: Practical applications of psychodramatic methods.* A comprehensive handbook covering the use of action approaches in both therapy and education. Springer Publishing Co., Inc., 200 Park Ave. S., New York, N.Y. 10003.

CHESLER, MARK, and FOX, ROBERT. *Role-playing methods in the classroom.* One of the classics in the field. 1966. Science Research Associates, Palo Alto, Calif. 94301.

CONTEMPORARY DRAMA SERVICE. *Can of squirms.* A unique kit of role-playing ideas. $5.00 plus $.35 postage. Arthur Meriwether, Inc., P. O. Box 457, Downers Grove, Ill. 60615.

HENRY, MABEL W. *Creative experiences in oral language.* Especially valuable to elementary school teachers. $2.75. National Council of Teachers of English, 1111 Kenyon Rd., Urbana, Ill. 61801.

SHAFTEL, FANNIE R., and SHAFTEL, GEORGE. *Role playing for social values.* One of the most useful guides to role playing in schools. Includes several dozen unfinished "problem stories" on various themes especially appropriate for elementary children. $8.95. Prentice-Hall, Inc., Englewood Cliffs, N.J. 07632.

SPOLIN, VIOLA. *Improvisation for the theater.* A collection of over 200 theater games useful as training or warm-up exercises. Northwestern University Press, Evanston, Ill. 60201.

7

SIMULATIONS AND SIMULATION GAMES

Jack E. Cousins

Excitement and interaction are not gone from all schools in the United States. Scenes like the following are taking place all across the nation:

In a junior high school in Baton Rouge, Louisiana, a social studies supervisor and a visitor are talking to some students in a ninth grade class. These students have finished some simulation activities and are beginning an activity called *Rutlee and the Beach*. When asked what they liked about the activities, one boy replies, "Well, in this class I can say what I think, and if I opened my mouth in any other class in this school, boy, I'd really get it!"

A tenth grade geography class in Boulder, Colorado, is in the final stages of an activity called *Farming*. They have been given the outcome cards, which tell these "farmers" what has happened to them in the years 1933, 1934, and 1935. Shouts of dismay, anger, happiness erupt from the students. Finally one boy, with great feeling, blurts, "Boy—well—this is kinda hard to say. Now, we've got a feeling and under-

Jack E. Cousins is Associate Professor of Education, University of Colorado, Boulder, Colorado.

standing for the land, I think. We've worked this land for fifty years and I don't think I'm going to leave. I don't care what the banks and the government do, I'm not going to leave my land."

In a parochial school located in Minneapolis, Minnesota, an all-girl tenth grade group sits quietly while the teacher, a nun, explains an activity which is about to begin. Not a word comes from the girls while the work is explained. The girls then begin to engage in the work. Slowly, but very surely, interaction within the small groups begins to develop. It continues until the entire class is ringing with excitement and spontaneous learning. The sister does not interfere, but rather moves from group to group to ask leading questions, answer others and in general to keep the situation alive.

These scenes, each occurring with very different groups, are characteristic of what happens when teachers use simulations or simulation games. There appears to be a rapidly growing movement among educators to use simulations with students from elementary grades through the university. It seems, to use the words of Dennis Benson (1971), that "a fad is sweeping the land" (p. 10). Publisher after publisher is producing boxes of materials which make up the ingredients of something called simulations, simulation games or educational games. Why are teachers enthusiastically making extensive use of these activities? Is this just another fad (characteristic of American education) that will pass on in a few years, or have teachers discovered something that promises to answer some real needs in our schools? And, just what are simulations anyway?

A MATTER OF DEFINITION

The terms "simulations," "simulation games" and "educational games" are used in a variety of ways by various authorities. Despite varying usages, there does seem to be considerable agreement in the literature about simulations. The definitions developed here are not intended to be universally acceptable and are offered only to add clarity to this discussion.

According to William Nesbitt (1971), "simulation is a selective representation of reality, containing only those elements of reality that the designer deems relevant to his purpose" (pp. 4-5). Another way of defining simulations is to say that they are models or sets of submodels which replicate some phenomenon of the real world (Klietsch *et al.*, p. 10). In other words, simulations are attempts to take a part or parts of physical and/or social situations and reduce them in size and complexity so that essential elements can be recreated in classroom settings for educational purposes. Clark Abt (1970), who uses the term "game" when discussing simulations, says that when a game is reduced to its formal essence it "is an activity among two or more independent decision makers seeking to achieve their objectives in some limiting context" (p. 6). These activities or models of reality contain only those elements which are considered essential for learning to occur and which are essential in order to establish the limiting context about which Abt has written.

The use of games seems to grow out of the very natural ways in which children learn about the world. It is not unusual to see several children about six years of age pretending to be adults. If one observes carefully, it is readily apparent that these children are role-playing adult problems. This play is not aimless. It is really, to some degree, preparation for the roles children will assume in due time. Even though they may be incorrect, these children play adult roles as they (the children) perceive them.

A six-year-old boy, for example, assumes the role of father who has just entered the house after a day at his work. He indicates he is angry since the boss gave him some extra work to do. The "father" shouts at the "mother" and sends his "son" to his room for leaving his toys in the living room. Play? To be certain, but on the other hand, based on a child's observation of the real world. These children are, in a very natural way, preparing for the adult world. Perhaps educators can take this natural tendency and, rather than engaging in negative situations, help youth role-play the adult work as it could be. Unfortunately, this natural tendency to learn by playing seems to be lost by the time most children are firmly into their adolescent years. Is this natural, or does the adult world (including the schools) cause children to abandon play as a means of learning? Abt (1970) puts it this way:

> The world of the child and the young adolescent, like that of primitive man, is a dynamic world, full of emotion, imagination and physical action. Yet the opportunities for students' expressive action in the schools have yielded to strong pressures from adults for emphasis on abstraction; when students have tried to relate abstract thoughts to concrete action, adults have frequently felt their need for action and participation in a world which has

become increasingly specialized and in which action has come to be the province of specified occupational groups (p. 4).

Simulation seems to offer educators rich opportunities to regain the natural tendency to learn by enjoyable involvement.

In Denver, Colorado, United Airlines operates a large flight training center. Within this facility are located simulators which are used extensively in the programs which train pilots of large commercial aircraft. Those flight simulators, developed from the Link Trainers of World War II, provide the student pilots opportunities to practice in a real way most of the things involved in flying an actual airplane. Students simulate taxiing, talking to control towers, taking off, cruising and landing the aircraft. In other words, the essential components of flying large aircraft have been reduced in size and recreated in a learning situation, but without the risks involved in using actual airplanes. Simulated experience enables the students to learn in a much safer and less time-consuming way than actual air experience. Two important ideas relative to simulation are involved in this example. First, a model of reality has been reduced in size, and second, the essential elements of the problem (flying) have been included in a learning situation.

The description of flight training deals with simulation, but not with a simulation *game*. Flight training is not a gamelike activity, and the pilot does not assume any identity other than himself. Further, the trainees are not necessarily attempting to beat each other, or to win over one another. The situation does contain the problem or task to be performed, but it is not done in a gamelike fashion.

In the curriculum *Geography in an Urban Age*, there is an activity which can be identified as a simulation *game*. "Farming" requires that students assume the identity of farmers living in western Kansas in three historical periods: 1880-1882, 1919-1921 and1933-1935. Each "farmer," represented by a group of three to five students, is given certain resources of land and money. He must invest his resources in order to make a living for himself and his family. Each "farmer" attempts to make the greatest gain from his efforts. The realities of inconsistent rainfall, changing technology, unpredictable markets, world political conditions and unstable economic conditions are built into the activity. Each "farmer" invests his resources and, at the end of each year, receives an outcome card which tells him how well these efforts are rewarded. Outcome results are tabulated for each year in all three historical periods. Since outcome cards vary greatly for individual "farmers," the results are not always similar. One farmer may have a disastrous year while his neighbor has a successful one.

By keeping records of the outcomes, it can be easily inferred that one or two "farmers" have won the activity while others have lost. This is especially true in the 1930's, when most farmers lost their farms due to their inability to make mortgage payments. Such conditions within "Farming" seem to arouse gamelike competition among students. This activity is most appropriately called a *simulation game.* The realities of farming in different historical times are reduced and included in a learning situation so that a gaming atmosphere develops. Unlike the flight simulation, the role player assumes the identity of someone who lived in the times involved and, in the role, engages in problematic decision making.

One also finds, in this same curriculum, *Geography in an Urban Age,* an activity called "Metfab." In this simulation students are assigned roles as various members of the board of directors of a company called "Metfab," and as company officials, they must decide in which one of several cities a new plant is to be located. Students role-play the president, sales manager, personnel director, production manager and treasurer of the company. Sets of data are provided for each city under consideration, and each official must carefully analyze the data which are appropriate for his role. The "company board" must come to one decision and in the final analysis make a single choice. Since some data seem to conflict, extensive interaction develops within the various "companies" as they struggle to make the final decision. Compromises must be made, personal considerations recognized and power moves made within the "companies." Since, in a class of 25-30 students, there are likely to be five or six "companies," it is interesting to see that several cities have been chosen as the "best" site. Finally, selections are listed on the chalkboard and the various "companies" relate why and how their decision was reached. Although the atmosphere which develops in "Metfab" is gamelike, there can be no winner, even by inference. Since there is no winner, this activity is appropriately called a *simulation.*

There are other classroom activities which are more appropriately called by the simple term, *game.* For example, Chess is simply a game, as opposed to a simulation game, since there is little (if any) attempt to seriously recreate any part of reality. To be certain, a player could gain some insight into medieval society, but Chess for the most part remains only an intriguing game of strategy. "Propaganda," an activity designed to help students analyze various categories of persuasive statements, is also a desirable classroom game, but it is not a simulation game.

Actually, it is really not important whether one calls an activity a game, a simulation or a simulation game. But it is important to recognize that the various activities do accomplish different things as far as educational gain is concerned. All do, however, have one characteristic in common, and [that is they involve students in an interactive way; they provide students with opportunities to be dynamic, emotional and imaginative in very desirable ways] This characteristic is probably more important than concerns for informational cognitive gains.

One other simulation-type activity that must be mentioned here is role playing. Although this has been thoroughly discussed in the preceding chapter, I mention it here since role playing is a very important component in most simulations. Further, there are role-playing materials which also contain many elements of simulation, but which are not intended to be careful models of reality. *Hang-Up* is an activity in which participants role-play members of various racial groups. They are placed in certain social situations that, because of certain personal hang-ups (assigned with the roles), cause persons to become upset or frustrated. As these situations are presented, participants silently act out their "hang-ups" while the others in the group attempt to guess what they are. This activity is not an attempt to create an accurate model of reality, even though it is clearly recognized that such "hang-ups" do occur to people in similar situations. *Hang-Up* is intended to get people to openly discuss real hang-ups they have about persons of different racial, ethnic or social groups. One will often see such activities referred to as simulations, but in a rather technical sense they are role-playing activities. There are differences in these activities, but unless one wishes to be a purist about terminology, the identifiers are not as important as the contributions they make to education.

At this point, perhaps it would be helpful to summarize what has been a rather lengthy statement of definition. Activities generally identified by the word "simulation" actually represent a variety of related learning strategies. In a rather strict sense, *simulations* are models of reality simplified for classroom use. Such models usually require that participants assume the identity of another person. The models further require that the role-playing person solve some problem or reach some decision using information provided in the model itself. In another sense, simulation activities are often carried out in a gamelike atmosphere.

Other activities which, to a small degree, are based on reality and are intended to serve as initiators of group interaction, are not simulations. These are most often called *role-playing materials*. Perhaps the most convenient way to deal with these various terms is to simply call all such activities simulation games or learning games, and leave the technical terminology to researchers and developers. For the purposes of this chapter, we are concerned about materials that enable students to become actively involved in situations in which they interact with other students, with their own minds and with teachers. Throughout the remainder of this chapter the reader will probably notice that terms are used without consideration for consistency.

REASONS FOR USING SIMULATIONS

Generally, one cannot state that students learn more cognitive content of a traditional nature from simulation games than they do from conventional practices. On the other hand, students do seem to learn as much (Boocock and Schild, 1968; Lee and O'Leary, 1971; Shirts, 1971). And, as will be elaborated later, they do so with enthusiasm. Although these generalizations are supported by most of the research that has been reported to date, there have been a few exceptions which suggest that simulation may be more efficient as a means of teaching factual knowledge. Baker (1968), reporting a study he conducted with a pre-Civil War simulation, stated:

> The sum total of the evidence presented in this paper, on learning and on attitude change, seems rather clear; the traditional method of teaching American history to the above-average child in junior high school may be the most effective way. The simulation technique, which represents a break from currently accepted classroom procedures, is a potentially more efficient means of communicating historical facts, concepts, and attitudes to children at this age level (p. 142).

Another study reported by Fletcher (1971) supports the conclusions reached by Baker. Fletcher stated that, "if the teacher encourages the students to plan, so as to make effective use of the information which the games provide, the result is a substantial increase in the knowlege gained by the students" (p. 281). A very interesting finding in this same study indicated that, although general ability was related to the learning of facts and concepts, it (general ability) was not significantly related to learning of games strategies.

Thus, teachers who are using simulations can be certain that these activities do teach as much information as traditional approaches. They might also find that games do teach information more effectively.

"If games don't teach more, why should teachers upset the normal activities by incorporating them into the classroom situations?" is a question one hears quite often. This question is often accompanied with reasoning which goes as follows: "School is serious business and since games are enjoyable there seems to be little reason to use them in school." Abt (1970), commenting about such thinking, stated:

> We reject the somewhat Calvinistic notion that serious and virtuous activities cannot be 'fun.' If an activity having good educational results can offer, in addition, immediate emotional satisfaction to the participants, it is an ideal instructional method, motivating and rewarding learning as well as facilitating it (pp. 9-10).

Boocock and Schild (1968) support this position, but caution that some teachers may justify using games simply because it is assumed that games provide for "morale-building relaxation" from the serious business of learning (p. 19). An important point in all this is that simulations do provide for a relaxed atmosphere, but one in which learning does occur.

It has been consistently found that simulations motivate students. Both bright and average students are motivated by participating in these activities. Games *involve* students and it is seriously suggested that this involvement, especially when students enjoy the interaction with each other, is solid justification for using them. Further, it is suggested that the involvement of students is good reason for gaming even if traditional content goals are not reached. Rejected here is the idea that games are fine for the slow students, but a waste of time for the brighter ones. Evidence cited by Abt (1970) and Baker (1968) indicates that such reasoning is not sound. I contend that participation and involvement are in themselves justification enough for using simulations, and that this holds for all students. Boocock and Schild (1968) support this position:

> It is unquestionably true that games can generate great interest and involvement (although it is still an open question under what conditions this interest transfers to the study of related subject-matter by other methods).

But we also believe that games in themselves teach, that the players learn from their very participation in the game (p. 19).

What do games teach other than cognitive content? First, games seem to help students suffering from negative self-concepts develop more positive ideas about themselves. Apparently this phenomenon grows out of the fact that all students, regardless of ability, can participate in the simulation activities. Games, according to Clarice Stoll (1970), are "social democratizers" (p. 39). They demonstrate that each individual possesses special abilities which are all too often unknown to traditional teachers. Successful players who may be among the bright or very average often present pleasant surprises. Self-concept, probably the strongest determiner of success, both in school and in life out of school, is slowly evolved out of daily experiences. Students who have endless successions of failures in school develop negative ideas about self and about school. Games provide alternatives to these unrewarding school experiences. It has been noted that students normally identified as slow can, and do, participate in games on equal footing with bright classmates. It has also been observed that "slow" students inductively learn very complex processes and use them consistently throughout the simulation (Boocock and Schild, 1968, p. 157). Such successful experiences can help change negative ideas about self to more positive ones.

Emerging evidence indicates that simulations can also cause one's attitude toward others to change. Wishing to know if the game *Ghetto* would result in changes of attitude toward the poor, Samuel A. Livingston (1970) used the activity in an all-boy Roman Catholic school in Baltimore. He reported that the finding with the greatest statistical significance was that students' attitudes toward the poor were more favorable after the activity than they were before it (p. 19). It is interesting to note that this shift occurred even though there did not appear to be any increase in factual information relative to the poor (p. 12). Livingston suggests that shifts in attitude are a product of an intense involvement, although vicarious, in the role of some person facing very different life problems (p. 12).

Banks (1970), writing in relation to interracial attitudes—blacks toward whites; whites toward blacks—states that there is an urgent need for both groups to develop more positive attitudes toward each other (p. 2). He reports that black children both hate and admire whites and that white teachers often stereotype black students (pp. 2-8). After using simulations with inter-city youth, he concludes that, "simulation gives students an opportunity to learn from experience without paying the price that might result from unwise decisions made in real life" (pp. 57-58).

Paul DeKock (1969) experimented with the game of *Sunshine,* a simulation involving various ethnic groups. Income and living conditions vary quite graphically in this activity and one's rewards in life vary in direct proportion to his status. DeKock's students were pretested and posttested by a thirty-item racial attitudes test that was developed by a professional sociologist. As a result of his experimentation with *Sunshine,* he concludes that students participating did change their attitudes in positive directions. Not all students had an overall positive shift, but the vast majority of the scores moved in positive directions. DeKock attributes these positive changes to the nature of the simulation: it was fun and resulted in heavy involvement and interaction among the students (pp. 181-183).

Steven J. Kidder (1971) not only suggests that attitude changes do occur as a result of using the game *Ghetto,* but also suggests that attitude shifts are directly related to the intensity of student participation and involvement. He further suggests that students remember more over long periods of time in proportion to their involvement (p. 1).

It must be made quite clear that these studies are rather singular, in that they were conducted using one game with a limited number of subjects. However, when one examines study after study and reads of similar results, it appears safe to assume that simulations do, in fact, cause positive attitude changes. Further, it is very important to note that it is likely that these attitude changes are directly related to the amount and intensity of a student's involvement in the activity. Kidder (1971), discussing his findings, refers to Rokeach's idea that a necessary prerequisite to attitude change is a state of inconsistency. Kidder believes this occurs when a student role-plays someone whose life is inconsistent to his own (p. 44). In such a situation, the role player must closely examine *his own* real self as well as the self that he is attempting to play.

The Democracy Game was utilized by two researchers, Samuel A. Livingston (1970) and Karen C. Cohen (1969), in separate studies. Both researchers stated that students' attitudes toward politics were affected by participating in the game. It is difficult to say that the attitudes were either positive or negative, but it was observed by Livingston that "log rolling" was more acceptable to the students after, than before, the game. Cohen, in her conclusions, wrote:

What is overwhelmingly apparent, despite the limitations of this study due to the small number of students and the brief time span involved, is that their game involvement does set the students to thinking (as evidenced by the amount of attitude change) and that the students prefer the game experience to their regular classroom experience on a variety of dimensions (p. 17).

Without citing other evidence, it appears quite clear that participation in simulation does effect attitude change. It is further noted that attitude change is definitely related to the interaction and involvement which occurs when simulations are used. And, to repeat, students enjoy the activities.

What are the educational outcomes from simulations? Three major results have been presented in this chapter. First, students engaging in simulations will learn as much as students taught by traditional approaches. Furthermore, it can now be stated that there is some evidence, although slight at this time, which indicates that students can remember more information from simulations, especially over longer periods of time. The second important contribution is that gaming is highly motivational. Games motivate students with all ranges of abilities, not just the slow reader or culturally deprived. Third, games appear to be very valuable in effecting attitude change toward other ethnic or racial groups and toward little understood domains in society such as politics. The most important result is that students become involved in interaction with one another; even if the other three results were minimal, simulation would be desirable simply as a source of constructive interaction.

SUGGESTIONS FOR USING SIMULATIONS

Simulation is not the usual type of teaching strategy in which the teacher occupies center stage and dominates the action. Teachers must make some adjustments in order to get maximum educational benefit from the utilization of simulations.

First of all, no simulation game should ever be used without the teacher being thoroughly acquainted with the structure, procedures, roles and class organization necessary for conducting the game. Judith

Gillespie (1972) suggests that teachers should ask the following questions about a simulation before using it:

1. Is the game interesting?
2. Is the game workable in a classroom situation?
3. Does the game have a sound knowledge base?
4. What is the central problem to be explored?
5. What choices are there for players?
6. What are the rules?
7. How is the game organized?
8. What summary activities are suggested? (p. 15)

Having decided to use a game, teachers should not hesitate to change the guidelines in the manual. Use your imagination! If you wish to adapt the simulation to meet some unique educational goals, do it. Furthermore, don't be afraid to interrupt the game if you feel there is a need for informational input, or a question that should be faced. Students find it quite easy to change from a role they are playing to their own identity without losing the continuity of the game.

Another suggestion is that teachers should not overprepare students for simulation action. Provide only enough advance organization to initiate the activity. Certainly one should present the intended goals of the activity, but if this is overdone, there is a good chance that students will be "turned off" by their teacher's preparatory lecture. Students can inductively figure out many of the rules as the activity progresses. Supply additional rules and information as needs arise during the simulation itself.

The teacher's role in some simulations is quite well defined. If this is the case, play your role but don't interfere with the students any more than you must, and if you don't have a clearly defined role, be as unobtrusive as possible. This does not mean that teachers should abandon their responsibility, but it does mean that they should be wise enough not to be too noticeable during the actual simulation.

After the game is completed, the teacher should conduct a definite analysis of the simulation; otherwise, the educational gains may be lost. The intentions of the simulation, what students think they have learned and how they feel about the game and themselves should be thoroughly analyzed. "A game without discussion is of virtually no educational value" (Stoll, 1970). Discussions should focus on the ways students played their roles, whether information was learned, whether attitudes have changed and how students feel about the game and its relevancy. Extensive discussions about clever ways of winning should be minimal, but discussion about why certain strategies were more effective is legitimate. To be brief, students who have just completed a simulation should be given ample opportunity to share with each other and with their teacher the experiences they have just had.

Any experienced teacher knows that motivation is difficult to develop with many classes. Since each student learns different things in simulation exercises, teachers should *never, never* administer a common test to be used in determining grades. Certainly, one might wish to collect data about the information students learned, but it should be very clear to students that this data is not to be used in determining grades. If students feel they are being graded, there is a good chance they will come to see simulations as one more trick teachers play on them, and the motivation and enjoyment will quickly disappear. While simulations are in progress teachers can make observations which should provide much evaluative information. The following questions are suggested as guidelines:

1. Are students enthusiastic?
2. Are bright, slow and average students participating?
3. Do students readily learn the processes necessary to participate in the activity?
4. Are students using information provided in the game, and seeking additional information upon which to base decisions?
5. Does the game seem to contribute to the overall study of the subject matter?
6. Is the interaction conducive to helping students become thoroughly acquainted with each other?
7. If appropriate, does the game seem to help initiate attitude changes?

A SELECTED LIST OF COMMERCIAL GAMES

In order to provide teachers with some sources and initial simulations, the following games are reviewed. This list is not necessarily composed of the best games for all purposes. These were selected for their interactive nature, and for the fact that they come from a variety of producers.

Once you have tried these games, write the producers for complete lists of the games produced. (See the address list under Additional Materials.)

Starpower, Simile II, Price: $35.00

This simulation creates within the classroom a low-mobility, three-tiered society, structured around the distribution of wealth. The game is weighted so that one group of participants receives a larger number of high value chips than do members of the other two groups. As soon as this society is well established, the wealthiest group is given the opportunity and the power to restate the rules for the entire society. This condition almost inevitably leads to a situation in which the wealthiest group forms rules which make it virtually impossible for the "lower classes" to rise in the social order. When the lower classes realize that the wealthy have firmly consolidated their social position in authoritarian ways, it is usual for the rules to break down and for the lower classes to rebel against the authoritarianism of the wealthy.

Starpower encourages students to exchange ideas about the personal accumulation of wealth and the power that usually accompanies it. In the process students usually analyze their own values toward society, power and one's relationship to a total society. Teachers using *Starpower* should know that the rules are supposed to collapse and that rebellion by the "lower classes" is intended to take place. It is possible that specific final results will vary from class to class. Simile II also publishes an elementary version of this game entitled *Gunpowder.*

The Game of Farming, Macmillan,
Price: $29.95

This simulation, an agricultural investment activity, is a part of the curriculum *Geography in an Urban Age,* published by Macmillan. Students in groups of about two to four role-play western Kansas farmers in three historical periods: 1880-1882, 1919-1921 and 1933-1935. Each group role-playing an individual farmer must invest its limited resources in order to survive, a condition which leads to considerable interaction *within* the small groups. After each year's investment has been recorded on special forms, outcome cards are given each "farmer." These outcome cards show each "farmer" how well he has done during that year; since summer weather varies greatly in western Kansas, not all outcomes are the same. This causes considerable interaction *among* the small groups as they analyze why they received varying outcomes and as they prepare for the next year's planting.

As historical periods change, the complexities of the game increase and are strongly conditioned by domestic and world political and economic changes. Farming has significant cognitive content for history courses and it effectively utilizes economic concepts such as the market. It is a very effective simulation for creating an interactive environment and providing for student involvement. The curriculum *Geography in an Urban Age* includes many other simulation activities in the areas of cultural and political geography.

The Inter-Nation Simulation Kit,
Science Research Associates, Price: $60.00

The Inter-Nation Simulation Kit (INS) is an activity simulating the major features of the international political system. Originally designed for college students, INS has been used successfully by many high school teachers. Role playing is very important in inter-nation simulation, but students must do this within a set of programmed restraints. These restraints are included to provide realistic boundaries similar to those which operate in the real world. Since INS is a simulation rather than a game, it is definitely best to correlate it with appropriate content material. Players are divided into five, seven or ten teams, each team representing one nation. For each nation there are the following positions: head of state, foreign policy adviser, official domestic adviser, foreign affairs diplomat, domestic opposition leader and validator (a powerful individual or group whose support is essential if a government is to stay in power). In addition, each nation has a national council composed of the already named officials. Each nation's officials analyze changing world conditions and initiate strategies to generally strengthen their nation's capability to produce food and services, and strengthen its comparative position in international politics. INS is a rather complicated simulation, and in order to get maximum results, students must be thoroughly briefed about their country's background and objectives.

Each round, representing one actual year, takes approximately ninety minutes to play and the entire simulation is designed to cover six calendar years. It is very important that debriefings take place throughout the game, preferably at the conclusion of each round. INS provides rich opportunity for serious role playing and individual participation, but the users should become thoroughly familiar with the strategies involved before the actual simulation begins.

Napoli, Simile II, Price: $35.00

Napoli is a simulation of politics within the United States in which students role-play legislators in the nation of Napoli. This simulated United States, or Napoli, has eight states rather than the real fifty and has the Conservative and Liberal parties rather than the Republican and Democratic parties. Two political objectives face each legislator in Napoli. The first is to get bills passed that please his state, and the second is to get reelected. Individual legislators' chances for reelection are determined by the use of a probability formula that combines the performance for one's party and the performance for one's state. In order to meet both sets of demands, individual legislators must often make arrangements or deals with members of the other parties, and with legislators representing other states. Each legislator is encouraged to vote his conscience on all matters. After each round, each player is informed of his tentative chances for reelection.

In addition to the interaction involved in debating various bills, *Napoli* provides significant personal involvement in party caucuses and state caucuses. *Napoli* also provides many opportunities for students to change the procedures to more closely simulate particular local or state politics.

Sitte, Simile II, Price: $35.00

Sitte is a simulation designed to help students experience and think about the problems and potential of cities. Each student is assigned to a Spokesman Group that wants to make changes in the city. The five spokesman groups represent: business; disenfranchised; government; taxpayers association; and the ad hoc committee for parks and trees. In addition to the interest groups, at least two students are given roles as members of the mass media. The teacher is usually the director analyst, a role which may, however, be assigned to a student if proper preparation is made.

Each group has influence points which are used to get proposals passed that will improve the city in the directions approved by a particular group. However, each group has different goals, a situation that often results in conflict. Through group interaction students learn about pressure groups, log-rolling, honesty and dishonesty and government. They also learn that it is usually not possible to satisfy all pressure groups at the same time.

Normal playing time for *Sitte* is about four class periods, but it can take more time if students are encouraged to employ some creative ideas that quite often emerge. For example, mass media persons can develop radio news releases (on tape) and can develop newspapers which are quite elaborate. Interaction in *Sitte* is most pronounced among groups, but within each interest group students usually become quite involved on personal levels.

Crisis, Simile II, Price: $35.00

Crisis is a simulation about relations among six fictitious nations that vary in overall and military strength. The nations are faced with solving a problem which arises about a mining area that is of vital importance to the entire world. Each student is assigned a general role on a team of Chief Decision Makers and each team represents one of the six nations: Axiom, Burymore, Camelot, Dolchaveet, Ergosum and Fabuland. Countries have similar objectives but vary in overall strength and military power. The objectives are to obtain the rare element dematrium and to avoid destruction of your own nation and to keep yourself in office. Briefly stated, each nation tries to get some or total control of the mining area without upsetting the national political picture. Proposals and negotiations that take place in a world organization provide many opportunities for students to debate issues, execute original strategies and in general become personally involved. On a cognitive basis this game could be used in the study of the Middle East (petroleum), Latin America (copper), Africa (copper-diamonds) or Alaska (petroleum).

The length of *Crisis* depends on how events fall together. If a war breaks out, the game ends immediately. Otherwise, the activity should be continued until students are involved to the degree that they come to understand many of the complexities of international relations.

Ghetto, Western Publishing Company, Price: $20.00

Ghetto is a simulation game designed to help students gain insight into the lives of the urban poor. Participants, singly or in groups, are assigned the role of a fictitious person who has certain responsibilities such as children and certain liabilities such as a lack of marketable skills. Each role also carries with it a specific amount of education. The major objective is to improve the quality of your life in a "Ghetto." Each person may try to do this but group action is necessary if many real gains are to be made. Role players use their resources—in this game they are called "hour chips"—to improve their life conditions. If a female has several small children, she is given fewer hour chips, a condition based on the notion that she must spend some time caring for her children and thus has less time in which to earn a living. Conversely, a single male has more hour chips to invest in his life. Investments may be in education, welfare, jobs or "hustling." The latter, "hustling," is a general term for any form of petty crime. Outcomes are based on chance, and students quickly learn that individual efforts alone are inadequate if some persons are to enjoy an improved life style.

Ghetto can be played for various lengths of time, but should go through about eight rounds, representing eight actual years. It also can be played several times by the same students. In order to make maximum gain from replay, students should assume roles different from the ones assumed in the original play. Insights gained in early participation are very useful in subsequent play, but do not guarantee that one will live a better life. Ghetto is a simulation that deeply involves students. Teachers should encourage considerable casual interaction among participants throughout the entire activity. The first two or three rounds usually take much more time than later ones, since students must learn about the many complexities of the game in the initial stages.

Sunshine, Interact, Inc., Price: $10.00

Sunshine is a simulation that places students in the roles of citizens in a fictitious community called "Sunshine." Citizens are "born" into one of the six neighborhoods of Sunshine by the drawing of identity tags. Accidents of birth not only determine one's neighborhood but also establish whether he is black, white or brown. Each citizen of Sunshine has the challenge of improving his own self-image, a task which is more readily accomplished by some individuals (and groups) than by others.

Through the use of assignments and pressure cards (descriptions of situations usually affecting racial attitudes), the game activity moves Sunshine toward a racial crisis. The most obvious crisis is caused by the de facto segregation of Sunshine's public school system. Groups attempt to influence governmental agencies by such things as speech making and making proposals to the city council.

Sunshine, at first glance, appears to be a very complicated simulation but it is not difficult to use, since students catch on quickly and are able to move from one phase to another quite easily. Although *Sunshine* is designed to teach information about American minorities and about racial tensions, the simulation is rich in affective potentials. It is not possible to conduct the activity well without having students gather considerable factual data about various aspects of civil rights and race relations. This simulation is designed to be conducted over a three- to four-week time span, and it requires considerable material preparation in advance. Teachers should work through this simulation with a colleague or with a small group of students before attempting to play it with an entire high school class.

Hang-Up, Synectics Educational Systems, Price: $8.00

Based on Gordon Allport's book *The Nature of Prejudice,* this simulation is designed to focus attention on racial "hang-ups." Each participant is assigned a number of "hang-ups" that cause him personal concern, especially in situations where there is an interaction between blacks and whites. One's race is determined each time the dice are rolled: if the dice total an even number, one is black; if they total an odd number, he is white. The seriousness of one's "hang-ups" is conditioned by various social situations that are presented as one moves around the board. The real impact of the game is realized when a player is placed in a social situation that causes his or her "hang-up" to become important.

For example, a white is placed in an all-black hospital. When this occurs, the player affected by the situation acts out his "hang-up" before the group in pantomime fashion. Other members of the class try to identify the "hang-up" which is being acted out before them. They also try to identify any other prejudicial attitudes which may become evident as the pantomime is carried out. The value of this role-playing activity lies in its potential in identifying prejudices without threatening the actor. *Hang-up*, despite its attractiveness, should be handled carefully, especially in mixed groups where pantomime could insult sensitive students.

Propaganda, Wff 'N Proof Company,
Price: $6.00

Propaganda is an instructional game based on approximately fifty propaganda techniques. Designed to help students develop critical ways of analyzing information both in school and in mass media, *Propaganda* helps students distinguish between affective and cognitive elements of information.

   In *Propaganda*, students play themselves as they learn about and apply persuasion tactics. The game may be played in groups of two or three, or it may be played individually. Students are presented with statements in which propaganda techniques are used. These are then analyzed and labeled by the student. Some techniques encountered are: techniques of self-deception, techniques of exploration and techniques of maneuver. Under each technique category, numerous subcategories such as "rationalization," "tabloid thinking" and "prejudice" are used. As students encounter and identify various techniques, scores are compiled so that a winner can be identified. Students may challenge the game, in that classification of propaganda techniques may be changed by the group. As soon as *Propaganda* is explained to a group, the teacher can permit students to run the game by themselves, and it may be played many times by the same students.

System I, Instructional Simulations, Inc.,
Price: $9.85

System I is a game about games. Cognitive content of *System I* is selected by the teacher or by students and the teacher. The basic rationale for this game is that students prefer to learn through interaction and that, given problems to solve, students can learn effectively in a gaming atmosphere.

In a general sense, *System I* is designed to help students become familiar with the classification of information. This classification may be designed for social sciences or almost any other content area. It is a unique game, since teachers and students together help select the content and establish the rules. Although *System I* is very useful in teaching information, it provides for a classroom climate that makes learning once again enjoyable.

DEVELOPING YOUR OWN SIMULATIONS

Some teachers may wish to develop their own simulation activities, but hesitate to do so since they don't have the necessary background in simulation models. Such teachers should be brave enough to try their hands at developing simulations. R. Garry Shirts, Director of Simile II, and the developer of *Starpower,* believes that classroom teachers can develop good simulation activities:

> The main point here is that the teacher designed simulations, even when they are relatively less complex than commercial versions, may be just as instructive and valuable as those experiences which cost thousands of dollars to build and years to design. If you add to this the enjoyment and learning that results when one creates his own experience, then the answer to the frequently asked question, "Should we try to design our own simulation experiences?" becomes Yes, yes, most emphatically yes (p. 302).

This writer has worked with undergraduate students who have successfully designed simulations for use in junior and senior high schools. One student teacher, after conducting simulations with a class of seniors, permitted her students to develop a simulation of their own dealing with international relations. The results were extremely successful in motivating the class and in assisting students to acquire and effectively use information about various international situations.

Now that a case has been made for teacher designed simulations, teachers may still wish to know just how to go about designing their own games. First, become acquainted with as many commercially produced games as possible. Carefully examine them, asking the following questions: What is the problem? What roles must students play in this activity? What are the constraints placed on the role players? What informational background do participants need? Does this game represent some part of reality, and is it an accurate representation? What are the educational gains inherent in this game? Can I use it as it is? Can I adapt this game by changing some of its dimensions? This last question is the first step in designing your own simulations. In other words, teachers should not hesitate to redesign an existing game to suit particular needs. Perhaps some of the roles are not appropriate for your class—if so, change them! Perhaps the rules are not consistent with your notions of reality—change them! Finally, you may get some insights from your efforts that will lead to a significantly different game. For those readers who might wish to attempt some adapting, it is recommended that the following games be examined for adaptability: "Metfab" and "Millersburg," from Macmillan's *High School Geography*, can be readily changed for a variety of situations and classes. *Ghetto* is another simulation that can be adapted for studies about rural poor, even though it was designed for use in urban study courses.

A second step in designing your own simulations is to acquire and read Ray Glazer's paper *How to Design Education Games* (1969), which contains ten steps of game design:

1. Define overall objectives
2. Determine scope
3. Identify key actors
4. Determine actors' objectives
5. Determine actors' resources
6. Determine the interaction sequence among the actors
7. Determine the decision rules or criteria on the basis of which actors decide what resources and information to transmit or receive and what actions to take
8. Identify external constraints on actions of the actors
9. Formulate scoring rules or win criteria on the basis of the degree to which actors or teams achieve their objectives
10. In defining teaching objectives, always give operational definitions, what the student should be able to do or know after participating in the game.

These steps are carefully elaborated in Glazer's paper. In addition to the initial design ideas, Glazer also makes valuable suggestions about how one actually puts together the physical game. This paper is a *must* if one wishes to design games for his own use.

ADDITIONAL MATERIALS

The following sources are suggested for teachers who wish to acquire more information about the rationale for using simulations and games. William Nesbitt's *Simulation Games for the Social Studies Classroom* (1971) is the best initial book available. This volume is written to the classroom teacher rather than to those who wish to ponder theories and rationale. It is practical in that it includes basic ideas about simulation models and an annotated bibliography of proven simulations. If one wishes to go beyond the theoretical dimensions of the Nesbitt book, *Serious Games* by Clark Abt (1970) is suggested. Although somewhat more theoretical than Nesbitt's work, Abt's work is very readable. A third book quite valuable for teachers is *Simulation Games in Learning*, edited by Boocock and Schild (1968). This book covers a wide range of concerns relative to simulation—including theory, research and teacher designed games. One can spend large amounts of time pursuing journal articles and unpublished reports through the ERIC system, but the three mentioned books really cover most of the information essential for classroom teachers who want to be well prepared in the literature relative to simulation.

Publishers are producing games much more rapidly than teachers can be informed about them. In order to assist teachers in locating games, the following sources are recommended. First, the guide by Zuckerman and Horn, *The Guide to Simulation Games for Education and Training* (1973), is the comprehensive guide for the entire field of simulation. This guide includes activities for business, economics, politics, industry, spelling and arithmetic, as well as all the areas of social studies. The guide does *not offer* detailed analyses of the games. Descriptions are quite brief, and it is often difficult to determine whether the activities are worthwhile. But it is comprehensive and quite accurate when it comes to producers, addresses and costs. This guide has been revised recently, so readers should make sure they have the latest edition.

Teachers would be wise to acquire a copy of Paul Twelker's *A Basic Reference Shelf on Simulation and Gaming* (1970), which includes annotations about bibliographies, game producers, theoretical books, journals and newsletters. The paper is readily available and inexpensive, and is perhaps the most useful up-to-date resource on simulations for classroom teachers. The paper has been revised by Twelker and Kent Layden (1972). The revision is titled "Education Simulation/Gaming" and was published by the ERIC Clearinghouse on Educational Media and Technology at Stanford University.

A most recent paper by Steven J. Kidder, *Simulation Games: Practical References, Potential Uses, Selected Bibliography* (1971), may be acquired from the Center for Social Organization of Schools, Johns Hopkins University. It is also listed in the ERIC system. This paper contains a brief review of the best literature, a section on the potential of gaming and an excellent selected bibliography. It is the most up-to-date bibliography available today.

For teachers who wish detailed analyses and descriptions of simulations, the *Data Book,* published by the Social Science Education Consortium (1972), is recommended. The game reviews included here are not intended to be highly critical but are intended to give teachers accurate information about them. At this time, over forty games have been reviewed in the *Data Book.* These reviews will have substantial additions in the very near future. Included are costs, difficulties in conducting various games, intentions of the games and appropriateness for use in various types of classrooms.

In the past few years the number of organizations producing games has increased so rapidly that it is almost impossible to keep up to date about available simulations. For the assistance of those who would like to contact publishers, the following selected list is included. I do not necessarily recommend all the simulations produced by these publishers, but each producer listed is a proven developer of games and simulations, and many of their activities are very good. Other producers are also developing desirable simulations, but time and space simply do not permit the listing of all those developers that are at work in the general area of simulations.

ABT ASSOCIATES, INC., 55 Wheeler Street, Cambridge, Massachusetts 02138

ACADEMIC GAMES ASSOCIATES, INC., 430 East Thirty-Third Street, Baltimore, Maryland 21218

CHANGING TIMES EDUCATION SERVICE, 1729 H. Street, N.W., Washington, D.C. 20006

DENOYER-GEPPERT CO., 5235 Ravenswood Avenue, Chicago, Illinois 60640

ENTELEK, INC., 42 Pleasant Street, Newburyport, Massachusetts 01950

INSTRUCTIONAL SIMULATIONS, INC., 2147 University Avenue, St. Paul, Minnesota 55114

INTERACT, INC., P.O. Box 262, Lakeside, California 92040

JOINT COUNCIL ON ECONOMIC EDUCATION, 1212 Avenue of the Americas, New York, New York 10036

THE MACMILLAN CO., School Division, 866 Third Avenue, New York, New York 10002

MASCO, P.O. Box 382, Locust Valley, New York 11560

OLCOTT FORWARD, INC., 234 N. Central Avenue, Hartsdale, New York 10530

PSYCHOLOGY TODAY GAMES, Carmel Valley Road, Del Mar, California 92014

SCIENCE RESEARCH ASSOCIATES, INC., 259 East Erie Street, Chicago, Illinois 60611

SIMILE II, 1150 Silverado, La Jolla, California 92037

SYNECTICS EDUCATIONAL SYSTEMS, 121 Brattle Street, Cambridge, Massachusetts 02138

URBAN DYNE, 5659 S. Woodlawn Avenue, Chicago, Illinois 60637

URBAN SYSTEMS, INC., 1033 Massachusetts Avenue, Cambridge, Massachusetts 02138

WESTERN PUBLISHING CO., INC., School and Library Department, 850 Third Avenue, New York, New York 10022

WFF 'N PROOF COMPANY, Box 71-OE, New Haven, Connecticut 06501

References   7

ABT, CLARK C. *Serious games.* New York: Viking, 1970.

BAKER, EUGENE H. A pre-civil war simulation for teaching American history. In Sarene E. Boocock and E.O. Schild (Eds.), *Simulation games in learning.* Beverly Hills, Calif.: Sage, 1968.

BANKS, JAMES A. *Teaching the black experience.* Belmont, Calif.: Fearon, 1970.

BENSON, DENNIS. *Gaming: The fine art of creating simulation/learning games for religious education.* Nashville, Tenn.: Abington Audio Graphics, 1971.

BOOCOCK, SARENE E., and SCHILD, E.O. (eds.) *Simulation games in learning.* Beverly Hills, Calif.: Sage, 1968.

COHEN, KAREN C. The effects of two simulation games on the opinions and attitudes of selected sixth, seventh, and eighth grade students. Johns Hopkins University, May, 1969: ERIC 031 766.

DEKOCK, PAUL. Simulations and change in racial attitudes. *Social Education,* February, 1969, 181-183.

FLETCHER, JERRY L. Evaluation of learning in two social studies simulation games. In *Simulation & Games,* September, 1971, 259-286.

GILLESPIE, JUDITH A. Analyzing and evaluating classroom games. *Social Education,* January, 1972, 33-34, 94.

GLAZIER, RAY. *How to design educational games.* Cambridge: Abt Associates, 1969.

KIDDER, STEVEN J. Emotional arousal and attitude changes during simulation games. Johns Hopkins University, August, 1971: ERIC ED 054 513.

KLIETSCH, RONALD G., WIEGMAN, FRED, and POWELL, JIM R., JR. *Directory of educational simulations, learning games, and didactic units.* St. Paul: Authors at Macalester College Simulation Center, 1969.

LEE, ROBERT S., and O'LEARY, ARLENE. Attitude and personality effects of a three-day simulation. *Simulation and Games,* 1971, *14,* 309-347.

LIVINGSTON, SAMUEL A. Simulation games and attitude change: Attitudes toward the poor. The Johns Hopkins University, April, 1970: ERIC ED 039 151.

NESBITT, WILLIAM. *Simulation games for the social studies classroom.* New York: The Foreign Policy Association, 1971.

SHIRTS, R. GARRY. Simulations, games and related activities for elementary classrooms. *Social Education,* March, 1971, 300-304.

SOCIAL SCIENCE EDUCATION CONSORTIUM. *Social studies curriculum data book.* Boulder, Colo.: Social Science Education Consortium, 1972.

STOLL, CLARICE. Games students play. *Media and Methods,* October, 1970, 37-44.

TWELKER, PAUL A. *A Basic reference shelf on simulation and gaming.* ERIC: ED 041-487, 1970.

TWELKER, PAUL A., and LAYDEN, KENT. *Education simulation/gaming.* ERIC: ED 064-955, 1972.

ZUCKERMAN, DAVID W., and HORN, ROBERT. *The guide to simulation games for education and training.* Cambridge, Mass.: Information Resources, Inc., 1973.

8

BEYOND THE CLASSROOM

"Escape . . . The real classroom is outside!" urges a poster produced by
the Environmental Studies Program. Its advice is sound, and in recent
years more and more students and teachers are heeding it. In some
cases, students (and teachers) are taking the advice literally and dropping out of a classroom-bound system they feel can offer them little of
value, perhaps agreeing with Mark Twain, who said, "I never let school
interfere with my education." In other cases, students and teachers are
working together to fashion new educational experiences that take them
into the world outside the confines of the classroom.

WHY LEAVE THE CLASSROOM?

Until recent decades, when it became fashionable for young people to
spend most of the first third of their lives in school, young people did
most of their learning of how to live and what the world is like through
direct experience in their communities. At a very early age children were
expected to contribute significantly to the work of keeping the family

going. They learned the skills they needed for adult success by working alongside their parents or other adults. School was reserved for learning only those things that a person couldn't learn outside.

However, schools have more and more begun to include in their curricula subject matter that could more easily and effectively be learned otherwise. Instead of learning about our political system by attending rallies, committee meetings and party caucuses, a student takes a "course" in something known as "civics," in which he reads about the political system and discusses it in class (and tries to pass a test on it). The result is that students all too often make a distinction between what they learn in the classroom and the "real" world outside. A student who can recite fifty grammar rules and correctly fill in dozens of workbook pages continues to pair singular subjects and plural verbs when talking to his friends at the local hang-out. Or, an A student in science leaves garden tools outside overnight, not realizing that they will rust from the dew.

One reason, then, for providing students with experiences outside the classroom is to give them a chance to transfer what they have learned in the safe confines of the classroom to the world of reality. The classroom can be seen as a sort of sheltered environment, in which new behaviors can be learned and practiced without the penalties that failure might bring in the world outside. The classroom "micro-society" can give students a safe introduction to new knowledge or new behavior and a chance to try it out. But he then needs an opportunity to transfer the skills to the situation in which he ultimately needs to utilize them—the world of everyday life.

Activities outside the classroom also have the advantage of providing a wider diversity of experiences than are possible within the school. Some learning experiences are simply not possible in the classroom—physical or financial limitations make them impossible. The classroom-bound student who wants to experience what the inside of a canning factory is like has but one choice—to read about it. However, the vicarious experience of reading will be so much less effective in helping the student learn that he may feel he might as well have not wasted his time. We—and a host of other educators from John Dewey to Edgar Dale—feel that the more direct the learning experience, the more permanent the learning will be. Even in the mid-nineteenth century, Thoreau (1865) was suggesting that students

> ... should not play life, or study it merely, while the community supports them at this expensive game, but earnestly live it from beginning to end. How could youths better learn to live than by at once trying the experiment of living? Methinks this would exercise their minds as much as mathemat-

ics. If I wished a boy to know something about the arts and sciences, for instance, I would not pursue the common course, which is merely to send him into the neighborhood of some professor, where anything is professed and practised but the art of life; to survey the world through a telescope or a microscope, and never with his natural eye; to study chemistry, and not learn how his bread is made, or mechanics, and not learn how it is earned; to discover new satellites to Neptune, and not detect the motes in his eyes, or to what vagabond he is a satellite himself; or to be devoured by the monsters that swarm all around him, while contemplating the monsters in a drop of vinegar. Which would have advanced the most at the end of a

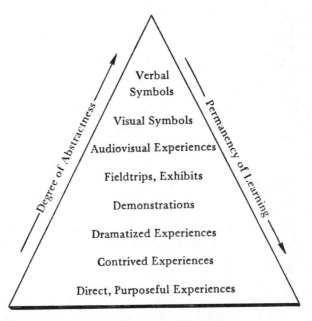

FIGURE 1. CONE OF EXPERIENCE (adapted from Dale, 1969)

month—the boy who had made his own jackknife from the ore which he had dug and smelted, reading as much as would be necessary for this—or the boy who had attended the lectures of metallurgy at the Institute in the meanwhile, and had received a Rodgers penknife from his father? Which would be most likely to cut his fingers? ... To my astonishment I was informed on leaving college that I had studied navigation!—why, if I had taken one turn down the harbor I should have known more about it (p. 43).

Dale (1969) has suggested the "Cone of Experience" above as a graphic means of comparing the relative effectiveness of several types of learning activities.

It is interesting to note that the approaches to learning that are utilized most frequently by most of us—verbal symbols (discussion, lecture) and visual symbols (reading)—are those that Dale claims lead to the least permanency of learning. On the other hand, direct experiences are the most effective. If we accept Dale's position, we will attempt to give students direct experiences with the subject matter as often as possible. For some educational goals we can provide these direct experiences in the classroom. But in a great number of cases, we must look beyond the classroom if we hope to provide direct experience.

ACTIVITIES OUTSIDE THE CLASSROOM

When choosing activities to help achieve educational objectives, the teacher's first question should be, "Can I give students direct experience with the subject matter?" If the direct experience can be provided within the confines of the classroom or school, fine. But if direct experience is possible only outside the school, the teacher should look for ways to make it available to students. Some possible approaches are suggested below. Only if a direct experience—inside or outside the classroom—is impossible (learning about the geological features of the moon through direct experience is an example) should the teacher resort to a more abstract experience—simulations, audiovisual presentations or reading.

Interactive Field Trips

The field trip has traditionally been a passive experience, accomplishing little of value except giving students and their teacher a chance to escape from the routine of daily life in the school. Usually students are cautioned not to talk or otherwise cause disturbance—as they shuffle along on a guided tour of the local city hall, a museum or a newspaper plant. The experience has rarely been any more involving than viewing a movie on the same topic—and often less effective because of the difficulty of seeing over the heads of other students on the tour. Yet, the field trip is potentially an effective learning experience—if students are allowed to become involved through interaction with the environment they are visiting. We are choosing to call this type of experience an *interactive field trip.*

Assume, for example, that your students are studying the rise of mass production in American industry. By fortunate circumstance, just two blocks down the street is a General Motors plant that assembles Chevrolet trucks. An excellent opportunity for your students to see mass production in action, you muse. If you call the plant's public relations department and ask for a tour of the plant for your students, you are likely to end up with a field trip of the traditional sort. Students will see some interesting things, but will have no personal involvement in the experience. On the other hand, you might ask the public relations department if it would be possible for your students to talk with some of the workers on the line—perhaps during a coffee break. The workers are likely to be delighted that someone is interested in their work and considers it valuable enough to bring a class of sixth-graders to look at and talk about. In addition, students will have a chance for human interaction to add personal significance to their tour of the plant. They can ask the workers whether they enjoy their work, how it feels to do the same repetitious job over and over, and so forth. Such an experience can have a profound effect on students' attitudes toward various occupational groups, as well as helping them in their own vocational exploration and understanding of mass production.

The key to planning an interactive field trip is to look for ways for students to interact with the human beings involved. Usually this consists of a chance to ask questions, but it can also extend to allowing students to participate in the process—sitting in the driver's seat, pressing the button at the right time, sliding down the fire pole or whatever. Actual participation may be difficult to accomplish with a big group. For this reason it might be useful to allow students to go on their own individual interactive field trips. A middle school we have worked with allows ninth-graders to spend two hours each Monday visiting some place that they would like to learn about. One student, for example, spends his time at the courthouse, where he is allowed to visit various offices, to do simple clerical tasks and to ask as many questions as he wants.

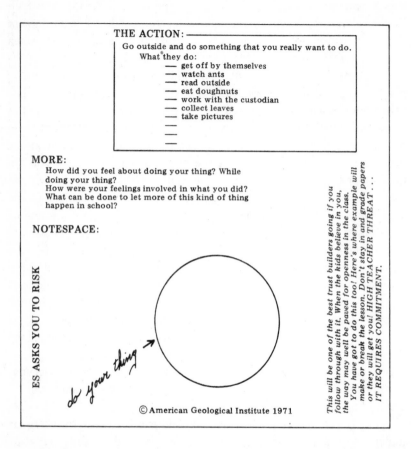

THE ACTION: ───────────
Go outside and do something that you really want to do.
What they do:
— get off by themselves
— watch ants
— read outside
— eat doughnuts
— work with the custodian
— collect leaves
— take pictures
—
—
—

MORE:
How did you feel about doing your thing? While doing your thing?
How were your feelings involved in what you did?
What can be done to let more of this kind of thing happen in school?

NOTESPACE:

This will be one of the best trust builders going if you follow through with it. When the kids believe in you, the way may well be paved for openness in the class. You have got to do this too! Here's where example will make or break the lesson. Don't stay in and grade papers or they will get you! HIGH TEACHER THREAT . . . IT REQUIRES COMMITMENT.

ES ASKS YOU TO RISK

do your thing →

© American Geological Institute 1971

The Environmental Studies Project of the American Geological Institute has been creating ideas for active-involvement experiences outside the classroom suitable for students at any grade level. Their Environmental Studies Packets (see the list of Additional Resources at the end of this chapter) comprise a set of cards; on each card is a suggested activity, along with follow-up possibilities and helpful hints to the teacher. Two such cards are reproduced here.

Exchange Programs

In a pluralistic society such as ours, students need frequent contact with

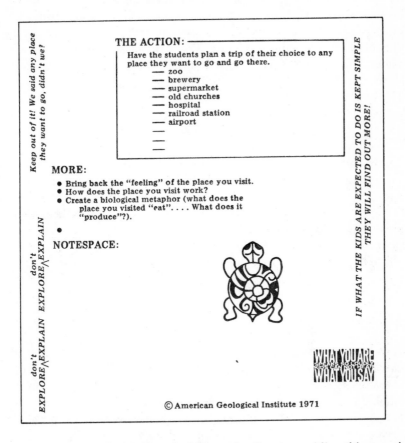

THE ACTION:
Have the students plan a trip of their choice to any place they want to go and go there.
— zoo
— brewery
— supermarket
— old churches
— hospital
— railroad station
— airport
—
—

MORE:
- Bring back the "feeling" of the place you visit.
- How does the place you visit work?
- Create a biological metaphor (what does the place you visited "eat". . . . What does it "produce"?).
-

NOTESPACE:

Keep out of it! We said any place they want to go, didn't we?

don't
EXPLORE∕EXPLAIN EXPLORE∕EXPLAIN
don't
EXPLORE∕EXPLAIN

IF WHAT THE KIDS ARE EXPECTED TO DO IS KEPT SIMPLE THEY WILL FIND OUT MORE!

WHAT YOU ARE
WHAT YOU SAY

© American Geological Institute 1971

people of different backgrounds. Many schools are providing this experience by establishing exchange programs between schools. A class in a suburban school might spend a week at an inner-city school, living with families of the inner-city students, who themselves are visiting the suburbs at the same time. A school in a small conservative town might arrange an exchange with a school in a cosmopolitan northern city.

Cross-Age Teaching

In numerous schools across America students leave behind not only their classroom but their role as students—as they devote themselves to the teaching of younger students. Fifth-graders are helping second-graders with arithmetic; high school students are conducting art lessons for third-graders; college students are tutoring sixth-graders with reading difficulties. The combinations are almost limitless, but all involve a student becoming "teacher" for a while. The benefits are far more significant than merely relieving some teacher of part of his work load. The older student who is serving as "teacher" learns not only subject matter but also interpersonal skills. He starts to understand more about the process of learning and thus gains skills he can use in his own learning.

In some schools, cross-age teaching is an informal process—with a student utilizing some of his unscheduled time to help younger students. In other schools, the process has become highly structured—with the "teachers" receiving a thorough orientation and obtaining school credit for their work. Gartner, Kohler and Riessman (1971) provide a current summary of the various approaches to cross-age teaching that are being utilized.

Shadowing

How can you give students direct experience and insight into what it's like to be a surgeon, a college professor, a bricklayer, a telephone operator, a union organizer or a beauty shop operator? It may not be feasible to let a student be a "surgeon-for-a-day." Yet, even though he may not be able to "walk in the other man's moccasins," he can walk in his footprints. That is what shadowing is all about.

The student literally "shadows"—that is, follows around—the person, whose role he is interested in learning more about. The experience can last for one day, a week or a month. Here are some general guidelines for a shadowing program in which college students shadowed a professor of their choice. They can easily be modified to suit shadows of any grade level.

1. The student and faculty member agree on a week (five days) for shadowing.
2. The student and faculty member agree on what situations will be private (e.g., shadow is asked to leave office because of confidential conversation).

3. The shadow attends meetings, conferences, classes; and listens to conversations, interviews, advising sessions and other daily activities of the faculty member. The shadow may travel with the faculty member on a consulting or speaking trip.

4. The faculty member shares his mail, decisions, problems and general thoughts with his shadow.

5. The faculty member attempts to inform the shadow of his areas of interest and expertise; he gives the shadow bibliographies and recommends books in his area. The shadow may read as many as three books during the week if he is interested.

6. It is recommended that the shadow spend at least four hours per day (twenty hours total) with the faculty member other than in classes, and that the shadow attend all of the faculty member's classes during the week.

7. The student will write a paper synthesizing his experiences on completion of the week and have it approved by the faculty member.

Sensitizing Modules

The concept of "sensitizing modules" was introduced by Simon (1970) and elaborated on by Kirschenbaum (1970). These are brief experiences that put the student into interaction with the environment in some way. For example, Simon suggests the following modules (particularly suitable for middle-class suburban students):

Sit in the waiting room of the maternity ward of (a large hospital). Strike up a conversation with other people in the waiting room. Try to distinguish which patients are charity cases and which are not. Spend 30 minutes in the emergency ward. Keep out of the way, but note carefully what happens.

Go to magistrate's court and keep a list of the kinds of cases brought before the magistrate. Who are his customers? How are they handled? What lesson about our economy can you learn here?

Wear old clothes and sit in the waiting room of the State Employment Office. Listen, observe, talk to the people sitting next to you. Read the announcements on the bulletin board, etc. Try to overhear an interview if possible (p. 29).

Kirschenbaum suggests a large number of module ideas, including the following:

Try to call City Hall with a complaint that your landlord did not give you heat, or has not repaired a roof leak, or that the toilet is not working. Better yet, find a neighbor with a real complaint and offer to help him get it fixed (p. 37).

In teaching elementary children the period of world exploration and the discovery of America, one teacher had her children go out and actually "discover" new parts of the city. One instruction was to "find a new faster route to the ball field." She stayed a half block behind them, but they had to do the discovering themselves. And the gap between Columbus and their own risk-taking world in the city was narrowed (p. 38).

One high school class studying the Second World War took a trip to a Veteran's Hospital where the students interviewed many of the patients (p. 38).

The "sensitizing module" can be almost any experience that puts the students—individually or in teams—in direct interaction with their environment. Insofar as possible, it should include the opportunity for the student to *do* something rather than passively looking, and should include the opportunity for interaction with other human beings.

On-the-Job Training

Some of the most exciting educational programs that we have visited have been designed to give the "non-college-bound" high school student practical vocational skills. Classroom-confined academic subjects are reduced to a minimum, and the student spends the greatest part of his day at a local business firm or industry, receiving on-the-job work experience. It is not hard to begin feeling as though it is the college-bound student who is suffering educationally—as well as psychologically. While students in the "lower tracks" are allowed to have direct experiences with the real world, the average and honors students are often forced to learn about the world second-hand. It is not surprising, then, that many of the students identified as potential dropouts are those with high ability and achievement scores. They are wise enough to realize that most of the "dropout" programs will give them a much more meaningful educational experience than what most classrooms filled with highly motivated students can offer.

It is unfortunate that practical work experiences are not provided for the "upper-track" student as well as the potential dropout. In our experience, a school which encourages—or even allows—the "good" students to learn a marketable skill and receive on-the-job experience is almost nonexistent. (One of the first exceptions will be described later in this chapter.) We feel that virtually every student should graduate from high school with a skill with which he can support himself and with at least one semester's experience in the world of work.

Schools Without Walls

An encouraging educational trend in recent years has been the establishment of a number of experimental programs that utilize the community as the classroom. Perhaps the best known of these is the Philadelphia Parkway Program. According to John Bremer (1970), the project's director:

> There is no school house, there is no separate building; school is not a place but an activity, a process. We are, indeed, a school without walls. Where do the students learn? In the city. Where in the city? Anywhere and everywhere. If students are to learn about television, they cannot do this apart from the studios and locations in which television is produced. So we use television studios and we use radio stations, and we use the museums, social service organizations, and we use the business community. The Philadelphia city government departments assist us—the Police Department, and the District Attorney's office to name only two. Parents help us. A large number of people help us and we are grateful. Everyone has a stake in education, everyone has a right and a duty to be involved, to participate. The community helps us in a great variety of ways; by providing us with meeting space, with resources, with instructors, even with total programs. And without the community's help we cannot do our job (pp. 4-5).

The Parkway Program was established as a four-year high school experience. It derived its students from previously existing schools in the city, who were chosen by lottery. Other programs "without walls" have been incorporated as alternatives *within* a preexisting high school. Below are excerpts from a description of Lexington (Massachusetts) High School's "Education Without Walls" program, which was established to serve volunteers from the regular school program:

> Some people would rather start their own business than read about management and marketing. Some people would rather be teachers' aides in a

Boston school than read *Up the Down Staircase.* Some people would rather make a film than watch one. Some people would rather read Eldridge Cleaver than Charles Dickens. Some people would rather find out what makes a criminal tick then study crime statistics. Some people would rather find out what makes themselves tick than serve detention. Some people find that their high school experiences are not meaningful. They have developed interests and needs that simply are not met in the traditional school curriculum. It was in recognition of these people that the Education Without Walls Program was devised.

WHAT IS "WITHOUT WALLS" EDUCATION?—Education is a total experience. The confines of the classroom and the limits of the academic disciplines are artificial. Man's natural curiosity cannot be contained within a school building. The community—indeed, the whole world—should be man's classroom. It is on this conception of education that Lexington's Education Without Walls Program is based.

HOW WAS THE EDUCATION WITHOUT WALLS PROGRAM CRE-ATED?—The framework of the Program was developed in a summer workshop in 1968. Participants included: High school teachers, students, administrators, and consultants from the local businesses and the community. During the school year 1968-1969, Education Without Walls began to take more definite shape, as teachers and students met frequently to discuss the Program. The specific form of Education Without Walls was refined in a summer workshop in 1969.

WHOM IS THE EDUCATION WITHOUT WALLS PROGRAM FOR?—Approximately 100 seniors have volunteered for the Education Without Walls Program for the school year 1969-1970. Next year, the Program will be expanded to include juniors as well as seniors. Eventually, the Program will be open to all high school students. In Education Without Walls are students of widely varied backgrounds, interests, "ability levels," aspirations, attitudes and needs. There is no "typical" EWOW student.

HOW WILL "EWOW" MEET THE DIVERSE NEEDS OF ALL OF ITS STUDENTS? In the morning—Mondays are devoted to a course designed to meet the universal desire of people to understand themselves. Students' own problems and questions form the basis for this Social Relations Course. A variety of interdisciplinary elective courses, based on the expressed interests of participating students, is offered on Tuesday through Friday. Students may also initiate their own individualized course, working with a teacher or a resource person from the community.

What are some of the elective courses being offered?

Film-making	American Music	The Psychology of
City and Suburb	Managing a Small Business	Violence
Freud and the Boys	The Black Man Revolts	

The Criminal Mind   Science for Decision-Making   Prisons, Jails and
Oceanography   Sociology   Reformatories
                   How to Use Your Money   Communist Theory

In the afternoon—Students may work at an occupation that will help to prepare them for a career. They may volunteer for service experiences in Lexington or in nearby communities or pursue independent research projects. Students may take courses offered in the High School outside of the Education Without Walls Program. They may observe or study occupations that interest them.

What will some of the students be doing in the afternoon?
Managing a Gas Station   Taking Flying Lessons   Research in
Studying a Foreign Language   Opening a Boutique   Science Museum
Elementary Teacher Aide

HOW WILL STUDENTS IN THE EDUCATION WITHOUT WALLS PROGRAM BE EVALUATED?—Students and staff members will agree on a contract—a statement of the student's goals for his Education Without Walls experience. The student's performance will be assessed according to his achievement of the goals to which he has agreed. Students will receive a written evaluation, as well as letter grades, for the morning elective course. Each student will receive a written evaluation of his overall performance in the Program on the combined observations of his teachers, his consultants and his employer.

Other high schools have offered modified "without walls" programs on a smaller scale—often only to seniors. The Cultural Enrichment Program at Horton Watkins High School in suburban St. Louis allows a senior (who is able to complete graduation requirements before his final semester) to work on a project away from the school. A more elaborate program is the Senior Seminar at Denver's East High School. Here are excerpts from a description of the program that appeared in the annual report of the Colorado Outward Bound School (1971):

For 93 seniors at Denver's East High School, the last semester of their senior year was unlike anything they had experienced before—in school or out. It began with two weeks on a remote stretch of beach on the Gulf of California in Mexico. With 8 teachers they sailed, hiked in the desert, climbed a high peak and each spent two very personal days alone—the sun, the ocean and the sea birds their only companions.

This was the unique beginning of a program called the Senior Seminar, designed to prove that learning is not restricted to the classroom, that experience is an effective and impressive teacher. The students were selected from volunteers to accurately reflect the student body of East. They were a mixture of middle class and ghetto, high achievers and dropouts.

Returning to Denver from their two weeks in Mexico, the students discovered that the entire city was to be their classroom and the people who worked and lived in that city their teachers. They studied Power and Politics by going to the State Legislature to participate in the actual business of running a state. They talked to lawmakers and lobbyists, to leaders of minority groups. They discovered first-hand how the democratic process works.

In the Urban Design module, another of the eight areas of investigation open to the students, they collected trash with city sanitation crews, visited Urban Renewal construction sites, talked with city planners and explored the challenges that face a growing city. "City problems like pollution never bothered me before," wrote one student. "Seminar turned me on to the fact that they are my problems too, and I better do something about them before it is too late."

Additional modules—Hispano Culture, Space Technology and Man, Urban Arts—exposed the students to the diverse personality of the city.

"My Indian mother couldn't speak any English, but we communicated with each other through the children. I never will forget them. I learned so much from them," was one girl's reaction to her week-long live-in with a Navajo family in the Southwest. Students became a part of their Indian families for the week, chopping wood, tending sheep and growing through their experiences. They followed up the live-in with a brief study of Indian anthropology at Prescott College in Arizona, and the very abrupt challenge of rock climbing and high rappel.

Floating the Yampa and Green Rivers of northwestern Colorado provided the culminating experience of the Seminar. Over the eons the rivers have carved from the land a geologic textbook of staggering proportions. Indian storage caves and petroglyphs gave a feeling of the timelessness of this ancient land. More recent history included stories of Spanish missionaries and explorers, and the outlaws Butch Cassidy and the Sundance Kid, who travelled through this remote and inaccessible region. Paleontology came to life in the Dinosaur Quarry, where the fossilized skeletons of long-extinct animals are being painstakingly excavated.

The experience of negotiating awesome rapids in the 7-man rubber rafts gave the greatest challenge. It was an exercise in group decision-making and discipline. A mistake in the planning or the execution of a route through the rapids meant an overturned raft and an unexpected swim in the cold rough water.

Statistics provide some insights into the success of the Seminar. It had a dropout rate of 2.2 percent, compared with 11.5 percent for the remainder of the Senior class at East. The program, while not designed specifically for potential dropouts, had 25 low achieving, poorly motivated "target" students. By the end of the Seminar, 17 of these 25 had applied and been accepted at colleges.

But what of the human effects—the statistically immeasurable results of this intensive five months of living and learning together? One student summed up: "The mountains, ocean, beach, solo, live-in, river, dancing, acting, plastic furniture, environmental disasters, city—these are only classifications and the minutest part of the experience. Each module gave new thoughts and ideas, each opened a new world to explore." Another wrote: "I've gotten closer than ever before to people in a learning situation. I've discovered new depths in feeling and understanding people. And I've learned a lot about life and myself. It's going to be that way—learning and growing—for the rest of my life."

And finally: "The Seminar has meant more to me than anything I've ever done in my life. I'm really sorry it's all over. But I'm also happy, because I've reached a point in my life where I understand a lot more things and now I feel I know where I'm going—and have the strength and determination to get there."

ONE SCHOOL'S APPROACH: CHERRY CREEK'S OFF-CAMPUS PROGRAMS

All too often books such as this one which propose a new approach to education urge that schools be changed or that teachers try new activities, without giving any assurance that the new approaches work in actual practice. So, the average reader quite justifiably asks with skepticism, "How do I know that this isn't just the romantic daydreaming of some fuzzy-thinking critic of education?" Having shared that frustration as readers of a number of best-selling books on education, sometimes written by journalists who have never taught a day in their lives yet who are disappointed that American education doesn't make students ecstatic, we have tried to limit our recommendations in this book to only those approaches which we—and other teachers—have successfully utilized. In keeping with this philosophy, we feel that we can best convey the possibilities for activities outside the classroom by describing the way one school district has made off-campus projects an integral part of its educational program.

The program we are going to describe is unique in that—to the best of our knowledge—it represents the first time a school district has *required* off-campus experiences for high school graduation (except, of course, in those schools-without-walls such as the Parkway Program, in which the total school program is based on interaction with the community). Other districts with programs that take students into the community have seen these experiences merely as frosting on the cake (as implied by the name itself of the Cultural Enrichment Program at Horton Watkins High School, which we mentioned earlier). Or, they have made the experiences into elective courses, such as East High School's Senior Seminar, which at least carries course credit. But the Board of Education of the Cherry Creek School District, serving an upper-middle-class suburb of Denver, considered out-of-school experiences so important that they passed Board of Education Policy #5127, which requires an "off-campus activity experience, i.e., work, exchange, outward bound, camp participation or a service activity experience ..." The policy, based on a rationale developed by Pino and Armistead (1969), will first affect the graduating classes of 1975. In the meantime, other students are free to participate in the programs voluntarily and for credit.

According to Albert R. Thompson, Director of Off-Campus Programs, Cherry Creek High School offers experiences of four basic types, which students can utilize to meet the new graduation requirement: teaching, service, exchange, or paid work or unpaid career exploration. We will describe each of these areas in detail.

Teaching

At the present time there are two ways a high school student at Cherry Creek can gain some direct experience with the role of teacher: the Mutually Aided Learning Project (MAL) and the Students Assisting Teachers Program (SAT). In the former, the high school student has eight subject areas—math, computers, science, fine arts, social studies, industrial arts, English and French—in which he or she can work with elementary school children. In charge of each subject area is one high school teacher. During the first few weeks of the MAL program, these teachers instruct the students in the use of the instructional material and techniques that they will use. After several training sessions, the high school students begin to work at the elementary school.

Under the supervision of one or two elementary teachers, high school students work with small groups of children, one hour a day, three days a week. Mondays and Fridays are generally reserved for lesson planning, conferences with elementary or high school teachers and further training. MAL is a regularly scheduled course that meets at specific and constant times each day. The "Learning Assistants," as the high school students are called, receive one hour per week of in-service training in their specific subject matter area from high school teachers and are observed on-the-job by a high school teacher at least once a week. To qualify, students must be either juniors or seniors, must have the approval of their parents and school counselor, and must submit an application to and be interviewed by one of the high school teachers involved or the project director. They receive one-half unit of credit per semester, which counts toward graduation.

The SAT program has the same requirements as those for the MAL program, except that freshmen and sophomores are also accepted. Unlike the MAL Learning Assistants, SAT participants are not responsible for the instruction of any specific group of children but instead act as teachers' aides. They help the teacher with a mutually agreed upon combination of instructional, clerical and custodial tasks, spending at least four hours per week in the elementary or junior high school they have been assigned to. SAT is an independently scheduled course that is put into the student's unscheduled or "free" time. The participants receive one hour of pre-service orientation from the program coordinator and receive no in-service training in a specific subject matter area. Once per semester they are observed on-the-job by the program coordinator. Like the MAL Learning Assistants, they receive one-half unit of credit for each semester's participation. High school students are strongly encouraged to take SAT before taking MAL, but that is not required.

Service

The second type of program through which students can meet Cherry Creek's requirement of an off-campus experience is nonpaid service activity. The Educational Participation in Communities (EPIC) Program seeks to involve students, faculty and parents in activities that encourage them to be actively concerned about other people. Students are trained to work in cooperation with existing agencies in the Denver metropolitan area, such as Head Start, Interfaith Task Force, Denver elementary schools, Ridge Home, Tri-County Health Department, Denver Museum of Natural History and others. Students are assigned to teams composed of fifteen to twenty students, one faculty member and interested parents. Each student must work at his assignment regularly, attend feedback sessions and operate upon the format established by the team of which he is a part. Unstructured or after-school time is used for the on-the-job experiences, involving at least four hours per week including feedback sessions. Students in grades nine to twelve can participate, if their application is approved by the program coordinator after being signed by the students' parents. For satisfactory completion of the course, one-half unit of credit is awarded.

Exchanges

Students in grades ten to twelve at Cherry Creek, who have the permission of their parents and approval of their teachers, can participate in one of a wide number of exchange programs—visits by Cherry Creek students to other high schools in Colorado or across the nation, with a return visit to Cherry Creek by students from the other school. Most exchanges last for one full week, but some may take only one day and others may run for as long as three weeks. The main purpose of the exchange program is to develop better human relations between Cherry Creek students and high school students from other communities that are significantly different in one or more respects from the socially homogeneous suburb that Cherry Creek High School serves.

Through advance discussions, rap sessions during exchanges and reports to the exchange class upon their return, participants expand their ability to relate to new people and situations, some of which are profoundly different from what the students have known before. A variety of schools are included to help Cherry Creek students appreciate and enjoy the personal touch of the small rural school, to expose them to the excitement and challenge of a school with a high percentage of students from minority groups, or to give them an opportunity to experience the educational style of independent, nonpublic schools. Exchanges have been arranged with, or are pending with, the following schools among others: Carthage (Missouri) High School, Craig (Alaska) High School, St. Louis High School in Hawaii, East High School in Denver, Evanston Township (Illinois) High School, John Marshall High School in Oklahoma City, Aspen (Colorado) High School and Ringstead (Iowa) High School.

Participants must pay their own travel expenses and school lunch costs when visiting another school, but are provided free room and board in the home of a student from the school they are visiting. In order to meet his or her off-campus activity experience requirement, a student must visit another school for a minimum of five days and host a student who is visiting Cherry Creek for an additional five days or more.

Work and Career Exploration

A fourth approach to meeting the requirement for off-campus experience allows the student to work part-time at a job related to his career interests. Some jobs are paid; others constitute volunteer work. The current offerings in this area at Cherry Creek are almost limitless: Co-operative Office Education, Distributive Education, Related Careers in Human Resources, Child Management Specialist, Cosmetology, Nurse's Assistant and Hospital Orderly, Health Careers, Cooperative Career Development Program, Medical Careers, Engineering Chemistry and Physics Careers. In addition, students may also meet the requirement by taking one of the following courses and arranging to work part-time at a job related to the course content: Commercial Art, Workshop in Precious Metals, Woodworking II, Cabinet Making, Advanced Metals II, Electronics III, Vocational Auto Mechanics, Engineering Drawing, Mechanical Drawing, Vocational Agriculture II and III, Ornamental Vocational Horticulture II, Major Appliance Repair II, Data Processing IV and Graphic Arts II.

Other Programs

Cherry Creek High School also offers a number of special programs which give students direct experience in the world outside the classroom:

MEXICAN CULTURE EXCHANGE TOUR.   Students spend two weeks during spring vacation touring historical, cultural and educational points of interest in Mexico under the guidance of teacher-chaperons. Preparation beforehand is required, and includes extensive readings in the Spanish language and five hours of lectures and group meetings.

INTRODUCTION TO COMMUNITY SERVICE AND SOCIAL STUDIES FIELD TECHNIQUES. This three-week summer course offers students a chance to become totally involved—on a twenty-four-hour-per-day, 7-day-a-week basis—in the multicultural life style of a rural community (near Cortez, Colorado) composed of Ute Indians, Spanish-speaking and An-glo-Americans. Students learn about the region through studying its ecology, geology, biology, history and culture, and through involvement in community service activities such as tutoring Head-Start children, excavating ancient Indian dwellings or serving as a cataloger in the Four Corners Museum.

HUMAN AND NONHUMAN ECOLOGY. This program involves partici-pants in an interdisciplinary study of the natural and human environ-ment, utilizing the Denver metropolitan area for a three-day study of urban ecology and then moving to the isolated setting of Pingree Park in the Roosevelt National Forest for an additional seven days. Sioux In-dian students from Pine Ridge, South Dakota, also participate, and help the other participants learn about Indian culture through studying their crafts, cooking, beliefs and total life study. The program is staffed by a team of Cherry Creek High School counselors and teachers from the science, social studies, art, English and mathematics departments.

FIND OUT. This program provides an opportunity for students to ex-plore a subject they are interested in while using educational methods other than the traditional classroom approach. In most cases, students involve themselves in experiences outside the school. One week is de-voted to this alternative program, and every student at Cherry Creek is eligible to participate, but participation is not mandatory. School is in session for those who don't wish to take part.

The major responsibility for planning a given activity is left to the student. He first arranges to meet with groups of other students and faculty with similar interests to see if projects can be combined into group experiences. But a student may elect to work individually. He then fills out an "intent form" explaining the educational value of the proposed activity and giving a brief description of it. A screening com-mittee considers the intent forms and either approves or disapproves them. Those groups or individuals with approved intent forms must then submit a formal proposal, which goes through a second screening committee. Those groups whose proposals are approved can then begin to make plans for their activity. Limitations on Find Out activities include the following: Students must spend the equivalent of one week of school engaged in the activity, they must have parental permission, they must have faculty sponsorship and they must undertake all of the expenses themselves. The proposed activity must be within the law and cannot expose the participants or the district to legal action. It must also be an educational experience that is beneficial to the student and can be shared with others and thus benefit them.

A total of 1,074 students participated in Find Out the first year it was offered. Their activities can be categorized as follows: Career Exploration (such as working with schools or hospitals, or visiting businesses), Independent or Small Group Activity (including learning to fly a plane, doing library or laboratory research, producing a film or play), Trips (including visits to colleges and universities, other schools in Colorado, the state penitentiary and reform school, Chicago (via train), Mexico and Hawaii), Outdoor Experiences (including winter survival techniques) and Large Group Experiences (including a crash course in jewelry making and a study of the court and criminal systems). Students' projects carried titles such as the following: "Weaving Lessons," "What Does It Take to Get an Airplane into the Air?" "Observing Procedures in a Veterinary Clinic," "Working with Denver Police Department," "Creating Toys and Games for Porter Hospital," "Working and Researching Project in Pre-Columbian Section in Denver Art Museum" and "Studying in Isolation and Solitude."

References   8

BREMER, JOHN. *The parkway program.* School District of Philadelphia, 1970.

DALE, EDGAR. *Audiovisual methods in teaching.* New York: Dryden, 1969.

GARTNER, ALAN, KOHLER, MARY, and RIESSMAN, FRANK. *Children teach children.* New York: Harper, 1971.

KIRSCHENBAUM, HOWARD. Sensitivity modules. *Media & Methods,* February, 1970, 36-38.

PINO, EDWARD, and ARMISTEAD, WALTER. Toward a more relevant and human secondary curriculum. *North Central Association Quarterly,* Winter, 1969, 43 (3), 269-276.

SIMON, SIDNEY. Sensitizing modules: A cure for "senioritis." *Scholastic Teacher,* September 21, 1970, 29, 42.

THOREAU, HENRY DAVID. *Walden—Essay on civil disobedience.* New York: Airmont Publishing Co., 1965.

Additional Resources   8

AMERICAN GEOLOGICAL INSTITUTE. *Environmental studies packets 1 and 2.* Sets of assignment cards, such as those reproduced on pages 240-241, which frequently take students into the environment outside the classroom. Appropriate for all grade levels and subject matters. $10.00 per set. Earth Sciences Educational Program, Box 1559, Boulder, Colo. 80302.

COX, DONALD WILLIAM. *The city as a school house.* A vivid description of Philadelphia's Parkway Program. $6.95. Judson Press, Valley Forge, Pa. 19481.

DALE, EDGAR. *Audiovisual methods in teaching.* A basic text, now almost a classic, that includes a superb rationale for use of direct experiences, including field trips. $13.00. Holt, Rinehart and Winston, 383 Madison Ave. New York, N.Y. 10017.

GARTNER, ALAN, KOHLER, MARY, AND RIESSMAN, FRANK. *Children teach children.* A summary of programs in cross-age teaching. $5.95. Harper and Row, 49 E. 33rd St., New York, N.Y. 10016.

LIPPITT, PEGGY, LIPPITT, RONALD, AND EISEMAN, JEFFREY. *The Cross-Age Helping Program.* Manual, filmstrip and two records. $60.00. Institute for Social Research, 426 Thompson St., Ann Arbor, Mich. 48106.

9

DESCRIBING CLASSROOM INTERACTION

A teacher's interaction with students extends far beyond classroom discussion, role playing and other structured forms of interaction. While we have provided many specific activities with rather detailed directions for their implementation, it is obvious that a majority of the time the teacher must draw on his own resources for interaction and teaching guidelines. For this reason, we do not urge an overnight change in total teaching style. Instead, we feel that a teacher can profit more from examining his teaching and by gradually introducing changes designed to lead to the desired teaching style. But, like golf, bowling and many other activities, teaching tends to defy self-analysis unless one is aided by observers who can "see" what one is doing and provide this information in a usable form. The instruments in this chapter were chosen to provide a means by which teachers can get the descriptive feedback necessary for constructive modification of their teaching.

Until recently it has not been possible to measure precisely what goes on between student and teacher and among members of classroom groups. Descriptions of classroom interaction have been couched in vague terms such as "open," "lively," "permissive," "authoritarian," "warm," or "restrained," without quantifiable data or an objective frame of reference to substantiate the observers' conclusions. Teachers have often claimed, "Today's discussion was terrific; the kids really got involved," without any way of verifying—beyond their personal impression—what actually occurred. Researchers have also found it difficult to pinpoint specific teacher behaviors that evoke certain pupil behaviors and contribute most to pupil growth, or to identify precisely the elements of classroom interaction involved.

CLASSROOM INTERACTION SCALES

Starting in the middle 1940s, however, with the work of Withall (1949) and his colleagues Anderson (1946) and Bales (1950), it became possible to classify different aspects of classroom interaction more precisely. A number of scales have been developed to measure specific aspects of interaction as it occurs within a particular classroom. Depending on the scale chosen, an observer—be he the teacher, a counselor, the principal or an outside resource person—can record particular kinds of behavior on the part of the teacher or students and how often certain kinds of behavior occur.

Development of these systems for describing interaction makes it possible to measure classroom interaction in addition to judging or evaluating it. Personal bias and frame of reference are reduced because a well-trained observer using these instruments obtains virtually the same data as any other well-trained observer using the same instrument. The description which the observer produces is, therefore, a fairly exact record of what occurred in the classroom. Evaluation and judgments of the events can be made later, based on whatever value system one wishes to apply.

Applications of Interaction Scales

Interaction scales have been used primarily to obtain data for research purposes. Specific variables, such as teacher criticism, can thereby be quantified and manipulated statistically. Using the Flanders System of Interaction Analysis, for example, Perkins (1965) found that teacher lecturing and criticizing were related to loss in reading comprehension.

Similarly, Soar (1967) found that when the teacher behaved in ways that made possible maximum freedom of expression on the part of students, students made the greatest gains in vocabulary. Thus, interaction scales can give a researcher specific information regarding the relationship between teacher behavior and pupil achievement.

The scales can also be used in pre-service and in-service teacher training programs to give teachers feedback on their actual classroom behavior and the response it evokes from the students. A professor or supervisor can use the scale to provide the trainee with concrete evidence of his ways of interacting with the class. He can then assess whether this is the most effective way to teach and can begin to modify his behavior accordingly. Some training programs go beyond merely using the scale as a feedback device. They also train teachers to use the various strategies that the scale measures. Teachers first learn the system and then role-play specific behaviors they wish to use, practice on and become proficient in. Flanders' research (1962) reveals that teachers who participated in his in-service training program made changes in spontaneous verbal responses which were statistically significant and consistent with the objectives of the training.

In addition to formal training programs, the scales can be used to give individual teachers feedback that is useful in determining if what they are actually doing in the classroom is what they want to do or think they are doing. An observer, such as a principal, counselor or subject-matter consultant, can measure the classroom interaction and provide the teacher with the data. Or, by tape-recording or videotaping a segment of classroom interaction and analyzing it afterwards, the teacher trained in the use of a scale can analyze his own behavior and that of the students to find areas of interaction that may need correcting. Likewise, the data can sometimes be fed back to the class itself for analysis and interpretation.

Choosing an Interaction Analysis Instrument

In choosing an interaction analysis instrument the teacher should keep in mind that: 1. all instruments focus on only a limited amount of classroom activity; 2. the behavior an instrument addresses was chosen because of the bias with which the instrument was constructed and is not necessarily more or less important than the behavior not covered by the instrument; and 3. instruments provide only a measure of what occurred—*judgments* regarding what occurred must be made after the measurement. Basically these instruments provide feedback that allows a teacher to determine if he is doing what he thinks he is doing or wants to do. Although most of the scales require a trained observer, this training is not extensive for personal use, and a teacher who understands the scale in question can analyze his own data.

From the dozens of scales available (Simon and Boyer, 1967) we have selected only five for inclusion here. These particular five scales were selected because, either alone or in combination, they provide data regarding most of the questions teachers have related to interactive approaches to education. Although they all are directed at interaction, each has particular strengths and weaknesses.

The Flanders System of Interactional Analysis provides the clearest picture of how student-centered a teacher's verbal behavior is and indicates whether students' freedom is being restricted or expanded. It is, perhaps, the easiest instrument to use, and we highly recommend it for the teacher looking at his behavior for the first time.

The Roark Dimensions of Psychological Distance are also easy to use, but they were chosen primarily because they deal directly with the question of meaning. A teacher who is attempting to determine whether a class is involved with issues of immediate concern to them would probably find this scale the most helpful.

The Hill Interaction Matrix provides the best global picture of classroom interaction but has the disadvantage of being the most difficult to use. If one is at the stage where it is important to know how a class is operating as a *group*, however, the HIM is the best choice and well worth the effort.

The Teaching Strategies Observation Differential was selected because it combines cognitive subject matter and classroom management concerns with the purer interactive aspects of teaching. It is the most comprehensive instrument described here, and also the only instrument which directly assesses flexibility in teaching style.

Since interactive education is based as much on the relationship of the people involved as it is on what they do, the Barrett-Lennard Relationship Inventory has been included. While observation seems to be the only way to determine what happened, it seems that the only way to ascertain what the events mean to the people involved is to ask them. For this reason we selected the Barrett-Lennard, a questionnaire, as the most desirable relationship measure.

We feel confident that the instruments described here will serve most self-improvement and training needs in interactive approaches to teaching. In the final analysis, however, one must decide what aspects of interaction are of most interest to him and then choose the appropriate instrument for the purpose.

References 9

ANDERSON, H.H., BREWER, J.E., and REED, M.F. Studies of teachers' classroom personalties, III: Follow up studies of the effects of dominative and integrative contacts on children's behavior. *Applied Psychology Monographs,* 1946, No. 11.

BALES, R.F. *Interaction process analysis.* Cambridge, Mass.: Addison-Wesley, 1950.

FLANDERS, N.A. Using interaction analysis in the inservice training of teaching. *Journal of Experimental Education,* June, 1962, **30,** No. 4, 313-315.

PERKINS, H.V. Classroom behavior and underachievement. *American Educational Research Journal,* 1965, **2,** 1-12.

SIMON, A.A. and BOYER, G.E. (Eds.) *Mirrors for behavior: An anthology of classroom observation instruments.* Philadelphia: Research for Better Schools, 1967.

SOAR, R.S. Pupil needs and teacher-pupil relationships: Experiences needed for comprehension in reading. In E.J. Smiden and J.B. Hough (Eds.), *Interaction analysis: Theory, research and application.* Reading, Mass.: Addison-Wesley, 1967.

WITHALL, J. Development of a technique for the measurement of socioemotional climate in classrooms. *Journal of Experimental Education,* 1949, **17,** 347-361.

THE FLANDERS SYSTEM OF INTERACTION ANALYSIS

ANNE RAMSEY, *Jefferson County (Colorado) Public Schools*

Developed by Ned A. Flanders, the Flanders System of Interaction Analysis (FSIA) is an observation instrument designed to examine teacher-student interaction in the classroom. It is the best-known and most widely used of the observation verbal instruments, and may be used at all grade levels and with all subject-matter areas. It provides teachers with objective feedback on their performance by observers coding the teacher's and students' behavior live, on-the-spot, as interaction occurs, using a preestablished category system.

The purpose of this system is to analyze the verbal influence within two categories—direct and indirect—according to the degree to which the teacher restricts or expands the students' freedom to perform. The ten classifications of verbal behavior isolated by Flanders can be charted as follows:

TEACHER BEHAVIORS

Indirect

1. Teacher accepts student's feelings
2. Teacher praises or encourages student
3. Teacher accepts or uses ideas of students
4. Teacher asks students questions

Direct

5. Teacher lectures
6. Teacher gives directions

Anne Ramsey is a counselor in the Jefferson County (Colorado) Public Schools.

7. Teacher criticizes or justifies his authority

STUDENT BEHAVIORS

8. Student responds to teacher's question
9. Student initiates a response

MISCELLANEOUS

10. Silence or confusion

The system tells what the teacher and students do in terms of both frequency and sequence. It can tell the teacher what preceded and followed every verbal behavior, as well as how much time he spent lecturing, criticizing, accepting feelings, praising, using students' ideas, giving directions and asking questions.

In order to use the system in the classroom, one trained observer is required to write down a number corresponding to one of the ten categories every three seconds, or more often if a change in speaker or behavior occurs. Only verbal behavior is coded in this system. The categories are mutually exclusive; that is, a single verbal behavior is classified in only one category. The intent of the act is ignored; only the actual act itself is recorded.

Observations are usually taken for at least a twenty-minute period of interaction. Observers make marginal notes of the kinds of things occurring in the classroom as they happen, and they draw a double line when changes occur in the class or in the subject under consideration. Numbers are recorded in vertical columns on a sheet of paper, beginning and ending each recording session with the category 10.

To bring the coded numbers into a meaningful form, a *matrix* is computed from the numbers after the observation (see Fig. 1). A matrix is made up of ten rows and ten columns corresponding to the ten major interaction analysis categories. The matrix is computed by recording pairs of numbers in the matrix, permitting analysis of the sequences of the class activity. Each number is treated as an initial member of a pair and a terminal member, the first number always functioning as the row number, the second as the column number. Each coding begins and ends with the number 10, in order to be able to record the first and last numbers of the interaction. A matrix should contain at least 400 tallies representing observation of a homogeneous activity period for at least twenty minutes (Flanders, 1963, p. 255).

The teacher's *I/D ratio*, the ratio of indirect or encouraging behavior to direct or restricting behavior, is computed by dividing the total of

FIGURE 1. MATRIX ANALYSIS (adapted from Ned A. Flanders, "Intent, Action and Feedback: A Preparation for Teaching," *Journal of Teacher Education*, Vol. 14, 1963, pp. 251-260). Used with permission of the *Journal of Teacher Education*.

Classification		Category	1	2	3	4	5	6	7	8	9	10	Total
Teacher Talk	Indirect Influence	1. Accepts Feelings											
		2. Praise											
		3. Accepts or Uses Student Ideas											
		4. Asks Questions											
	Direct Influence	5. Lectures											
		6. Gives Directions											
		7. Criticism											
Student Talk		8. Student Response											
		9. Student Initiation											
		10. Silence											
		Total											

Area E Extended Indirect Influence

Area G

Area F Extended Direct Influence

Content Cross

Area I

Area H

Area J

Area A Indirect Teacher Talk

Area B Direct Teacher Talk

Area C Student Talk

Area D

categories 1, 2, 3 and 4 by the total of categories 5, 6 and 7 (that is, dividing Area A by Area B). The teacher's *revised I/D ratio,* which is nearly content free and is a good indication of classroom climate, may be computed by dividing the total categories 1, 2 and 3 by the total of categories 6 and 7. The *percentage of teacher talk* is computed by dividing the totals of categories 1 through 7 (Areas A and B) by the totals of 1 through 10 (Areas A, B, C and D). The *percentage of student talk* is found by dividing the totals of categories 8 and 9 (Area C) by totals of categories 1 through 10 (Areas A, B, C and D) (Olson, 1970, p. 39).

Area E is the matrix area containing categories 1, 2 and 3. A tally in this area represents evidence that the teacher accepted student feelings, used praise or used student ideas for a period of longer than three seconds (represented by a 1-1, 2-2 or 3-3 tally), and is therefore called the *area of extended indirect (encouraging) influence* (Flanders, 1963, p. 255). Categories 2 and 3 have been found through usage to be a sort of catalyst of good social-emotional relationships in the classroom and to be associated with significantly higher student attitude scores (Flanders, 1959, p. 36).

Area F, the *area of extended direct (restricting) influence,* is a combination of category 6 (giving directions) and category 7 (giving criticism or self-justification). This area may reflect teacher problems with discipline, and criticism may indicate that students are not satisfactorily complying. Teacher domination of student activities is seen by a heavy loading in the 6-6 and 7-7 cells. High loading in the 6-6 cells alone merely indicates that the teacher is giving lengthy directions to the class (Flanders, 1963, p. 255).

Tallies when the student stops talking and the teacher begins are located in Area G (rows 8 and 9 and columns 1, 2 and 3), and in Area H (rows 8 and 9 and columns 6 and 7). Area G reflects teacher indirect influence and Area H reflects teacher direct influence in response to student talk. If the proportion of G to H versus A to B are quite different, the inference is that the teacher acts differently when the student stops talking than he ordinarily does, which may be an indication of the teacher's flexibility (Flanders, 1963, p. 255).

Area I, representing rows 4 and 5 and columns 8 and 9, tell what type of teacher statement brought about student participation. Classroom drill led by the teacher is seen by a high loading in the 4-8 and 8-4 cells. A contrast between the tallies in columns 8 and 9 is an indication of the frequency with which students respond to the teacher versus initiating their own ideas (Flanders, 1963, p. 257). Area J, containing categories 8 and 9, represents lengthy student statements or combinations of student-to-student interaction. A high frequency of tallies in Area C but not in Area J indicates short student responses. Frequencies in Area J are usually positively correlated with frequencies in Area E (Flanders, 1963, p. 257).

The area called the *content cross* involves all cells with a category 4 or 5 and reflects what happens before and after content-related behaviors of the teacher. This area is a reflection of teaching style. Heavy loading of the 4-5 cell indicates that the teacher answers all his own questions. Loading of the 4-9 cell indicates unexpected responses to teacher questions. Loading of the 3-5 cell represents the possible use of student ideas as a stepping stone for lectures by the teacher. Loading of the 3-4 cell represents use of student ideas as a basis for questioning (Olson, 1970, p. 42).

The extreme lowest row and extreme right column are called the *silence l.* The behaviors which follow silence or confusion are found across the bottom, and the behaviors preceding silence or confusion are found along the right side (Olson, 1970, p. 43).

Interaction Analysis has been widely used in both teacher training and inservice training. Flanders, using it in an inservice training program with teachers, found it useful in developing flexibility within the teachers' styles by allowing them to vary their direct and indirect influence and to adjust their behavior according to their plans or the situation (Flanders, 1962). The teachers involved in the inservice program with Flanders developed new concepts as tools for thinking about their behavior that helped them to describe both actions and to become proficient in assessing their own spontaneous behaviors. Teachers became more independent and self-directed by choosing their own behaviors to fit their own plans (Flanders, 1963, p. 254).

This system can be used to compare class periods, to compare teaching episodes, to focus on differing objectives or to compare teaching styles. Specific instructions for the use of the Flanders System of Interaction Analysis can be found in N.A. Flanders, *Interaction Analysis in the Classroom—A Manual for Observers* (University of Michigan, 1965); E. Amidon and N.A. Flanders, *The Role of the Teacher in the Classroom* (Amidon and Associates, 1963); or Miles C. Olson, *Learning Interaction Analysis: A Programmed Approach* (Educational Consulting Associates, 1970).

References   Ramsey

AMIDON, E., and FLANDERS, NED A. *The role of the teacher in the classroom.* Amidon and Associates, 1963.

FLANDERS, NED A. Intent, action and feedback: A preparation for teaching. *Journal of Teacher Education,* 1963, **14**, 251-260.

FLANDERS, NED A. *Interaction analysis in the classroom—A manual for observers.* University of Michigan, 1965.

FLANDERS, NED A. Teacher-pupil contacts and mental hygiene. *Journal of Social Issues,* 1959, **15**, 30-39.

OLSON, MILES C. *Learning interaction analysis: A programmed approach.* Englewood, Colo.: Educational Consulting Associates, 1970.

DIMENSIONS OF
PSYCHOLOGICAL DISTANCE

ALBERT E. ROARK, *University of Colorado*

The scales and dimensions described here were developed to study and teach interaction skills in intensive groups. Thus, they are particularly useful for describing interaction in personally involving group discussions. They are verbal dimensions ostensibly, but the user can include any type of interaction desired. The basis for the development of the scales was the concept of *psychological distance.*

All preliminary work in the original development of the scales and isolation of the dimensions indicated that psychological distance in

Albert E. Roark is at the School of Education, University of Colorado, Boulder, Colorado.

human interaction is determined by the interaction of several variables and could not be attributed to any one factor. Pursuing this thought further in informal research and in observation of group interaction of many types led to the isolation of four dimensions of interaction which seemed to influence psychological distance most. Psychological distance is used here as a global concept indicating the degree to which the interaction is relevant to and influenced by the *self* of the participants.

There have been several previous useful attempts at categorizing group interaction in terms relevant to understanding classroom groups (Bales, 1950, 1970; Amidon and Flanders, 1963; Hill, 1965; and Goldman, 1962). However, none of these approaches has been primarily focused on the concept of psychological distance. Also, there have been many scales developed to determine the *quality* of the interaction which takes place (see Truax, 1970, and Carkhuff, 1969, for references). In addition, many scales have been constructed in accordance with particular psychological theories or approaches. None of these scales or conceptualizations is particularly useful if the task is to distinguish personally meaningful classroom discussions from subject-matter-oriented discussions or encounter groups or guidance groups. Also, it is difficult to determine from most of these approaches whether the amount of interaction the group is reputed to have actually occurs. Most important, they do not provide the practitioner with particularly useful ways to improve his functioning on a psychological distance dimension.

The four dimensions are: *Meaning, Spatial* (Locus of Interaction), *Time* (Temporal) and *Response Type* (see Fig. 2). The first three are considered to be structural dimensions which in a sense provide an outline of the interaction without considering its substance. The Response Type dimension fills in this outline; it does not explain it (theoretical dimension) or tell how good it is (qualitative dimension). It is not necessary, however, to be able to explain group interaction or tell how good it is in order to describe it. These dimensions are considered to be equally applicable to groups of any type or theoretical orientation. Although their use is being discussed in terms of teaching, they are applicable to any type of human interaction. The scales are tentative and are included only to further describe the dimensions and to provide guidelines for use of the dimensions in teaching.

Ratings of interaction may be made in many different ways. The rater may observe the interaction for specified lengths of time and then make the ratings based on his judgment of the interaction for the total time observed. Or, ratings can be made by rating the interaction at

Figure 2. Dimensions of Psychological Distance

				Personal	
	1	**2**	**3**	**4**	**5**
MEANING	theoretical — Psychological, mathematical, sociological theory, etc.	abstract — Love in general, geometry, inferences from observations	objective — Specific descriptions of events, objects or relationships	cognitive — *Personal* beliefs, ideas or interpretations	experiencing — (*current*) feelings, emotions or attitudes
	1	**2**	**3**	**4**	**5**
TEMPORAL	historical futuristic indefinite — Beyond the person's life span. No specific time implied	personal history-future — Within the person's past or projected future	related to present — Having a direct bearing on current events	situational present — Directly a part of the person's present	experiential present — Reporting what is being experienced at the moment
	1	**2**	**3**	**4**	**5**
LOCUS OF INTERACTION	objects — Books, school subjects, trees, automobiles, etc.	events — Occurrences which have not been objectified, games, weddings, etc.	people — People in general, events in which people are central	significant others — People significant in the discussant's life, e.g. parents, teachers	person→person(s) present — Person or persons directly involved in the group interaction
	1	**2**	**3**	**4**	**5**
RESPONSE TYPE	advice direction information Structuring remarks	labeling — In reference to people or events, especially of people present. "You are..." statements.	reaction[2]	reflection clarification — Response meant to convey or promote understanding	personal response[2]

[1] Extensive descriptions of the categories are not included, although they would be necessary for research purposes and for teaching purposes. The writer's experience has been that after a brief discussion of the categories, most teachers and counseling students have very little difficulty with these scales.

[2] A reaction is meant to include defensive, attacking, etc. statements. Response statements are meant to include the typical "I feel . . ." statements regardless of phrasing, so long as they are directly and openly expressed.

predetermined intervals and then averaging the ratings to arrive at an overall rating for the total period observed. The unit of interaction rated can thus vary from a period of several minutes to a single complete thought unit. The following are examples of ratings of single exchanges.

Classroom setting:

STUDENT: "I don't understand how Sullivan's concepts differ from Snygg and Combs' at this point."

PROFESSOR: "It's mostly a matter of how much stress is placed on the importance of interpersonal behavior."

RATINGS: *Meaning* = 1, theoretical
Temporal = 1, indefinite   Average rating = 1
Locus of Interaction = 1, objects
Response Type = 1, information

The next illustration demonstrates how a different response from the professor would be rated.

PROFESSOR: "Do you see them as pretty much the same at this point?"

RATINGS: *Meaning* = 4, personal
Temporal = 1, indefinite   Average rating = 2.5
Locus of Interaction = 1, objects
Response Type = 4, clarifying

If the student responded, "I'm just confused and disgusted, I study and study and I still can't make any sense out of it. I'm ready to give up," the rating would be 5 on all dimensions. The average rating for the interaction would be 3.75, arrived at by averaging the ratings for the professor's responses and the student's responses on all dimensions.

The next illustration demonstrates how an angry confrontation in the same general setting would be rated.

Classroom Setting:

STUDENT: "Mr. Jones, you just don't understand! And, I don't think you care! You are just like all the other teachers!"

RATINGS: *Meaning* = 4, personal, cognitive
Temporal = 5, experiential present   Average rating = 4
Locus of Interaction = 5, persons present
Response Type = 2, labeling

The following illustration is included to show how a response to feelings followed by an expression of feelings would be rated.

Encounter group setting:

FACILITATOR: "Barbara's remark seems to have upset you."

PARTICIPANT: "I'm scared. I'm afraid that I may be like that too and that really scares me."

RATINGS:	Facilitator	Student	Average for Exchange
Meaning	5	5	
Temporal	5	5	
Locus of Interaction	5	5	
Response Type	4	5	

Approx. 5 (4.9)

These are very obvious interactions, but they do illustrate the relative ease of rating. Also, it can be seen that the scales are appropriate for many different types of analysis including the construction of profiles.

From a training viewpoint, the scales can be used in a prescriptive manner, either singly or in combination, to correct or improve a trainee's functioning. They can also be useful in providing feedback to teachers on how they function in a variety of interpersonal situations. The use of the scales in training situations in conjunction with measures of the quality of the interaction as recommended by Truax (1970) and Carkhuff (1969) has been particularly successful.

A teacher is obviously free to draw his own conclusions from the scales and to determine for himself what uses they may have. The following discussion is meant only as an introductory guide to their use.

The further to the right a classroom discussion falls on any of the first scales, the more personal and intense it is likely to be and the closer it is psychologically. In general, this is also true of the Response Type scale but not to the same extent and in some cases perhaps not at all. The Response Type dimension, to a certain extent, incorporates qualitative characteristics that interact considerably with other features of the interaction in question, so that the same degree of generalization cannot be made. For example, a personal response is generally considered to lead to more intense group interaction, but if the case is one in which a person of authority is used to overpowering people, a hostile reaction by a person who finally got the courage to point this out may in fact lead to more intense interaction. This should not be seen as negating our main point: that the further to the right a response occurs on any of the dimensions, the more intimate, meaningful and intense the interaction will be. In terms of psychological distance, the further to the right the closer the response.

For purposes of general classification, the following rating parameters may be used: Average classroom discussions, average rating of 2 or lower, with the *Meaning* and *Locus of Interaction* scales not being above 3; Guidance groups, 2.25-3.00, with the *Meaning* and *Temporal* scales not going below 2; Counseling groups, 3.25-4.25, with the *Meaning* and *Temporal* scales averaging close to 4; Encounter groups, 4.5-5.0 (if any dimension averages below 4, the definition of encounter group should be questioned). We have advocated elsewhere in this book that the teacher structure class discussions which are closer psychologically than average, particularly that the *Meaning* rating be kept close to an average of 3 if possible. Classroom interaction of the type described in Chapter Five might often qualify for a rating of 5 on each of the dimensions.

By comparing his ratings with that of the group which he is leading (or with the desired type of group), a teacher can determine on what dimension he is contributing and on what dimensions he is deviating in a detracting manner. Thus, a teacher can engage in an analysis of both the group's and his own behavior and make specific adjustments. Group development can also be studied by doing periodic ratings of the group's interaction. The net effect of the continuous use of these dimensions for teacher and group behavior analysis is to reduce the mystique surrounding group work and to substitute understanding of groups in terms of specific observable behavior.

References   Roark

Amidon, E.J., and Flanders, N.A. *The role of the teacher in the classroom: A manual for understanding and improving teachers' classroom behavior.* Minneapolis: Amidon, 1963.

Bales, R.F. *Interaction process analysis.* Reading, Mass.: Addison-Wesley, 1950.

Bales, R.F. *Personality and interpersonal behavior.* New York: Holt, 1970.

Carkhuff, R.R. *Helping and human relations,* Vols. I and II. New York: Holt, 1969.

GOLDMAN, L. Group guidance: Content and process. *Personnel and Guidance Journal,* 1962, **40,** 518-522.

HILL, W.F. *HIM: Hill Interaction Matrix.* University of Southern California: Youth Study Center, 1965.

TRUAX, C.B. An approach to counselor education. *Counselor Education and Supervision,* 1970, **10,** 4-15.

THE TEACHING STRATEGIES
OBSERVATION DIFFERENTIAL

RONALD D. ANDERSON, *University of Colorado*
JOSEPH A. STRUTHERS, *Boulder Valley (Colorado) Public Schools*
HELEN H. JAMES, *Southern Illinois University*

The hundreds of different observation systems which have been used in classrooms in recent years vary greatly in terms of the scope of behaviors and group characteristics observed. The Teaching Strategies Observation Differential (TSOD) is an example of an instrument which is designed to provide a measure of the overall teaching strategy or style used by a teacher, including both verbal and nonverbal interactions between teacher, students and the physical materials which constitute the classroom environment. The need for a broader instrument of this type has been spurred by the development of new curricular programs in which students are expected to work intensively with materials other

As with many research efforts, the development of the instrument described herein extended over a considerable period of time with many persons involved in various ways. The development of the original of three versions of the instrument, and its rationale, was the work of Joseph A. Struthers. Further developmental work resulting in two other versions was conducted by Ronald D. Anderson and several graduate students at the University of Colorado. One of them, Helen H. James, was involved in the development of all three versions. Others who contributed to its development were Daniel Bauman, Edward DeAvila, Thomas Gier, Jerry G. Horn and particularly Arthur L. White.

than traditional books, papers and pencils (e.g., the use of centimeter rods and attribute blocks in mathematics, and elementary school science programs with extensive materials for individual student use but with minimal reading materials).

The many observation systems available also vary greatly in terms of their state of development. The TSOD is an example of one which is in the very earliest stage of development; information about it has never been published until now, and it has been used in a research setting only.

It should be stated at the outset that the need for this instrument, its development and use are all governed by the frame of reference of the developers, their conceptions of what events are significant to the learning process and their beliefs about teachers' roles. Any classroom observer and any systematic observation instrument selects out of a complex system those events deemed significant and hence are theory laden either through stated or unstated assumptions. The educational objectives and approaches to learning generally encouraged through the modern curriculum development projects are basic to the rationale of this observation instrument.

The instrument was developed to give a single rating of a teacher's style, representing his position on a continuum which, described in very general terms, has extremes defined as follows: 1. *expository—direct* teaching and 2. *inductive—indirect* teaching. The former is represented by this diagram:

$$(S) \longleftrightarrow (T) \longleftrightarrow (E)$$

which shows interactions between the teacher (T), the student (S) and the environment (E). E is a broad category including materials such as centimeter rods, paint brushes, globes, or chemicals, and natural phenomena that might be studied in a science class. The arrows represent interactions between the components. In this mode of teaching, the teacher serves in the role of interpreter, explaining and describing the environment to the learners. This approach can include such activities as asking questions and reinforcing correct answers, answering student questions, citing authoritative sources, demonstrating through the manipulation of equipment and narrative explanation.

The inductive-indirect approach is represented by the following diagram:

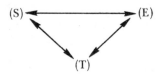

This diagram uses the same symbols as those used to depict interactions under the inductive-indirect mode. In this mode the teacher acts to place the student in direct contact with the environment. The teacher responds to questions in such a way as to cause the student to search for his own answers. The essential ingredient in this mode of teaching is the direct student reception of input from the environment and other students without the teacher's interpretation.

The instrument based on this model of teaching passed through several versions during its initial development. In all versions, a rating of teaching style on a numerical scale was given for each one-minute interval. The determination of whether an inductive-indirect or expository-direct function is being served requires the observation of a sizable amount of behavior and an inference on the part of the observer.

A set of descriptors was formulated to aid the observer in making the overall rating of teaching style during each one-minute interval. These descriptors, or operational definitions, were formalized and used as the basis for making the ratings on a ten-point scale. The descriptors are *examples* of behaviors which illustrate a position on the scale and are given *only* as a guide to marking the intervals of the instrument. Other incidents necessitate an additional interpretation by the observer. Note that movement along the scale from one to ten represents movement from an area of student passivity through an area of overlap of expository-direct and inductive-indirect techniques to an area of student autonomous activity. The descriptors are as follows:

I. Noneducational Activities
   O_1 *Noneducational activities beyond the teacher's control.* This category includes class interruptions, such as announcements on the intercom, which are not under the control of the teacher. This zero rating is not averaged into the overall rating.

O₂ *Teacher controllable noneducational activities.* This category includes managerial tasks (e.g., taking roll), off-subject discourse and other activities which the observer judges to be "noneducational" but are normally expected to be susceptible to teacher influence.

II. Direct Verbal

In this category, the students are either passive or at most responding only in a limited verbal way to teacher stimuli.

1. *Facts:* e.g., direct exposition of content as in lectures by the teachers. Students are involved only as listeners.

2. *Direction or opinion:* e.g., direct instruction on "how to" or direct influence on class activities through stated opinions. The students are involved only as listeners but the teacher's talk is presumed to be a prelude to student activity.

3. *Limiting questions:* questions structured for a definite and specific answer, or for which only *the* "correct" answer is accepted. Student involvement is limited to one-word or phrase response to teacher questions.

III. Direct Nonverbal

In this category, student activity is heavily teacher dominated but includes nonverbal activity as well as verbal.

4. *Demonstration:* direct instruction using equipment, books, chalkboard, etc. either before the whole class or in a manner as would affect most of the class, e.g., showing several individuals or small groups "how a reaction must be obtained." The student's role is that of observer as well as listener, but interaction with the teacher is limited to simple clarification of teacher verbalization.

5. *Student exercises:* students are following the directions of a recipe (presented either orally or in visual form) in working with materials such as laboratory equipment, maps or tools. The student's activities are determined by the teacher in a manner that results in student's thought and actions being directed toward prespecified or "correct" results.

IV. Indirect Verbal

This category is characterized by verbal interactions between teacher and students, and between students and students, which go beyond simple and limited response to teacher stimuli. The students' verbalization influences the pattern of the interaction.

6. *Teacher questions:* questions of an open-ended nature which are probing and necessitate individual student thought and for which variations in response are accepted. Students play a major role in determining the pattern of the verbal interaction.

7. *Teacher response:* teacher is responding to student questions or comments. The response may or may not be demanded by the student verbalization and it may itself be a question, but it is in direct response to student's questions or comments.

8. *Teacher guidance:* teacher guidance of interstudent discussion, planning or presentation to stimulate and keep it thought-provoking and to avoid shallowness and tangential trivia. The interaction is largely between students, and the teacher serves only in the role of moderator or consultant.

V. Indirect nonverbal

This category is characterized by student work that is not limited to verbal activity, but includes work with materials. In addition, the activity is not teacher-dominated but gives the student varying degrees of autonomy.

9. *Teacher-planned investigations:* student investigations in which the problems pursued are determined by the teacher, laboratory manual or guide rather than by the student. Outcomes, however, are not prespecified, i.e., no specific "recipe" is followed and all students do not necessarily follow the same routine.

10. *Student-planned investigations:* student investigations in which the student participates in determining the specific problem he will pursue. The investigation is student-planned and conducted and the teacher's guidance is limited to monitoring, encouragement and reference help.

A segment of an observer's record sheet is reproduced below.

At the end of each one-minute interval, the observer records a rating for that interval by circling the appropriate number on the ten-point scale. This number does *not* necessarily describe the actual behaviors in accord with the numbered items above. For example, the observer might judge that about one half of the minute interval was best described by 4 and the other half best described by 2. In this case, he would circle 3 on the record sheet, since it would be most indicative of the overall approach of the one-minute interval. The "doodle space" is used in various ways by observers to aid themselves in this determination. At the end of the observation session, the mean of the ratings of the

Interval (one minute)	Doodle Space	Rating									
1	0_10_2	1	2	3	4	5	6	7	8	9	10
2	0_10_2	1	2	3	4	5	6	7	8	9	10
3	0_10_2	1	2	3	4	5	6	7	8	9	10
4	0_10_2	1	2	3	4	5	6	7	8	9	10
5	0_10_2	1	2	3	4	5	6	7	8	9	10
6	0_10_2	1	2	3	4	5	6	7	8	9	10
7	0_10_2	1	2	3	4	5	6	7	8	9	10
8	0_10_2	1	2	3	4	5	6	7	8	9	10

one-minute intervals is computed and used as an overall indicator of the teacher's style during that class. It should be emphasized that the end product is a single numerical indicator of the overall style of teaching and *it is not possible to determine from this rating what specific behaviors occurred during the class session,* even though the descriptors given above were used as the basis for making the ratings. In addition, it should be pointed out that this rating is not a measure of the *effectiveness* with which this style was employed.

Rotating the observer's record sheet ninety degrees so that the progression of time is indicated along the base will provide a teaching behavior × time profile throughout the period of observation. It not only depicts the general progression of behavior, which may be pattern specific for individuals or subject matter, but indicates degree of deviation toward either extreme expository-direct or inductive-indirect behaviors. This "profile" record allows the interpreter to determine, for example, the versatile teacher from the giver of class exercises, both of whom might obtain an overall score of "5" when all one-minute interim tallies are averaged. This record of versatility or the lack of it may, in fact, be of greater importance to some consumers of the data than the overall mean score.

It should be noted that the focus of the observation shifts between the teacher and selected students; the categories of the instrument are defined in terms of the behaviors of both teachers and students. If the teacher is employing a teaching strategy in which the entire class is expected to attend to the teacher or that which the teacher determines, the observer is to focus on the teacher and his interactions with students. If the style employed is one in which the students are expected to work independently as individuals or small groups, the observer shifts his observation to six randomly selected students. Each of the six students is observed for one minute in a randomly selected order, with the pattern of observation being repeated as long as observation of this type of activity continues.

The requirement of close observation of both teacher and students necessitates either observation by observers who are actually in the classroom or a videotape recorder operator who is employing the necessary procedures for sampling student behavior. Thus far, the instrument has been used only with "live" observers. (An earlier version of the instrument was used successfully with videotape recordings.)

When employed in the initial stages of a study of elementary school social studies, the instrument yielded a Hoyt interrater reliability of .88 when used by two observers, each observing the same two classes of sixteen different teachers. In a previous study of elementary school science, an earlier but only slightly different version of the instrument yielded a Hoyt interrater reliability which ranged between .89 and .97 for seven different pairs of raters, with an average interrater reliability of .94.

THE HILL INTERACTION MATRIX

DONALD L. JOHNSON, *Student Life Center, University of Colorado*

The Hill Interaction Matrix (HIM) conceptualizes verbal interaction on two dimensions: content (*what* is being discussed) and process (*how* it is being discussed). The originator of this instrument, Wm. Fawcett Hill, suggests that interaction falls into four content categories and five process categories. These intersect each other to form a twenty-cell matrix. Following is a diagram of the matrix with its content and process categories labeled (Fig. 3).

THE *HIM* SYSTEM

The HIM will be presented in some detail. The intent is to give the reader a simplified yet complete enough understanding of the matrix for practical analysis in a classroom or small group setting. After a general description of each of the content and process dimensions, a cell-by-cell description with examples will be presented.

Content Dimensions

The content dimension of the interaction is concerned with the subject matter being discussed. Four categories cover all the possibilities.

TOPIC. Any subject *other* than the group (or dyad—see details on this under the "group-dyad" heading) itself, a member (person) of the dyad or group, or a relationship within the group or dyad would be categorized in the topic column of the matrix. In terms of *what* is being discussed, topic subjects would always be outside the dyad or the group. Discussion about general interest topics, ideas and things are good examples of "topic" subjects. Most classroom settings would have a heavy concentration of "topic" matter being discussed. Social "small talk" and socializing generally fit here, too.

GROUP OR DYAD. A dyad is simply another way of saying a pair (in this case, two persons.) Hill originally designed the matrix to categorize the verbal interaction occurring with a small group. But the categorization fits equally well for the dyad. Statements like, "When shall we meet again?" "Is what we're talking about getting us anyplace?" or, "It seems like we haven't been listening to each other for the last few minutes," would be group or dyadic in nature. The "thing" being talked about is the group or dyad per se.

Donald L. Johnson is a counseling psychologist at the Student Life Center, University of Colorado, Boulder, Colorado.

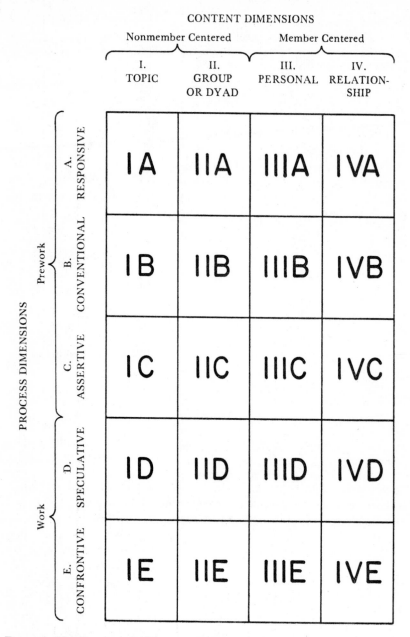

FIGURE 3. HILL INTERACTION MATRIX (adapted from Wm.
Fawcett Hill, 1965, with permission)

PERSONAL. The focus of discussion is upon the group member as an individual. Such things as a member's personality, characteristics, traits, problems, etc., are discussed. In the personal category, the concept of a "topic person" (the one being discussed) is a useful one. Focus can be by the topic person (when he talks about himself) or by another group member (when he talks about the topic person).

RELATIONSHIP. In this context, the description "what is being talked about" in describing the content dimension can be misleading. Very often in this case verbal interaction that is classified as "relationship" does not talk *about* a relationship between two people, or one person and the rest of the group (in a small group setting).

In the relationship column, "what" is being talked about is the feelings and thoughts that two people have about each other. At first glance many "relationship" statements would seem to overlap with those previously defined as personal statements. In the personal category, there is a topic person and the focus of discussion stays on that person. Relationship discussions, on the other hand, are characterized by a reciprocal exchange or a direct discussion of the existing relationship between people.

It is important to note that often a topic will be the *vehicle* by which one talks of group, personal or relationship information. This is especially true of the personal and relationship categories. As an example:

JOHN: I never have been able to talk with my mother.

MARY: Have you always had trouble with her?

JOHN: Even when I was a little kid I felt closer to my father.

While John's mother (in this case, a topic) is part of what is being discussed, this is only a vehicle through which John is giving information about himself. It would therefore be classified in the personal category.

On the other hand, interpersonal exchanges that have an argumentative tone to them can seem to be personal even when they fit into the topic category. One must carefully try to determine what is being argued about in these cases. Only when one argues *about* a person (group member) does the interaction properly fit into the personal category. When members are arguing (fighting) *with* each other, and *not* about some subject matter, then the categorization is relationship. When the argument is about the group, then it fits under group. Otherwise, arguments about topics fit under the topic category.

Note again the matrix presented earlier (Fig. 3). Notice that topic and group columns are labeled "nonmember centered" (member referring to a dyad partner or a small group participant). The thing being discussed is either a topic or the group per se, not the individual involved.

Personal and relationship content columns are "member centered." The thing talked about is either oneself or opinions about one another. Notice also that Roman numerals are used to label the various columns.

Process Dimensions

Process categorization is concerned with the *manner* in which one discusses something. We examine at this point *how* something is being discussed rather than *what* is being discussed. There are five categories (representing rows on the matrix) that will be discussed here: responsive, conventional, assertive, speculative and confrontive.

RESPONSIVE. This category represents the most simple interaction and consists of little more than acknowledgement of a message received (yep, nope, or a grunt). It is most often evidenced in settings such as mental hospitals with very passive patients. For most practical purposes the lower sixteen cells of the matrix encompass all the verbal interactions in a classroom or small group.

CONVENTIONAL. Discussion is carried on in a typically socially appropriate manner. The conversation is at a "safe" noninvolved level. Verbal interaction that would often be thought of as small-talk or chit-chat is typical of this row of the HIM. The conversation is usually polite and friendly. If one were to think in terms of people trying to solve problems, such a context or orientation has *not* been established in conventional level conversation. The level of discussion could probably best be called descriptive, rather than problem solving.

ASSERTIVE. Very often the assertive category is distinguished by a hostile and/or attacking tone. Assertive statements are often argumentative. However, this is not always the case. For instance, defeatism is usually classified as assertive. One of the characteristics distinguishing the assertive category is that the interaction tends to shut off discussion rather than enhance it. Speakers tend to be finalistic in their pronouncements and do not appear to be open to consider another point of view. Exchanges then tend to be one-way rather than two-way.

SPECULATIVE. Speculative interaction is characterized by cooperative two-way open communication. A problem (or desire for understanding) context has been introduced into the interaction. Rather than closing off communication, there is an implicit invitation in the interaction to examine and seek understanding together. The key word here is *discuss.* The tone of the discussion is one of tentativeness.

CONFRONTIVE. The key word to characterize the confrontive category might well be *clarify.* Statements tend to draw upon what has already been said and to clarify, resolve, evaluate, etc., A confrontive statement is characteristically backed up with some form of documentation. The speaker gives support to his opinions. A confrontive statement is also one that opens rather than closes interaction doors. The speaker takes full responsibility for his thoughts and feelings. While negative feelings and ideas may at times be expressed, the overall tone is one of an attempt to be helpful, rather than harmful, and work for resolution of conflict or problems. (*Note:* It is not necessary that the conclusions, clarifications, etc., of a speaker be correct for them to be classified as confrontive. But especially in the categories of group, personal and relationship, the statements are usually documented.)

Referring again to the general outline of the matrix, you will note that the conventional and assertive categories are labeled as "prework" while the speculative and confrontive categories are labeled as "work" categories. This labeling reflects a value judgment by the developer of the system. It is felt that problem-solving activities (and the most meaningful levels of communication) take place at the work level rather than at the prework level.

Cells of the Matrix

This should give you a basic introduction to the various dimensions of the system. The following are examples of the sixteen principal cells of the matrix. Movement will be across the rows of the matrix, starting with conventional.

IB, TOPIC CONVENTIONAL. In this cell, discussion is about things outside of the group. This type of interaction is common. Discussion about the weather, a sports event, community activity, grades, etc., are usually of this sort. Examples:

> "That's the same movie I saw last week."
> "Did you see Jim yesterday?"
> "Alcohol is a dehydrating agent."
> "Would you like a cigarette?"
> "Whose car were you in yesterday?"

IIB, GROUP-DYAD CONVENTIONAL. In this cell, things such as details of meeting times, social and recreation plans, structuring of how to use time, etc., are discussed. Examples:

> "What time shall we meet next week?"
> "What shall we talk about?"
> "Let's get together for coffee later on today."

IIIB, PERSONAL CONVENTIONAL. A group member talks about himself in a conventional manner. The interaction is nonproblem-oriented. The speaker discusses his background, plans, likes, dislikes, etc. Examples:

> "I'm from the midwest originally."
> "I have about as many friends as most people, I guess."
> "I think I'll take a job with the YMCA."
> "I get headaches almost every day."

IVB, RELATIONSHIP CONVENTIONAL. Group members show that they like each other by praising, joking, sparring back and forth, etc. The tone is friendly. Examples:

> "You really said that well."
> "I really like your new hairdo."
> "I certainly enjoyed our talk the other day."

IC, TOPIC ASSERTIVE. In this cell, a member talks about a topic outside of the group in an assertive way. He talks as though his mind is made up and nothing will change it. People don't seem to listen to each other. Examples:

> "Labor unions are so crooked, they're worse than big business."

"All conservatives are a bunch of fools, they don't have any brains at all.

IIC, GROUP-DYAD ASSERTIVE. Members act unhappy with the *way* the group or dyad is operating. Examples:

"We're wasting so much time in this conversation, I'm getting tired of it."
"This is a terrible place to try and talk, it's ridiculous to go on unless we move somewhere else."

IIIC, PERSONAL ASSERTIVE. The topic person makes assertive statements about himself, or is supported by such statements by other group members. He shuts out incoming information about himself. Examples:

"Why should I change, no one cares anyway."
"Nobody is going to push me around, just let them try it."
"That's right, don't let them push you around."
"I might as well give up, there's no hope for me."
(*Note:* Defeatism is defined as a special form of assertion.)

IVC, RELATIONSHIP ASSERTIVE. In this cell, anger is evidenced toward each other, a fighting atmosphere prevails. Examples:

"I've got just as much right to talk as you do, now shut up."
"You can't insult me, I just consider the source."
"You make me sick, why don't you just listen carefully to yourself for a few minutes, maybe you'd die of boredom."

ID, TOPIC SPECULATIVE. This kind of interaction is characterized by exchange of opinion and information much like that heard in a classroom discussion where participants are seeking to gain knowledge or information. Examples:

"What do you suppose causes people to become alcoholics?"
"What was the impact of the President's speech upon you?"
"I didn't think he dealt with the most important issues."

IID, GROUP-DYAD SPECULATIVE. Statements are made in an attempt to understand, improve or make better that which happens in the group.

The major goal is analysis, in a cooperative way so that the group can be more useful. Examples:

> "Have you noticed how we don't get angry with each other as often as we used to?"
>
> "I think we ought to spend more time talking about personal impressions of each other."

IIID, PERSONAL SPECULATIVE. Here, a problem context of some kind has been established and people are working toward understanding of the topic person. The topic person can either speculate about himself, or the group member can do so. Examples:

> "I don't know what to do to solve this problem, can you help?"
>
> "Maybe you like to suffer and set it up so that people reject you."
>
> "What are some of the situations where you run into this kind of problem?"

IVD, RELATIONSHIP SPECULATIVE. In this cell, group members speculate about how they view one another. A member may show that he wants to know how he is seen by another person. Requests for information and the information given, however, is fairly tentative and is not documented. Examples:

> "I wish I knew how you felt about me."
>
> "I suppose I react negatively to you because you are so much like my sister."
>
> "Fred, are you comfortable around me?"

IE, TOPIC CONFRONTIVE. In this cell, states tend to clarify and "pull together" various things that have been discussed. Rather than adding a new dimension to the ongoing discussion, a IE remark has the effect of clearing away the nonessentials and confronting the members with the essence of the ideas being discussed. Examples:

> "That's probably why we resent the professors: they can do all the things we say we don't really care about, but that we probably really want to do."
>
> "Wouldn't it be a joke on us to discover that the qualities we like in other people are the qualities we like in ourselves? That makes friendship really self-love, doesn't it?"

IIE, GROUP-DYAD CONFRONTIVE. IIE Interaction is characterized by statements or questions which analyze, diagnose or suggest solutions for group process problems. Documentation is given. Examples:

> "I've noticed that one of the things we do is agree with each other all the time. Maybe that's why we both feel dissatisfied."
>
> "We haven't been able to help each other much, have we? All we do is fight."

IIIE, PERSONAL CONFRONTIVE. In this cell are statements that are an open, honest effort to get and give information. Feedback is usually documented. The speaker shows that he is willing to be direct and take responsibility for what he says. Examples:

> "Ever since I've been able to remember I've been unable to tolerate selfishness. I'm beginning to think that I've felt this way because I'm really selfish myself. Do you see me doing selfish things?"
>
> "You want your fiancée's time all to yourself; that's selfish."
>
> "You say you're often taken advantage of, yet you seem to leave yourself wide open, like you wanted it to happen. When you were dating Frank you seemed to be inviting him to walk all over you."

IVE, RELATIONSHIP CONFRONTIVE. In this cell, the members talk about the way they feel about each other and their relationship in a confrontive way. Members examine the way they react to each other. Examples (documentation) are given. One dimension is honesty and another an evident desire to help and improve the relationship. Examples:

> "Jim, whenever I ask you a question, you act like you're mad at me. Do I say things that rub you the wrong way?"
>
> "I don't know why, but I feel uneasy around you most of the time. It's like you're always trying to please me."
>
> "I always feel like you're willing to help me. You often give me ideas that have been very valuable in handling some of my problems."

Use of the HIM

The HIM has proven to be a useful tool in evaluating classroom or small group interaction. It can give a clear picture of how the group in question is interacting. How a group *should* interact becomes a situational and a somewhat academic problem. For instance, as mentioned previously, an implicit value system exists in the HIM structure. It suggests that interaction in the lower right-hand quadrant of the principal sixteen cells of the matrix is "good" interaction. This is especially true for an encounter type setting. It seems reasonable, however, to always evaluate interaction in terms of the specific situational characteristics of the class or group. For example, what are the goals of a group? If the goals are personal problem solving and personal growth (as in the activities suggested in Chapter Five of this book), one would logically expect the most productive interaction to occur in the member-centered columns (III and IV). On the other hand, in a setting where content or subject learning is the principal goal, time would most productively be spent in columns I and II. In either case, the format of the matrix would suggest that work level (D and E) interaction vis-à-vis *process* will generally be more productive than prework level (A, B and C) interaction.

Research suggests that in terms of the HIM conceptual system, it is often necessary for a group to spend some time "finding its bearings" in the "prework" categories (Liebroder, 1962). But at the same time, groups judged most productive move toward the "work" categories. There is some evidence to suggest that productive groups spend some time in almost all of the cells of the matrix and tend to move over the matrix during a session. For instance, after a heavy "work" period, there is a tendency to spend some time in the conventional category, being more light (almost like refueling). Productive groups seem to be capable of spending a good deal of time in the work categories, and do so, however.

References   *Johnson*

HILL, WM. FAWCETT. *HIM: Hill Interaction Matrix* and *HIM: Hill Interaction Matrix Scoring Manual.* University of Southern California:Youth Studies Center, 1965.

LIEBRODER, M.N. *Effects of therapist style of interaction in psychotherapy groups.* (Unpublished Doctoral dissertation) University of Utah, 1962.

THE BARRETT-LENNARD
RELATIONSHIP INVENTORY

BARBARA STILTNER, *Graduate Assistant, University of Colorado*

In contrast to the interaction observation systems which use an outside observer's objective report of interpersonal relations, the Barrett-Lennard Relationship Inventory relies on the subjective report of the individuals involved in the interaction. The inventory is based on the philosophy that how the individual perceives a relationship in which he is involved with another person is more important in determining how that relationship will influence him than another person's judgment of that relationship. The assumption is that it is difficult for the third person to observe the individual and infer what meaning the relationship has for that individual.

The Barrett-Lennard Relationship Inventory (BLRI) was developed originally in 1959 with the aim of measuring five different aspects of the therapist-client relationship. Based on Carl Rogers' statement (1957) of the necessary and sufficient conditions of therapy, the inventory was later refined to include the following four aspects of the therapeutic relationship: empathy, congruence, level of regard and unconditionality of regard. (See Chapter One, pp. 8-9 and Chapter Two, pp. 40-41 for an explanation of these conditions.) The Barrett-Lennard distinguishes between level of regard, which is the tendency of the feeling reactions of one person toward another at any one time, and unconditionality of regard, which is the consistency or lack of consistency of a person's feeling reactions toward another. Unconditionality of regard is evi-

Barbara Stiltner is a graduate assistant at the University of Colorado, Boulder, Colorado.

denced in the ability of the helping person to react in a consistent
manner to the individual regardless of his current behavior.

In its present form (Form OS-M-64; Litwack et al., 1968, pp. 416-
420), the inventory contains sixty-four statements evenly divided among
the four dimensions of relationships and presented in an alternating
format. Sample questions include:

_____ 1. He respects me as a person. (level of regard)

_____ 2. He wants to understand how I feel. (empathy)

_____19. He wants me to be a particular kind of person. (unconditional-
ity)

_____29. I feel that he disapproves of me. (level of regard)

_____36. He expresses his true impressions and feelings with me. (congru-
ence)

The pronouns can be varied depending on the sex of the therapist or the
sex of the client. The above questions are taken from the client form for
a male therapist. Items are stated in both positive and negative forms.
Items 1, 2 and 36 above are positively stated, and items 19 and 29 are
negatively stated. Each item is answered on a scale from $+3$ (strongly
agree) to -3 (strongly disagree). In scoring the inventory, the negatively
stated items are reversed to give a consistent direction to the composite
score. Scores are computed for the individual scales or dimensions and
for the total inventory. On the individual scales the scores can range
from -48 to $+48$, and on the total inventory from $+192$ to -192.
Frequently the BLRI is completed by both individuals involved in the
relationship—by the receiver of help as he sees his helper, and by the
helper as he thinks the receiver will respond. In the original research
Barrett-Lennard (1962) found that there was a tendency for therapists to
see the relationship as slightly more positive than their clients saw it.

Several studies evaluating the BLRI have been conducted. Generally the reliability of the total score and its subscales ranges from .75 to
.94 with split half methods (Litwack *et al.*, 1968, p. 418). As most of the
values reported are in the upper part of this range, the reliability of the
inventory is satisfactory for most uses. Several investigators have tried to
determine whether the subscales are actually measuring discrete aspects
of interpersonal relations or one main factor. Using a sample of college
students who completed the inventory in reference to their relationships
with their mothers, Mills and Zytowski (1967) found that there appeared

to be a strong underlying factor which accounted for a large part of the variance. This indicates that the inventory is measuring a general factor in relationships rather than four separate factors. In a similar study, Walker and Little (1969) found that there was a close relationship between the empathy and congruence subscales, indicating that they were not measuring separate factors. Both of these studies were conducted using nontherapy relationships, indicating that there may also be less differentiation in the four subscales when teacher-student relationships are considered.

Despite the fact that there appears to be some difference between therapy relationships and other helping relationships as measured by the BLRI, there is support for its use in looking at interpersonal relationships which may affect a student's learning. The instrument has been applied in a number of coeducational situations. Hollenbeck (1965) found that the way college students reported their relationships with their parents was related to their adjustment and was minimally related to school achievement. Schlesinger (1967) found that high school students' conception of their ideal teacher as reported on the BLRI was related to academic ability. In comparing two groups of open and less open teachers, Emmerling (1961) found very significant differences in perception of teacher-student relationship as reported by the students (ninth through twelfth grades) of these teachers. Thompson (1967) found a relationship between the quality of teacher-student relationships as reported by seventh- and eighth-grade students and the teacher's effectiveness based on administrator ratings. Mason and Blumberg (1969) found significant differences in the way high school seniors completed the inventory for the teacher from whom they had learned the most and the way they completed it for the teacher from whom they had learned the least. However, Mason (1970) found that there was no relationship between high school teachers' classroom behavior as observed using the Flanders System of Interaction Analysis and students' completion of the BLRI.

Although the evidence supporting a relationship between the student-teacher relationship as measured by the BLRI and student achievement and adjustment is not conclusive, there is enough support to indicate that more positive relationships may be associated with better adjustment and achievement. Further support comes from two sources. Aspy (1965), using a different measure of the dimensions of relationships, found a clear relationship between the conditions offered by a teacher and third-graders' reading achievement. In addition, there is a

large body of evidence indicating that change in therapy is related to the
level of interpersonal relationships offered by the therapist, including the
indication that when the therapist offers low levels the patient may
change for the worse.

In using the inventory in the classroom, best results will be obtained
by asking the student to fill it out anonymously. This allows students the
freedom to answer as they truly feel rather than as they think the teacher
might like them to. However, it still allows the teacher to assess the
average level of his or her relationship with students and to study the
range of scores from the lowest to the highest. A large range of scores
may indicate either that he is reacting differently to different students
or that different students have different expectations of what they would
like from him as a teacher.

The scores on the subtests are of interest to the teacher as well. By
comparing these, teachers can determine areas of particular strength in
their relating to students and also determine weaker areas. However,
caution should be exercised in interpreting the subscale scores on an
absolute basis. It is wise for the teacher to study the items and the
definitions of the subscales to determine his own conception of his ideal
teaching style and relationship to students. For example, Mr. Stoller, a
twelfth-grade mathematics teacher, may decide that while empathy is of
high importance to his style of teaching, unconditionality is not congruent with his style. Therefore, he would be more concerned if his
students saw him as uniformly low on the empathy scale than if they
saw him as uniformly low on the unconditionality of regard scale.

In interpreting results from the BLRI in terms of classroom behavior change, a teacher again needs to study both the subscale definitions
and the individual items to determine specific ways in which he may
adjust his teaching style in order to relate to students in a more helpful
way. Unfortunately, little research using the inventory and an observation analysis instrument in the same classroom has been conducted. This
type of research could help define specific teaching behaviors used by
those teachers who have positive scores on the BLRI. However, analysis
of the inventory items can lead to an intuitive conception of those
behaviors which lead to more positive relationships with students.

further application with students is to ask them to complete the
inventory twice, once for the way they perceive the actual relationship
with their teacher and once for the way they perceive the ideal teacher-
student relationship. This gives the teacher an additional point of comparison against which to consider his students' responses. He may also

complete the inventory as he perceives his relationship with his students and then compare his responses to theirs. Teachers may also complete the inventory considering their relationship with their principal. Again, the principal should be allowed to consider responses on the inventory in light of his own conceptions of the relationship he would like to have with teachers. Additionally, teachers who work closely with each other may want to complete the inventory considering their relationships with each other. Clark and Culbert (1965) used this approach in a T group setting, having each member consider his relationship with one member each time he completed the inventory.

In using the inventory, rather than or in addition to other methods of studying classroom interaction, the teacher is indicating that he values the perceptions of his students and that he is willing to consider these perceptions in continually striving to improve his teaching style. This, in itself, is an important statement of intention to students.

For additional information concerning the BLRI consult Barrett-Lennard (1962). Form OS-M-64 appears in Litwack et al., 1968. Because Form OS-M-64 was designed for use with adults, precautions should be taken to ensure that all students can understand the items. With a small group of students it would be feasible to read the inventory to students and allow them to respond either verbally or in writing. Emmerling (1961, Form OS-M-HS) and Thompson (1967) have made revisions more suited to high school students. Teachers may also wish to construct their own versions.

References   Stiltner

ASPY, DAVID N. *A study of three facilitative conditions and their relationships to the achievement of third grade students.* (Unpublished doctoral dissertation) University of Kentucky, 1965, Dissertation Abstracts International, 1969, 1853-A.

BARRETT-LENNARD, G.T. Dimensions of therapist response as causal factors in therapeutic change. *Psychological Monographs,* 1962, Vol. 76, No. 43, whole No. 562.

BLUMBERG, ARTHUR. Supervisory behavior and interpersonal relations. *Educational Administration Quarterly,* Spring, 1968, Vol. IV, No. 2, 34-35.

CLARK, JAMES V., and CULBERT, SAMUEL A. Mutually therapeutic perception and self-awareness in a T group. *Journal of Applied Behavioral Science,* 1965, Vol. 1, No. 2, 180-194.

EMMERLING, FRANK C. *A study of the relationships between personality characteristics of classroom teachers and pupil perceptions of these teachers.* (Unpublished doctoral dissertation) Auburn University, 1961, Dissertation Abstracts International, 1961.

HOLLENBECK, GEORGE. Conditions and outcomes in the student-parent relationship. *Journal of Consulting Psychology,* 1965. Vol. 29, No. 3, 237-241.

HOLLENBECK, GEORGE. *The use of the relationship inventory in the prediction of adjustment and achievement.* (Unpublished doctoral dissertation) The University of Wisconsin, 1961, Dissertation Abstracts International, 1961, 2063.

LITWACK, LAWRENCE, GETSON, RUSSELL, and SALTZMAN, GLENN (Eds.). *Research in counseling.* Itasco, Ill.: Peacock Publishers, 1968, 416-420 (Appendix C).

MASON, JACK L. Study of the relationships between the behavioral styles of classroom teachers and the quality of teacher-student interpersonal relations. *Educational Leadership,* October, 1970, Vol. 28, 49-56.

MASON, JACK L., and BLUMBERG, ARTHUR. Perceived educational value of the classroom teachers and the quality of teacher-pupil interpersonal relations. *Journal of Secondary Education,* March, 1969, Vol. 44, 135-139.

MILLS, DAVID H., and ZYTOWSKI, DONALD G. Helping relationship: A structural analysis. *Journal of Counseling Psychology,* 1967, Vol. 14, No. 3, 193-197.

ROGERS, CARL. The necessary and sufficient conditions of therapeutic personality change. *Journal of Consulting Psychology,* 1957, Vol. 21, 95-103.

SCHLESINGER, TOM. *Four attitudinal dimensions of counseling relationships as perceived by students in relating to a real and an ideal teacher.* (Unpublished doctoral dissertation) University of Massachusetts, 1967, Dissertation Abstracts International, 1967, 2992-A.

THOMPSON, JACK M. *The relationship between Carl Rogers' helping relationship concept and teacher behavior.* (Unpublished doctoral dissertation) University of California, Berkeley, 1967, Dissertation Abstracts International, 1968.

WALKER, B.S., and LITTLE, D.F. Factor analysis of the Barrett-Lennard Relationship Inventory. *Journal of Counseling Psychology,* 1969, Vol. 16, No. 6, 516-521.

Appendix

Supporting Evidence from Research

In a sense, all research in education involves interpersonal interaction, and even when we consider only that research which might be directly relevant to the thrust of this book, the amount is staggering. For this reason, only a few selected studies and analyses of research are presented here.

Carkhuff (1969) has discussed and summarized most of the research that has been done regarding empathy, positive regard and genuineness, in addition to the small amount of research on concreteness of expression. His feeling—and ours—is that there can be little doubt from the research evidence and the experience of practitioners that these factors are crucial in helping relationships, including teaching.

Perhaps even more significant are the strong indications from research cited by Carkhuff and Berenson (1967) that the quality of interpersonal relationships determines whether the relationships will be for better or for worse. That is, there is evidence from the research they cite that if the level of empathy, positive regard and congruence is too low in a helping relationship such as teaching, the person being helped (taught) will also begin to function at a lower level. The relationship will actually harm the students, rather than help them. This is a sobering thought. Normally we feel that at least the students are no worse off than they were before, even if we are not successful in our efforts to help them. This research suggests that we may not only not help, but we may do harm in the process.

So far, we have discussed empathy, positive regard, congruence and concreteness of expression as abstract concepts and have said little about what teacher behaviors have been associated with an ideal relationship. The similarity between what is conceptualized as an ideal therapeutic relationship and an ideal teaching relationship is remarkable. Even more remarkable is that in the study by Fiedler (1950) which originally explored the concept of an ideal therapeutic relationship, therapists with different theoretical backgrounds showed a substantial similarity in their concepts. In the study by Tyler (1964) based on Fiedler's original concepts, college professors with different backgrounds and a medical doctor arrived at a surprisingly similar definition of an ideal teaching relationship. The general dimensions were identified as follows: ideal relationships involve good communication, in an emotionally close, co-worker or peer type relationship; the least ideal relationships involve no communication and superior status of the teacher, in an emotionally distant relationship. The specific statements involved supported these generalizations. The similarity between the conceptualizations in this study and the concepts of empathy, congruence and positive regard are clear. The overlap from other standpoints is also extensive. Truax and Tatum (1966) show that constructive personality change in preschool children is linked to the same variables, and use these findings as evidence that an ideal therapeutic relationship is just a specific form of an ideal relationship.

The effects of good interpersonal relationships are revealed in many different ways. An extensive study involving over seven hundred students and twenty-seven teachers indicated that the teacher was the single most important person in the student's school life and that if he thinks his teacher dislikes him he is likely to dislike school and be dissatisfied with himself. In addition, it was found that children with low social positions tend to achieve below their ability level. The implication is that a student's social position is an important determinant of his school success and that teachers are particularly important persons in students' perception of their position in school (Lewis, 1964).

Regardless of other types of gains or outcomes, to many people the acid test for any variable tends to be, "Does it improve academic achievement?" While the importance of interpersonal relations is probably only tangentially related to what is ordinarily categorized as academic achievement, there is considerable evidence of the positive effect of good interpersonal relationships on academic achievement. Aspy (1971) reports positive correlations of improvements on standardized tests with the conditions of empathy, genuineness and positive regard. Lewis, Lovell and Jessee (1965) found that sixth-grade students who perceive their relationship with their teacher to be similar to an ideal therapeutic relationship make greater academic gains than those who do not feel they have this type of relationship with their teacher.

Walberg (1969) found significant relationships between classroom climate and learning. This is an especially important study because the analysis of the data is sophisticated and because the number of students involved (3,700) makes the findings more likely to be representative of everyday classroom results. This is a complicated study and offers many clues for further research and additional interpretations of the findings; it can serve as a source of ideas for the teacher looking for research leads.

Mason and Blumberg (1969) found that students judged the quality of their relationships to be better in the classrooms in which they learned the most. Soar (1968) found that while warmth in interpersonal relationships is probably indicated in all teaching relationships, the amount of indirectness for optimal pupil growth seems to vary; teacher criticism seems to be inversely related to pupil growth. Christensen (1960) found teacher warmth to be positively related to pupil achievement in vocabulary and arithmetic.

The questions that must be considered first are: how valid are the data reported in these studies, and how valid are the conclusions we have drawn? Only a thorough analysis far beyond the scope and purpose of this book could adequately deal with the data. You are free to examine the original source of the data and draw your own conclusions. To us, our conclusions seem valid, but we expect to revise and improve them as we learn more about human interaction and teaching. Finally, we need to ask, "What does it all mean?" To us, it means—as we have stressed throughout this book—that interpersonal interaction in education is far more important than is usually recognized, and that to improve education we need to improve the relationships that take place between the persons involved.

References   Appendix

Aspy, D.N. Toward a technology which helps teachers humanize their class-rooms. *Educational Leadership:* Research Supplement, 1971, **29**, 626-628.

Carkhuff, R.R. *Helping and human relations.* New York: Holt, 1969.

Carkhuff, R.R., and Berenson, B.G. *Beyond counseling and therapy.* New York: Holt, 1967.

Christensen, C.M. Relationships between pupil achievement, pupil affect-need, teacher permissiveness. *Journal of Educational Psychology,* 1960, **51**, 169-174.

Fiedler, F. The concept of an ideal therapeutic relationship. *Journal of Consulting Psychology,* 1950, **14**, 235-245.

Lewis, G.M. Interpersonal relations and school achievement. *Children,* 1964, **11**, 235-236.

Lewis, W.A., Lovell, J.T., and Jessee, B.E. Interpersonal relationship and pupil process. *Personnel and Guidance Journal,* 1965, **44**, 396-401.

Mason, J., and Blumberg, A. Perceived educational value of the classroom and teacher-pupil interpersonal relationships. *Journal of Secondary Education,* 1969, **44**, 135-138.

Soar, R.S. Optimum teacher-pupil interaction for pupil growth. *Educational Leadership,* 1968, **26**, 275-280.

Truax, C.B., and Tatum, C.D. An extension from the effective psychotherapeutic model to constructive personality change in preschool children. *Childhood Education,* 1966, **42**, 456-462.

Tyler, L.J. The concept of an ideal teacher-student relationship. *Journal of Educational Research,* 1964, **58**, 112-117.

Walberg, H.J. Predicting class learning: An approach to the class as a social system. *American Education Research Journal,* 1969, **6**, 529-542.

Index